PUBLIC HEALTH AND HYGIENE

PUBLIC HEALTH AND HYGIENE

Dr. Afroze Eqbal

RANDOM

RANDOM PUBLICATIONS

NEW DELHI - 110 002 (INDIA)

Public Health and Hygiene

ISBN 978-93-51117-36-0

Published in 2015 in India by

RANDOM PUBLICATIONS

4376-A/4B, Gali Murari Lal, Ansari Road
New Delhi-110 002
Phone: +9111-43580356, 23289044
E-mail: randomexports@gmail.com; sales@randompublications.com; info@randompublications.com

Reprinted 2022

Type Setting by: Friends Media, Delhi-110089
Digitally Printed at: Replika Press Pvt. Ltd.

Preface

Public health is "the science and art of preventing disease, prolonging life and promoting health through the organized efforts and informed choices of society, organizations, public and private, communities and individuals." It is concerned with threats to health based on population health analysis. The population in question can be as small as a handful of people, or as large as all the inhabitants of several continents (for instance, in the case of a pandemic). The dimensions of health can encompass "a state of complete physical, mental and social well-being and not merely the absence of disease or infirmity", as defined by the United Nations' World Health Organization. Public health incorporates the interdisciplinary approaches of epidemiology, biostatistics and health services. Environmental health, community health, behavioural health, health economics, public policy, insurance medicine and occupational safety and health are other important subfields. The focus of public health intervention is to improve health and quality of life through the prevention and treatment of disease and other physical and mental health conditions, through surveillance of cases and health indicators, and through the promotion of healthy behaviours. Promotion of hand washing and breastfeeding, delivery of vaccinations, and distribution of condoms to control the spread of sexually transmitted diseases are examples of common public health measures.

Modern public health practice requires multidisciplinary teams of public health workers and professionals including physicians specializing in public health/community medicine/infectious disease, psychologists epidemiologists, biostatisticians, medical assistants or Assistant Medical Officers, public health nurses, midwives, medical microbiologists, environmental health officers / public health inspectors, pharmacists, dental hygienists, dietitians and nutritionists, veterinarians, public health engineers, public health lawyers, sociologists, community development workers, communications experts, bioethicists, and others. Hygiene, is a set of practices performed for the preservation of health. Whereas in popular culture and parlance it can often mean mere 'cleanliness', hygiene in its fullest and original meaning goes much beyond that to include all circumstances and practices, lifestyle issues, premises and commodities that engender a safe and healthy environment. While in modern medical sciences there is a set of standards of hygiene recommended for different situations, what is considered hygienic or not can vary between different cultures, genders and etarian groups. Some regular hygienic practices may be considered good habits by a society while the neglect of hygiene can be considered disgusting, disrespectful or even threatening. Sanitation in its current US popular meaning is often (incorrectly) taken to be merely the hygienic disposal and treatment by the civic authority of potentially unhealthy human waste, such as household garbage and sewage, and the maintenance of the sewerage and drainage infrastructure. In the UK the term 'sanitation' has unfortunately come closer to meaning water and waste plumbing and disposal, and it is not used to include garbage collection and disposal. The full and proper meaning of 'sanitation' is closer to the full meaning of 'hygiene' and includes the control of water and air quality; vectors; healthful housing; safe products; safe food and working conditions. The more recent broad term 'environmental health' equates to the original meaning of sanitation.

Written in engaging, non-technical language, this valuable textbook explains in clear terms the multidisciplinary strategies and methods for measuring, assessing, and promoting public health.

I thank all members of my team who have helped in the preparation of the book. My special thanks go to "Random Publications" who have published the book.

— Dr. Afroze Eqbal

Contents

Chapter 1

Health

Health is the level of functional or metabolic efficiency of a living organism. In humans, it is the general condition of a person's mind and body, usually meaning to be free from illness, injury or pain (as in "*good health*" or "*healthy*"). The World Health Organization (WHO) defined health in its broader sense in 1946 as "a state of complete physical, mental, and social well-being and not merely the absence of disease or infirmity." Although this definition has been subject to controversy, in particular as lacking operational value and because of the problem created by use of the word "complete," it remains the most enduring. Other definitions have been proposed, among which a recent definition that correlates health and personal satisfaction. Classification systems such as the WHO Family of International Classifications, including the International Classification of Functioning, Disability and Health (ICF) and the International Classification of Diseases (ICD), are commonly used to define and measure the components of health.

Systematic activities to prevent or cure health problems and promote good health in humans are undertaken by health care providers. Applications with regard to animal health are covered by the veterinary sciences. The term "healthy" is also widely used in the context of many types of non-living organizations and their impacts for the benefit of humans, such as in the sense of healthy communities, healthy cities or healthy environments. In addition to health care interventions and a person's surroundings, a number of other factors are known to influence the health status of individuals, including their background, lifestyle, and economic, social conditions, and spirituality; these are referred to as "determinants of health." Studies have shown that high levels of stress can affect your health.

Determinants

Generally, the context in which an individual lives is of great importance for both his health status and quality of their life. It is increasingly recognized that health is maintained and improved not only through the advancement and application of health science, but also through the efforts and intelligent lifestyle choices of the individual and society. According to the World Health Organization, the main determinants of health include the social and economic environment, the physical environment, and the person's individual characteristics and behaviours.

More specifically, key factors that have been found to influence whether people are healthy or unhealthy include the following:

- Income and social status
- Social support networks
- Education and literacy
- Employment/working conditions
- Social environments
- Physical environments
- Personal health practices and coping skills
- Healthy child development
- Biology and genetics
- Health care services
- Gender
- Culture

An increasing number of studies and reports from different organizations and contexts examine the linkages between health and different factors, including lifestyles, environments, health care organization, and health policy – such as the 1974 Lalonde report from Canada; the Alameda County Study in California; and the series of World Health Reports of the World Health Organization, which focuses on global health issues including access to health care and improving public health outcomes, especially in developing countries. The concept of the "*health field,*" as distinct from medical care, emerged from the Lalonde report from Canada. The report identified three interdependent fields as key determinants of an individual's health. These are:

- Lifestyle: the aggregation of personal decisions (i.e., over which the individual has control) that can be said to contribute to, or cause, illness or death;

- Environmental: all matters related to health external to the human body and over which the individual has little or no control;
- Biomedical: all aspects of health, physical and mental, developed within the human body as influenced by genetic make-up.

The maintenance and promotion of health is achieved through different combination of physical, mental, and social well-being, together sometimes referred to as the *"health triangle."* The WHO's 1986 *Ottawa Charter for Health Promotion* further stated that health is not just a state, but also "a resource for everyday life, not the objective of living. Health is a positive concept emphasizing social and personal resources, as well as physical capacities."

Focusing more on lifestyle issues and their relationships with functional health, data from the Alameda County Study suggested that people can improve their health via exercise, enough sleep, maintaining a healthy body weight, limiting alcohol use, and avoiding smoking. The ability to *adapt* and to *self manage* have been suggested as core components of human health.

The environment is often cited as an important factor influencing the health status of individuals. This includes characteristics of the natural environment, the built environment, and the social environment. Factors such as clean water and air, adequate housing, and safe communities and roads all have been found to contribute to good health, especially to the health of infants and children. Some studies have shown that a lack of neighbourhood recreational spaces including natural environment leads to lower levels of personal satisfaction and higher levels of obesity, linked to lower overall health and well being. This suggests that the positive health benefits of natural space in urban neighbourhoods should be taken into account in public policy and land use.

Genetics, or inherited traits from parents, also play a role in determining the health status of individuals and populations. This can encompass both the predisposition to certain diseases and health conditions, as well as the habits and behaviours individuals develop through the lifestyle of their families. For example, genetics may play a role in the manner in which people cope with stress, either mental, emotional or physical. For example, obesity is a very large problem in the United States that contributes to bad mental health and causes stress in a lot of people's lives. (One difficulty is the issue raised by the debate over the relative strengths of genetics and other factors; interactions between genetics and environment may be of particular importance.)

Potential Issues

There are a lot of types of health issues common with many people across the globe. Disease is one of the most common. According to GlobalIssues.org, approximately 36 million people die each year from non-communicable (not contagious) disease including cardiovascular disease cancer, diabetes, and chronic lung disease (Shah, 2014). As for communicable diseases, both viral and bacterial, AIDS/HIV, tuberculosis, and malaria are the most common also causing millions of deaths every year (2014). Another health issue that causes death or contributes to other health problems is malnutrition. One of the groups malnutrition affects most is young children. Approximately 7.5 million children under the age of 5 die from malnutrition, and it is usually brought on by not having the money to find or make food (2014).

Bodily injuries are also a common health issue worldwide. These injuries, including broken bones, fractures, and burns can reduce a person's quality of life or can cause fatalities including infections that resulted from the injury or the severity injury in general (Moffett, 2013).

Some contributing factors to poor health are lifestyle choices. These include smoking cigarettes, which according to LIVESTRONG.com kills 443,000 people each year (2013). It also can include a poor diet, whether it is overeating or an overly constrictive diet. Inactivity can also contribute to health issues and also a lack of sleep, excessive alcohol consumption, and neglect of oral hygiene (2013). There are also genetic disorders that are inherited by the person and can vary in how much the affect the person and when they surface (2013).

The one health issue that is the most unfortunate because the majority of these health issues are preventable is that approximately 1 billion people lack access to health care systems (Shah, 2014). It is easy to say that the most common and harmful health issue is that a lot of people do not have access to quality remedies.

Mental Health

The World Health Organization describes mental health as "a state of well-being in which the individual realizes his or her own abilities, can cope with the normal stresses of life, can work productively and fruitfully, and is able to make a contribution to his or her community". Mental Health is not just the absence of mental illness.

Mental illness is described as 'the spectrum of cognitive, emotional, and behavioural conditions that interfere with social and emotional well-being and the lives and productivity of people. Having a mental illness can seriously impair, temporarily or permanently, the mental functioning of a person. Other terms include: 'mental health problem', 'illness', 'disorder', 'dysfunction'. (Hungerford et al. 2012).

Roughly a quarter of all adults 18 and over in the US suffer from a diagnosable mental illness. Mental illnesses are the leading cause of disability in the US and Canada. Examples include, schizophrenia, ADHD, major depressive disorder, bipolar disorder, anxiety disorder, post-traumatic stress disorder and autism.

Many teens suffer from mental health issues in response to the pressures of society and social problems they encounter. Some of the key mental health issues seen in teens are: depression, eating disorders, and drug abuse. There are many ways to prevent these health issues from occurring such as communicating well with your child or a teen suffering from mental health issues. Also, remember that mental health can be treated and be attentive to your child's behavior.

Maintaining Health

Achieving and maintaining health is an ongoing process, shaped by both the evolution of health care knowledge and practices as well as personal strategies and organized interventions for staying healthy known as Lifestyle Management.

Diet

An important way to maintain your personal health is to have a healthy diet. A healthy diet includes a variety of plant-based and animal-based foods that provide nutrients to your body. Such nutrients give you energy and keep your body running. Nutrients help build and strengthen bones, muscles, and tendons and also regulate body processes (i.e. blood pressure). The food guide pyramid is a pyramid-shaped guide of healthy foods divided into sections. Each section shows the recommended intake for each food group (i.e. Protein, Fat, Carbohydrates, and Sugars). Making healthy food choices is important because it can lower your risk of heart disease, developing some types of cancer, and it will contribute to maintaining a healthy weight.

Exercise

Physical exercise enhances or maintains physical fitness and overall health and wellness. It strengthens muscles and improves the cardiovascular system.

Role of Science

Health science is the branch of science focused on health. There are two main approaches to health science: the study and research of the body and health-related issues to understand how humans (and animals) function, and the application of that knowledge to improve health and to prevent and cure diseases and other physical and mental impairments. The science builds on many sub-fields, including biology, biochemistry, physics, epidemiology, pharmacology, medical sociology. Applied health sciences endeavour to better understand and improve human health through applications in areas such as health education, biomedical engineering, biotechnology and public health.

Organized interventions to improve health based on the principles and procedures developed through the health sciences are provided by practitioners trained in medicine, nursing, nutrition, pharmacy, social work, psychology, occupational therapy, physical therapy and other health care professions. Clinical practitioners focus mainly on the health of individuals, while public health practitioners consider the overall health of communities and populations. Workplace wellness programmes are increasingly adopted by companies for their value in improving the health and well-being of their employees, as are school health services in order to improve the health and well-being of children.

Self-care Strategies

Personal health depends partially on the active, passive, and assisted cues people observe and adopt about their own health. These include personal actions for preventing or minimizing the effects of a disease, usually a chronic condition, through integrative care. They also include personal hygiene practices to prevent infection and illness, such as bathing and washing hands with soap; brushing and flossing teeth; storing, preparing and handling food safely; and many others. The information gleaned from personal observations of daily living – such as about sleep patterns, exercise behavior, nutritional intake and environmental features – may be used to inform personal decisions and actions (*e.g.*, "I feel tired in the morning so I am going to try sleeping on a different pillow"), as well as clinical decisions and treatment plans (*e.g.*, a patient who notices his or her shoes are tighter than usual may be having exacerbation of left-sided heart failure, and may require diuretic medication to reduce fluid overload).

Personal health also depends partially on the social structure of a person's life. The maintenance of strong social relationships, volunteering, and other social activities have been linked to positive mental health and also increased longevity. One American study among seniors over age 70, found that frequent volunteering was associated with reduced risk of dying compared with older persons who did not volunteer, regardless of physical health status. Another study from

Singapore reported that volunteering retirees had significantly better cognitive performance scores, fewer depressive symptoms, and better mental well-being and life satisfaction than non-volunteering retirees.

Prolonged psychological stress may negatively impact health, and has been cited as a factor in cognitive impairment with aging, depressive illness, and expression of disease. Stress management is the application of methods to either reduce stress or increase tolerance to stress. Relaxation techniques are physical methods used to relieve stress. Psychological methods include cognitive therapy, meditation, and positive thinking, which work by reducing response to stress. Improving relevant skills, such as problem solving and time management skills, reduces uncertainty and builds confidence, which also reduces the reaction to stress-causing situations where those skills are applicable.

Occupational Health

In addition to safety risks, many jobs also present risks of disease, illness and other long-term health problems. Among the most common occupational diseases are various forms of pneumoconiosis, including silicosis and coal worker's pneumoconiosis (black lung disease). Asthma is another respiratory illness that many workers are vulnerable to. Workers may also be vulnerable to skin diseases, including eczema, dermatitis, urticaria, sunburn, and skin cancer. Other occupational diseases of concern include carpal tunnel syndrome and lead poisoning.

As the number of service sector jobs has risen in developed countries, more and more jobs have become sedentary, presenting a different array of health problems than those associated with manufacturing and the primary sector. Contemporary problems such as the growing rate of obesity and issues relating to stress and overwork in many countries have further complicated the interaction between work and health.

Many governments view occupational health as a social challenge and have formed public organizations to ensure the health and safety of workers. Examples of these include the British Health and Safety Executive and in the United States, the National Institute for Occupational Safety and Health, which conducts research on occupational health and safety, and the Occupational Safety and Health Administration, which handles regulation and policy relating to worker safety and health.

Public Health

Public health is "the science and art of preventing disease, prolonging life and promoting health through the organized efforts and informed choices of society, organizations, public and private, communities and individuals." It is concerned with threats to health based on population health analysis. The population in question can be as small as a handful of people, or as large as all the inhabitants of several continents (for instance, in the case of a pandemic). The dimensions of health can encompass "a state of complete physical, mental and social well-being and not merely the absence of disease or infirmity", as defined by the United Nations' World Health Organization. Public health incorporates the interdisciplinary approaches of epidemiology, biostatistics and health services. Environmental health, community health, behavioural health, health economics, public policy, insurance medicine and occupational safety and health are other important subfields.

The focus of public health intervention is to improve health and quality of life through the prevention and treatment of disease and other physical and mental health conditions, through surveillance of cases and health indicators, and through the promotion of healthy behaviours. Promotion of hand washing and breastfeeding, delivery of vaccinations, and distribution of condoms to control the spread of sexually transmitted diseases are examples of common public health measures. Modern public health practice requires multidisciplinary teams of public health workers and professionals including physicians specializing in public health/community medicine/infectious disease, psychologists epidemiologists, biostatisticians, medical assistants or Assistant Medical Officers, public health nurses, midwives, medical microbiologists, environmental health officers / public health inspectors, pharmacists, dental hygienists, dietitians and nutritionists, veterinarians, public health engineers, public health lawyers, sociologists, community development workers, communications experts, bioethicists, and others.

Objectives

The focus of a public health intervention is to prevent and manage diseases, injuries and other health conditions through surveillance of cases and the promotion of healthy behaviours, communities and environments. Many diseases are preventable through simple, non-medical methods. For example, research has shown that the simple act of hand washing with soap can prevent many contagious diseases. In other cases, treating a disease or controlling a pathogen can be vital to preventing its spread to others, such as during an outbreak of infectious disease, or contamination of food or water supplies. Public health communications programmes, vaccination programmes, and distribution of condoms are examples of common public health measures. Measures such as these have contributed greatly to the health of populations and increases in life expectancy.

Public health plays an important role in disease prevention efforts in both the developing world and in developed countries, through local health systems and non-governmental organizations. The World Health Organization (WHO) is the international agency that coordinates and acts on global public health issues. Most countries have their own government public health agencies, sometimes known as ministries of health, to respond to domestic health issues. For example in the United States, the front line of public health initiatives are state and local health departments. The United States Public Health Service (PHS), led by the Surgeon General of the United States, and the Centres for Disease Control and Prevention, headquartered in Atlanta, are involved with several international health activities, in addition to their national duties. In Canada, the Public Health Agency of Canada is the national agency responsible for public health, emergency preparedness and response, and infectious and chronic disease control and prevention. The Public health system in India is managed by the Ministry of Health & Family Welfare of the government of India with state owned health care facilities.

There is a great disparity in access to health care and public health initiatives between developed nations and developing nations. In the developing world, public health infrastructures are still forming. There may not be enough trained health workers or monetary resources to provide even a basic level of medical care and disease prevention. As a result, a large majority of disease and mortality in the developing world results from and contributes to extreme poverty. For example, many African governments spend less than US$10 per person per year on health care, while, in the United States, the federal government spent approximately US$4,500 per capital in 2000. However, expenditures on health care should not be confused with spending on public health. Public health measures may not generally be considered "health care" in the strictest sense. For example, mandating the use of seat belts in cars can save countless lives and contribute to the health of a population, but typically money spent enforcing this rule would not count as money spent on health care.

History

Early History

Public health has early roots in antiquity. From the beginnings of human civilization, it was recognized that polluted water and lack of proper waste disposal spread communicable diseases (theory of miasma). Early religions attempted to regulate behavior that specifically related to health, from types of food eaten, to regulating certain indulgent behaviours, such as drinking alcohol or sexual relations. Leaders were responsible for the health of their subjects to ensure social stability, prosperity, and maintain order.

By Roman times, it was well understood that proper diversion of human waste was a necessary tenet of public health in urban areas. The ancient Chinese medical doctors developed the practice of variolation following a smallpox epidemic around 1000 BC. An individual without the disease could gain some measure of immunity against it by inhaling the dried crusts that formed around lesions of infected individuals. Also, children were protected by inoculating a scratch on their forearms with the pus from a lesion.

During the 14th century Black Death in Europe, it was believed that removing bodies of the dead would further prevent the spread of the bacterial infection. This did little to stem the plague, however, which was most likely spread by rodent-borne fleas. Burning parts of cities resulted in much greater benefit, since it destroyed the rodent infestations . The development of quarantine in the medieval period helped mitigate the effects of other infectious diseases.

In 1485 the Republic of Venice established a Permanent Court of supervisors of health with special attention to the prevention of the spread of epidemics in the territory from abroad. The three supervisors were initially appointed by the Venetian Senate. In 1537 it was assumed by the Grand Council, and in 1556 added two judges, with the task of control, on behalf of the Republic, the efforts of the supervisors.

However, according to Michel Foucault, the plague model of governmentality was later controverted by the cholera model. A Cholera pandemic devastated Europe between 1829 and 1851, and was first fought by the use of what Foucault called "social medicine", which focused on flux, circulation of air, location of cemeteries, etc. All those concerns, born of the miasma theory of disease, were mixed with urbanistic concerns for the management of populations, which Foucault designated as the concept of "biopower". The German conceptualized this in the *Polizeiwissenschaft* ("Police science").

Modern Public Health

The 18th century saw rapid growth in voluntary hospitals in England. The latter part of the century brought the establishment of the basic pattern of improvements in public health over the next two centuries: a social evil was identified, private philanthropists brought attention to it, and changing public opinion led to government action.

The practice of vaccination became prevalent in the 1800s, following the pioneering work of Edward Jenner in treating smallpox. James Lind's discovery of the causes of scurvy amongst sailors and its mitigation via the introduction of fruit on lengthy voyages was published in 1754 and led to the adoption of this idea by the Royal Navy. Efforts were also made to promulgate health matters to the broader public; in 1752 the British physician Sir John Pringle published *Observations on the Diseases of the Army in Camp and Garrison*, in which he advocated for the importance of adequate ventilation in the military barracks and the provision of latrines for the soldiers.

With the onset of the Industrial Revolution, living standards amongst the working population began to worsen, with cramped and unsanitary urban conditions. In the first four decades of the 19th century alone, London's population doubled and even greater growth rates were recorded in the new industrial towns, such as Leeds and Manchester. This rapid urbanisation exacerbated the spread of disease in the large conurbations that built up around the workhouses and factories. These settlements were cramped and primitive with no organised sanitation. Disease was inevitable and its incubation in these areas was encouraged by the poor lifestyle of the inhabitants. Unavailable housing led to the rapid growth of slums and the per capita death rate began to rise alarmingly, almost doubling in Birmingham and Liverpool. Thomas Malthus warned of the dangers of overpopulation in 1798. His ideas, as well as those of Jeremy Bentham, became very influential in government circles in the early years of the 19th century.

Public Health Legislation

The first attempts at sanitary reform and the establishment of public health institutions were made in the 1840s. Thomas Southwood Smith, physician at the London Fever Hospital, began to write papers on the importance of public health, and was one of the first physicians brought in to give evidence before the Poor Law Commission in the 1830s, along with Neil Arnott and James Phillips Kay. Smith advised the government on the importance of quarantine and sanitary improvement for limiting the spread of infectious diseases such as cholera and yellow fever.

The Poor Law Commission reported in 1838 that "the expenditures necessary to the adoption and maintenance of measures of prevention would ultimately amount to less than the cost of the disease now constantly engendered". It recommended the implementation of large scale government engineering projects to alleviate the conditions that allowed for the propagation of disease. The Health of Towns Association was formed in Exeter on 11 December 1844, and vigorously campaigned for the development of public health in the United Kingdom. Its formation followed the 1843 establishment of the Health of Towns Commission, chaired by Sir Edwin Chadwick, which produced a series of reports on poor and insanitary conditions in British cities.

These national and local movements led to the Public Health Act, finally passed in 1848. It aimed to improve the sanitary condition of towns and populous places in England and Wales by placing the supply of water, sewerage, drainage, cleansing and paving under a single local body with the General Board of Health as a central authority. The Act was passed by the Liberal government of Lord John Russell, in response to the urging of Edwin Chadwick. Chadwick's seminal report on *The Sanitary Condition of the Labouring Population* was published in 1842 and was followed up with a supplementary report a year later.

Vaccination for various diseases was made compulsory in the United Kingdom in 1851, and by 1871 legislation required a comprehensive system of registration run by appointed vaccination officers.

Further interventions were made by a series of subsequent Public Health Acts, notably the 1875 Act. Reforms included latrinization, the building of sewers, the regular collection of garbage followed by incineration or disposal in a landfill, the provision of clean water and the draining of standing water to prevent the breeding of mosquitoes. So began the inception of the modern public health.

In the U.S., the first public health organization based on a state health department and local boards of health was founded in New York City in 1866.

Epidemiology

The science of epidemiology was founded by John Snow's identification of a polluted public water well as the source of an 1854 cholera outbreak in London. Dr. Snow believed in the germ theory of disease as opposed to the prevailing miasma theory. He first publicized his theory in an essay, *On the Mode of Communication of Cholera*, in 1849, followed by a more detailed treatise in 1855 incorporating the results of his investigation of the role of the water supply in the Soho epidemic of 1854.

By talking to local residents (with the help of Reverend Henry Whitehead), he identified the source of the outbreak as the public water pump on Broad Street (now Broadwick Street). Although Snow's chemical and microscope examination of a water sample from the Broad Street pump did not conclusively prove its danger, his studies of the pattern of the disease were convincing enough to persuade the local council to disable the well pump by removing its handle.

Snow later used a dot map to illustrate the cluster of cholera cases around the pump. He also used statistics to illustrate the connection between the quality of the water source and cholera cases. He showed that the Southwark and Vauxhall Waterworks Company was taking water from sewage-polluted sections of the Thames and delivering the water to homes, leading to an increased incidence of cholera. Snow's study was a major event in the history of public health and geography. It is regarded as the founding event of the science of epidemiology.

Disease Control

With the pioneering work in bacteriology of French chemist Louis Pasteur and German scientist Robert Koch, methods for isolating the bacteria responsible for a given disease and vaccines for remedy were developed at the turn of the 20th century. British physician Ronald Ross identified the mosquito as the carrier of malaria and laid the foundations for combating the disease. Joseph Lister revolutionized surgery by the introduction of antiseptic surgery to eliminate infection. French epidemiologist Paul-Louis Simond proved that plague was carried by fleas on the back of rats, and the Americans Walter Reed and James Carroll demonstrated that mosquitoes carry the virus responsible for yellow fever. With onset of the epidemiological transition and as the prevalence of infectious diseases decreased through the 20th century, public health began to put more focus on chronic diseases such as cancer and heart disease. Previous efforts in many developed countries had already led to dramatic reductions in the infant mortality rate using preventative methods. In Britain, the infant mortality rate fell from over 15% in 1870 to 7% by 1930.

In the United States, public health worker Dr. Sara Josephine Baker established many programmes to help the poor in New York City keep their infants healthy, leading teams of nurses into the crowded neighborhoods of Hell's Kitchen and teaching mothers how to dress, feed, and bathe their babies.

Dramatic increases in average life span in the late 19th century and 20th century, is widely credited to public health achievements, such as vaccination programmes and control of many infectious diseases including polio, diphtheria, yellow fever and smallpox; effective health and safety policies such as road traffic safety and occupational safety; improved family planning; tobacco control measures; and programmes designed to decrease non-communicable diseases by acting on known risk factors such as a person's background, lifestyle and environment.

Another major public health improvement was the decline in the "urban penalty" brought about by improvements in sanitation. These improvements included chlorination of drinking water, filtration and sewage treatment which led to the decline in deaths caused by infectious waterborne diseases such as cholera and intestinal diseases.

Recent

Large parts of the developing world remained plagued by largely preventable or treatable infectious diseases and poor maternal and child health, exacerbated by malnutrition and poverty. The WHO reports that a lack of exclusive breastfeeding during the first six months of life contributes to over a million avoidable child deaths each year. Intermittent preventive therapy aimed at treating and preventing malaria episodes among pregnant women and young children is one public health measure in endemic countries.

Each day brings new front-page headlines about public health: emerging infectious diseases such as SARS, rapidly making its way from China to Canada, the United States and other geographically distant countries; reducing inequities in health care access through publicly funded health insurance programmes; the HIV/AIDS pandemic and its spread from certain high-risk groups to the general population in many countries, such as in South Africa; the increase of childhood obesity and the concomitant increase in type II diabetes among children; the social, economic and health effects of adolescent pregnancy; and the public health challenges related to natural disasters such as the 2004 Indian Ocean tsunami, 2005's Hurricane Katrina in the United States and the 2010 Haiti earthquake.

Since the 1980s, the growing field of population health has broadened the focus of public health from individual behaviours and risk factors to population-level issues such as inequality, poverty, and education. Modern public health is often concerned with addressing determinants of health across a population. There is a recognition that our health is affected by many factors including where we live, genetics, our income, our educational status and our social relationships; these are known as "social determinants of health." A social gradient in health runs through society. The poorest generally suffer the worst health, but even the middle classes will generally have worse health outcomes than those of a higher social stratum. The new public health advocates for population-based policies that improve health in an equitable manner.

Public Health 2.0

Public Health 2.0 is a movement within public health that aims to make the field more accessible to the general public and more user-driven. The term is used in three senses. In the first sense, "Public Health 2.0" is similar to "Health 2.0" and describes the ways in which traditional public health practitioners and institutions are reaching out (or could reach out) to the public through social media and health blogs.

In the second sense, "Public Health 2.0" describes public health research that uses data gathered from social networking sites, search engine queries, cell phones, or other technologies. In the third sense, "Public Health 2.0" is used to describe public health activities that are completely user-driven. An example is the collection and sharing of information about environmental radiation levels after the March 2011 tsunami in Japan. In all cases, Public Health 2.0 draws on ideas from Web 2.0, such as crowdsourcing, information sharing, and user-centred design.

Education and Training

Education and training of public health professionals is available throughout the world in Medical Schools, Veterinary Schools, Schools of Nursing, Schools of Public Health, and Schools of Public Affairs. The training typically requires a university degree with a focus on core disciplines of biostatistics, epidemiology, health services administration, health policy, health education, behavioural science and environmental health. The National Commission for Health Education Credentialing (NCHEC) offers a national certification, Certified Health Education Specialist, C.H.E.S., for those who meet the eligibility requirements.

Schools of Public Health

In the United States, the Welch-Rose Report of 1915 has been viewed as the basis for the critical movement in the history of the institutional schism between public health and medicine because it led to the establishment of schools of public health supported by the Rockefeller Foundation. The report was authored by William Welch, founding dean of the Johns Hopkins Bloomberg School of Public Health, and Wycliffe Rose of the Rockefeller Foundation. The report focused more on research than practical education. Some have blamed the Rockefeller Foundation's 1916 decision to support the establishment of schools of public health for creating the schism between public health and medicine and legitimizing the rift between medicine's laboratory investigation of the mechanisms of disease and public health's nonclinical concern with environmental and social influences on health and wellness.

Even though schools of public health had already been established in Canada, Europe and North Africa, the United States had still maintained the traditional system of housing faculties of public health within their medical institutions. A $25,000 donation from businessman Samuel Zemurray instituted the School of Public Health and Tropical Medicine at Tulane University in 1912 conferring its first doctor of public health degree in 1914. The Johns Hopkins School of Hygiene and Public Health became the an independent, degree-granting institution for research and training in public health, and the largest public health training facility in the United States, when it was founded in 1916. By 1922, schools of public health were established at Columbia, Harvard and Yale on the Hopkins model. By 1999 there were twenty nine schools of public health in the US, enrolling around fifteen thousand students.

Over the years, the types of students and training provided have also changed. In the beginning, students who enrolled in public health schools typically had already obtained a medical degree; public health school training was largely a second degree for medical professionals. However, in 1978, 69% of American students enrolled in public health schools had only a bachelor's degree.

Degrees in Public Health

Schools of public health offer a variety of degrees which generally fall into two categories: professional or academic. The two major postgraduate degrees are the Master of Public Health (M.P.H.) or the Master of Science in Public Health (MSPH). Doctoral studies in this field include Doctor of Public Health (DrPH) and Doctor of Philosophy (Ph.D.) in a subspeciality of greater Public Health disciplines. DrPH is regarded as a professional leadership degree and Ph.D. as more of an academic degree.

Professional degrees are oriented towards practice in public health settings. The Master of Public Health, Doctor of Public Health, Doctor of Health Science (DHSc) and the Master of Health Care Administration are examples of degrees which are geared towards people who want careers as practitioners of public health in health departments, managed care and community-based organizations, hospitals and consulting firms among others. Master of Public Health degrees broadly fall into two categories, those that put more emphasis on an understanding of epidemiology and statistics as the scientific basis of public health practice and those that include a more eclectic range of methodologies. A Master of Science of Public Health is similar to an MPH but is considered an academic degree (as opposed to a professional degree) and places more emphasis on quantitative methods and research. The same distinction can be made between the DrPH and the DHSc. The DrPH is considered a professional degree and the DHSc is an academic degree.

Academic degrees are more oriented towards those with interests in the scientific basis of public health and preventive medicine who wish to pursue careers in research, university teaching in graduate programmes, policy analysis and development, and other high-level public health positions. Examples of academic degrees are the Master of Science, Doctor of Philosophy, Doctor of Science (ScD), and Doctor of Health Science (DHSc). The doctoral programmes are distinct from the MPH and other professional programmes by the addition of advanced coursework and the nature and scope of a dissertation research project.

In the United States, the Association of Schools of Public Health represents Council on Education for Public Health (CEPH) accredited schools of public health. Delta Omega is the honour society for graduate studies in public health. The society was founded in 1924 at the Johns Hopkins School of Hygiene and Public Health. Currently, there are approximately 68 chapters throughout the United States and Puerto Rico.

Public Health Programmes

Today, most governments recognize the importance of public health programmes in reducing the incidence of disease, disability, and the effects of aging and other physical and mental health conditions, although public health generally receives significantly less government funding compared with medicine. In recent years, public health programmes providing vaccinations have made strides in promoting health, including the eradication of smallpox, a disease that plagued humanity for thousands of years.

The World Health Organization (WHO) identifies core functions of public health programmes including:

- providing leadership on matters critical to health and engaging in partnerships where joint action is needed;
- shaping a research agenda and stimulating the generation, translation and dissemination of valuable knowledge;
- setting norms and standards and promoting and monitoring their implementation;
- articulating ethical and evidence-based policy options;
- monitoring the health situation and assessing health trends.

In particular, public health surveillance programmes can:

- serve as an early warning system for impending public health emergencies;
- document the impact of an intervention, or track progress towards specified goals; and
- monitor and clarify the epidemiology of health problems, allow priorities to be set, and inform health policy and strategies.
- diagnose, investigate, and monitor health problems and health hazards of the community

Public health surveillance has led to the identification and prioritization of many public health issues facing the world today, including HIV/AIDS, diabetes, waterborne diseases, zoonotic diseases, and antibiotic resistance leading to the reemergence of infectious diseases such as tuberculosis. Antibiotic resistance, also known as drug resistance, was the theme of World Health Day 2011. Although the prioritization of pressing public health issues is important, Laurie Garrett argues that there are following consequences. When foreign aid is funneled into disease-specific programmes, the importance of public health in general is disregarded. This public health problem of stovepiping is thought to create a lack of funds to combat other existing diseases in a given country.

For example, the WHO reports that at least 220 million people worldwide suffer from diabetes. Its incidence is increasing rapidly, and it is projected that the number of diabetes deaths will double by the year 2030. In a June 2010 editorial in the medical journal *The Lancet*, the authors opined that "The fact that type 2 diabetes, a largely preventable disorder, has reached epidemic proportion is a public health humiliation." The risk of type 2 diabetes is closely linked with the growing problem of obesity. The WHO's latest estimates highlighted that globally approximately 1.5 billion adults were overweight in 2008, and nearly 43 million children under the age of five were overweight in 2010. The United States is the leading country with 30.6% of its population being obese. Mexico follows behind with 24.2% and the United Kingdom with 23%. Once considered a problem in high-income countries, it is now on the rise in low-income countries, especially in urban settings. Many public health programmes are increasingly dedicating attention and resources to the issue of obesity, with objectives to address the underlying causes including healthy diet and physical exercise.

Some programmes and policies associated with public health promotion and prevention can be controversial. One such example is programmes focusing on the prevention of HIV transmission through safe sex campaigns and needle-exchange programmemes. Another is the control of tobacco smoking. Changing smoking behavior requires long-term strategies, unlike the fight against communicable diseases, which usually takes a shorter period for effects to be observed. Many nations have implemented major initiatives to cut smoking, such as increased taxation and bans on smoking in some or all public places. Proponents argue by presenting evidence that smoking is one of the major killers, and that therefore governments have a duty to reduce the death rate, both through limiting passive (second-hand) smoking and by providing fewer opportunities for people to smoke. Opponents say that this undermines individual freedom and personal responsibility, and worry that the state may be emboldened to remove more and more choice in the name of better population health overall.

Simultaneously, while communicable diseases have historically ranged uppermost as a global health priority, non-communicable diseases and the underlying behavior-related risk factors have been at the bottom. This is changing however, as illustrated by the United Nations hosting its first General Assembly Special Summit on the issue of non-communicable diseases in September 2011.

Many health problems are due to maladaptive personal behaviours. From an evolutionary psychology perspective, over consumption of novel substances that are harmful is due to the activation of an evolved reward system for substances such as drugs, tobacco, alcohol, refined salt, fat, and carbohydrates. New technologies such as modern transportation also cause reduced physical activity. Research has found that behavior is more effectively changed by taking evolutionary motivations into consideration instead of only presenting information about health effects. Thus, the increased use of soap and hand-washing to prevent diarrhea is much more effectively promoted if its lack of use is associated with the emotion of disgust. Disgust is an evolved system for avoiding contact with substances that spread infectious diseases. Examples might include films that show how fecal matter contaminates food. The marketing industry has long known the importance of associating products with high status and attractiveness to others. Conversely, it has been argued that emphasizing the harmful and undesirable effects of tobacco smoking on other persons and imposing smoking bans in public places have been particularly effective in reducing tobacco smoking.

Applications in Health Care

As well as seeking to improve population health through the implementation of specific population-level interventions, public health contributes to medical care by identifying and assessing population needs for health care services, including:

- Assessing current services and evaluating whether they are meeting the objectives of the health care system
- Ascertaining requirements as expressed by health professionals, the public and other stakeholders
- Identifying the most appropriate interventions
- Considering the effect on resources for proposed interventions and assessing their cost-effectiveness
- Supporting decision making in health care and planning health services including any necessary changes.
- Informing, educating, and empowering people about health issues

Implementing Effective Improvement Strategies

To improve public health, one important strategy is to promote modern medicine and scientific neutrality to drive the public health policy and campaign, which is recommended by Armanda Solorzana, through a case study of the Rockefeller Foundation's hookworm campaign in Mexico in the 1920s. Soloranza argues that public health policy can't concern only politics or economics. Political concerns can lead government officials to hide the real numbers of people affected by disease in their regions, such as upcoming elections. Therefore, scientific neutrality in making public health policy is critical; it can ensure treatment needs are met regardless of political and economic conditions.

The history of public health care clearly shows the global effort to improve health care for all. However, in modern-day medicine, real, measurable change has not been clearly seen, and critics argue that this lack of improvement is due to ineffective methods that are being implemented. As argued by Paul E. Farmer, structural interventions could possibly have a large impact, and yet there are numerous problems as to why this strategy has yet to be incorporated into the health system. One of the main reasons that he suggests could be the fact that physicians are not properly trained to carry out structural interventions, meaning that the ground level health care professionals cannot implement these improvements. While structural interventions can not be the only area for improvement, the lack of coordination between socioeconomic factors and health care for the poor could be counterproductive, and end up causing greater inequity between the health care services received by the rich and by the poor. Unless health care is no longer treated as a commodity, global public health can ultimately not be achieved. This being the case, without changing the way in which health care is delivered to those who have less access to it, the universal goal of public health care cannot be achieved.

10 Essential Public Health Services

The 10 Essential Public Health Services codify the responsibilities of public health agencies and institutions.

Purposes of Public Health

Organized according to the "three fundamental purposes of public health"— assessment, policy development, and assurance—the essential services include the following:

Assessment

1. Monitor health status to identify community health problems.
2. Diagnose and Investigate health problems and health hazards in the community.

Policy Development

1. Inform, Educate, and Empower people about health issues.
2. Mobilize community partnerships to identify and solve health problems.
3. Develop policies and plans that support individual and community health efforts.

Assurance

1. Enforce laws and regulations that protect and ensure public health and safety.
2. Link people to needed personal health services and assure the provision of health care when otherwise unavailable.

3. Assure a competent public and personal health care workforce.
4. Evaluate Effectiveness, Accessibility, and Quality of Personal and Population-Based Health Services.
5. Research for New Insights and Innovative Solutions to Health Problems.

History

In 1988, the Institute of Medicine (IOM) released an assessment of the U.S. public health system titled, *The Future of Public Health.* The report described the network of county, state, and national public health agencies as being in "disarray" and prompted a national discussion about the state of public health in the country. Questioning the ability of existing public health systems to provide essential services, the report sought to establish a comprehensive framework delineating the "three fundamental purposes of public health." These purposes included "assessment, policy development, and assurance." Though health policy academicians identified with and understood the IOM framework, policy makers found its highly conceptual language difficult to apply. Therefore, as part of President Clinton's 1994 healthcare reform efforts, a federal working-group was tasked with reviewing and supplementing the framework. Under the auspices of both the Centre for Disease Control and Prevention's (CDC) Public Health Practice Programme Office and the Office of Disease Prevention and Health Promotion, the group sought to

1. explain what public health is,
2. clarify the role of public health within the larger healthcare system and
3. provide accountability by linking public health performance to health outcomes.

These efforts culminated in the publication of *The Essential Services of Public Health* in late 1994.

The report was well received. Public health agencies and professional organizations began to align guidelines and employ self-assessment tools in support of the ten Essential Services. The CDC launched a number of research projects aimed at developing strategies for measuring how well public health agencies provided the services. Many of these studies were the first of their kind and ushered in an era of health agency monitoring and assessment.

In 2002, the CDC and several national public health associations launched the National Public Health Performance Standards

Programme (NPHPSP). With the goal of developing a consensus-based set of performance standards for state and local public health delivery systems, the NPHPSP adopted the Essential Public Health Services as "the fundamental framework" underpinning its assessment strategy. The NPHSP consists of three instruments— The State Public Health System Assessment, The Local Public Health System Assessment, and The Local Public Health Governance Assessment—and covers the gamut of public health action as described by the Essential Public Health Services.

Ten Essential Public Health Services

Monitor Health Status to Identify Community Health Problems

It is essential for public health organizations to monitor the health status of populations in order to identify trends and to target health resources. Components of this service include: utilization of appropriate tools to interpret and disseminate data to audiences of interest; collaboration in integrating and managing public health; and accurate and periodic assessment of the community's health status. Specifically, public health organizations can monitor the health status of their populations by creating a disease reporting system, community health profiles, and health surveys. For example, the Los Angeles Department of Public Health completes a Los Angeles County Health Survey (LACHS) every two to four years to obtain population-based data. This information is used for public health assessment and planning and for evaluating changes in health over time in Los Angeles County.

Diagnose and Investigate Health Problems and Health Hazards in the Community

In order to appropriately allocate public health resources, it is essential to diagnose and investigate health problems and hazards in the community. Components in this service include: population-based screening of diseases; access to public health laboratories capable of completing rapid screening and high volume testing; and epidemiologic investigations of disease outbreaks and patterns of disease. The Los Angeles County Health and Examination Survey (LA HANES) was piloted in 2011 and aims to establish a profile description of health outcomes of residents of Los Angeles County (e.g. adult obesity and cardiovascular disease is monitored via collection of physical measurements such as blood pressure and body mass index). These survey results will inform public education and chronic disease prevention efforts. Emergency preparedness is also an essential component of public health organizations. Teams must be available and prepared to combat natural disasters, severe weather, outbreaks, bioterrorism, mass casualties and chemical emergencies.

Inform, Educate, and Empower People About Health Issues

Once public health priorities have been established through monitoring and investigation of health problems in the community, educational activities that promote improved health should be disseminated. Components in this service include: both the availability of health information and educational resources and the presence of health education and health promotion programmes. This can be achieved through media advocacy and social marketing. An example of this is the Eat Less, Weigh Less campaign executed by the Los Angeles County Department of Public Health that aims to increase awareness about appropriate portion sizes using advertisements on buses, billboards and social media. It is also essential to establish health education and health promotion programme partnerships with organizations in the community, such as schools, churches and employment facilities.

Mobilize Community Partnerships to Identify and Solve Health Problems

Public health organizations on the local, state and national level can mobilize community partnerships to identify and solve health problems. Components of this service include: building coalitions to utilize the full range of available resources; convening and facilitating partnerships that will undertake defined health improvement projects; and provide assistance to partners and communities to solve health problems. Of particular importance is identification of potential stakeholders who will contribute to or benefit from public health activities. First 5 LA is a community partner who supports targeted programmes that address the needs of Los Angeles County children ages zero to five and their families. They work closely with the Los Angeles County Department of Public Health to improve the physical and emotional health of this population. It is important to note that many of these stakeholders may not be considered to be health-related at first glance. For example, organizations involved in urban planning may be influential in improving the health of its residents. This could include increasing the walkability of a community or the number of parks or bike trails in a neighbourhood.

Develop Policies and Plans That Support Individual and Community Health Efforts

Policies can be effective in modifying human behavior and reducing negative health outcomes. Components in this service include:

development of policy to guide the practice of public health; alignment of resources and strategies for community health efforts; and systematic health planning strategies to guide community health improvement. In response to increasing rates of obesity and cardiovascular disease, the New York City Board of Health passed a ban on the sale of sodas and other sugary drinks larger than 16 ounces at restaurants, street carts and movie theaters. In addition to policies that can support health efforts, laws can reduce negative health outcomes.

For example, dram shop liability is a law that holds the owner or server at a bar or restaurant where a patron consumed their last alcoholic beverage responsible for injuries or deaths caused as a result of alcohol-related incidents. A systematic review completed by the Task Force on Community Preventive Services, found strong evidence of the effectiveness of this law in reducing alcohol-related harms.

Enforce Laws and Regulations That Protect and Ensure Public Health and Safety

It is important that individuals and organizations comply with existing laws and regulations in order to ensure the overall health and safety of the general public. Components of this service include: reviewing, evaluating, and revising laws and regulations put in place to protect the health and safety of the public; educating persons and organizations about these laws and regulations to improve compliance and encourage enforcement of them; and enforcing actions that protect the health of the public (e.g., protection of drinking water; enforcement of clean air standards; enforcement of laws prohibiting the sale of alcoholic and tobacco products to minors, of laws concerning seat belt and child safety seat use; mandating childhood immunizations; facilitating timely follow-ups in the event of hazards and outbreaks of exposure-related diseases; monitoring quality of health services; conducting the timely review of new drugs, biologics, and medical devices; ensuring food safety; and enforcing housing and sanitation codes).

Link People to Needed Personal Health Services and Assure the Provision of Health Care When Otherwise Unavailable

Having access to care when it is needed is important in helping individuals prevent and avoid unfavourable health outcomes and medical costs. At the local level, components of this service include: identifying populations that face barriers to accessing health services and addressing their personal health needs, assuring the linkage of these populations to appropriate health services by coordinating provider services, and developing and implementing interventions that address the barriers they face in attempting to access care. At the state and governance levels, components of this service include: assessing access to and availability of state health services; partnering with public, private, and non-profit sectors to provide a coordinated system of health care; assuring access to this coordinated health care system by using outreach efforts that link individuals to the health services they need; developing and implementing a continuous improvement process to assure the equitable distribution of resources for those in greatest need of these services. The National HIV/AIDS Strategy (NHAS) employs this service idea as one of the action steps for achieving increased access to care and improved health outcomes for people living with HIV.

Assure a Competent Public and Personal Health Care Workforce

Health care workers and staff who are competent (i.e., skilled in the core principles of public health practice) are more likely to provide care and other services more effectively and efficiently compared to those who are not. Components of this service include: making sure that the workforce meets the health needs of the population, maintaining public health workforce standards by developing and implementing efficient licensure and credentialing processes and incorporating core public health competencies into personnel systems, and adopting continuous quality improvement methods and long-term learning opportunities for public health workforce members.

In two 2002 reports, the Institute of Medicine (IOM) recommended instituting a certification examination as a way of ensuring minimum competence in public health. Web-based training strategies may be useful in providing the long-term learning opportunities that many current and upcoming public health workers need in order to serve as well-informed advocates of public health and safety.

Evaluate Effectiveness, Accessibility, and Quality of Personal and Population-Based Health Services

Given scarce resources, it is important to keep track of whether or not programmes and/or policies end up producing intended outcomes. Components of this service include: assessing the accessibility, quality and effectiveness of services and programmes delivered; providing policymakers with the information they need in order to make well-informed decisions regarding the allocation of scarce resources; tracking efficiency, effectiveness, and quality of services analysing data on health status and service utilization; and striving to improve the public health system's capacity to well serve the population. Cost-effectiveness analysis has been proposed as one possible strategy for informing policymakers on how best to allocate health care resources.

Research for New Insights and Innovative Solutions to Health Problems

Through research, the health and health care problems that individuals face can be better understood, and therefore be better and more appropriately addressed given the evidence provided by such research efforts. Components of this service include: fostering the development of a continuum of innovative solutions for health programming in terms of both practical field-based efforts as well as academic efforts, establishing a consortium of research institutions and other institutions of higher learning to encourage more collaborative and cross-cutting efforts, and ensuring the public health system's capacity to perform timely epidemiological and health policy analyses.

Chapter 2

Hygiene

Hygiene (which comes from the name of the Greek goddess of health, Hygieia), is a set of practices performed for the preservation of health. Whereas in popular culture and parlance it can often mean mere 'cleanliness', hygiene in its fullest and original meaning goes much beyond that to include all circumstances and practices, lifestyle issues, premises and commodities that engender a safe and healthy environment.

Figure: *Washing one's hands, a form of hygiene, is the most effective way to prevent the spread of infectious disease.*

While in modern medical sciences there is a set of standards of hygiene recommended for different situations, what is considered hygienic or not can vary between different cultures, genders and etarian groups. Some regular hygienic practices may be considered good habits by a society while the neglect of hygiene can be considered disgusting, disrespectful or even threatening.

Sanitation in its current US *popular* meaning is often (incorrectly) taken to be merely the hygienic disposal and treatment by the civic authority of potentially unhealthy human waste, such as household garbage and sewage, and the maintenance of the sewerage and drainage infrastructure. In the UK the term 'sanitation' has unfortunately come closer to meaning water and waste plumbing and disposal, and it is not used to include garbage collection and disposal. The full and proper meaning of 'sanitation' is closer to the full meaning of 'hygiene' and includes the control of water and air quality; vectors; healthful housing; safe products; safe food and working conditions. The more recent broad term 'environmental health' equates to the original meaning of sanitation.

Concept of Hygiene

Hygiene is an old concept related to medicine, as well as to personal and professional care practices related to most aspects of living. In medicine and in home (domestic) and everyday life settings, hygiene practices are employed as preventative measures to reduce the incidence and spreading of disease.

In the manufacture of food, pharmaceutical, cosmetic and other products, good hygiene is a key part of quality assurance i.e. ensuring that the product complies with microbial specifications appropriate to its use. The terms cleanliness (or cleaning) and hygiene are often used interchangeably, which can cause confusion. In general, hygiene mostly means practices that prevent spread of disease-causing organisms. Since cleaning processes (e.g., hand washing) remove infectious microbes as well as dirt and soil, they are often the means to achieve hygiene.

Other uses of the term appear in phrases including: *body hygiene, personal hygiene, sleep hygiene, mental hygiene, dental hygiene,* and *occupational hygiene,* used in connection with public health. *Hygiene* is also the name of a branch of science that deals with the promotion and preservation of health, also called hygienic. Hygiene practices vary widely, and what is considered acceptable in one culture might not be acceptable in another.

Medical Hygiene

Medical hygiene pertains to the hygiene practices related to the administration of medicine, and medical care, that prevents or minimizes disease and the spreading of disease.

Medical hygiene practices include:

- Isolation or quarantine of infectious persons or materials to prevent spread of infection.
- Sterilization of instruments used in surgical procedures.
- Use of protective clothing and barriers, such as masks, gowns, caps, eyewear and gloves.
- Proper bandaging and dressing of injuries.
- Safe disposal of medical waste.
- Disinfection of reusables (i.e. linen, pads, uniforms)
- Scrubbing up, hand-washing, especially in an operating room, but in more general health-care settings as well, where diseases can be transmitted

Most of these practices were developed in the 19th century and were well established by the mid-20th century. Some procedures (such as disposal of medical waste) were refined in response to late-20th century disease outbreaks, notably AIDS and Ebola.

Home and Everyday Life Hygiene

Home hygiene pertains to the hygiene practices that prevent or minimize disease and the spreading of disease in home (domestic) and in everyday life settings such as social settings, public transport, the work place, public places etc. Hygiene in home and everyday life settings plays an important part in preventing spread of infectious diseases. It includes procedures used in a variety of domestic situations such as hand hygiene, respiratory hygiene, food and water hygiene, general home hygiene (hygiene of environmental sites and surfaces), care of domestic animals, and home healthcare (the care of those who are at greater risk of infection).

At present, these components of hygiene tend to be regarded as separate issues, although all are based on the same underlying microbiological principles. Preventing the spread of infectious diseases means breaking the chain of infection transmission. The simple principle is that, if the chain of infection is broken, infection cannot spread. In response to the need for effective codes of hygiene in home and everyday life settings the International Scientific Forum on Home Hygiene has developed a risk-based approach (based on Hazard Analysis

Critical Control Point (HACCP), which has come to be known as "targeted hygiene". Targeted hygiene is based on identifying the routes of spread of pathogens in the home, and applying hygiene procedures at critical points at appropriate times to break the chain of infection.

The main sources of infection in the home are people (who are carriers or are infected), foods (particularly raw foods) and water, and domestic animals (in western countries more than 50% of homes have one or more pets). Additionally, sites that accumulate stagnant water—such as sinks, toilets, waste pipes, cleaning tools, face cloths—readily support microbial growth, and can become secondary reservoirs of infection, though species are mostly those that threaten "at risk" groups. Germs (potentially infectious bacteria, viruses etc.) are constantly shed from these sources via mucous membranes, faeces, vomit, skin scales, etc. Thus, when circumstances combine, people become exposed, either directly or via food or water, and can develop an infection. The main "highways" for spread of germs in the home are the hands, hand and food contact surfaces, and cleaning cloths and utensils. Germs can also spread via clothing and household linens, such as towels. Utilities such as toilets and wash basins, for example, were invented for dealing safely with human waste, but still have risks associated with them, which may become critical at certain times, e.g., when someone has sickness or diarrhea. Safe disposal of human waste is a fundamental need; poor sanitation is a primary cause of diarrhea disease in low income communities. Respiratory viruses and fungal spores are also spread via the air.

Good home hygiene means targeting hygiene procedures at critical points, at appropriate times, to break the chain of infection i.e. to eliminate germs before they can spread further. Because the "infectious dose" for some pathogens can be very small (10-100 viable units, or even less for some viruses), and infection can result from direct transfer from surfaces via hands or food to the mouth, nasal mucosa or the eye, 'hygienic cleaning' procedures should be sufficient to eliminate pathogens from critical surfaces. Hygienic cleaning can be done by:

- Mechanical removal (i.e. cleaning) using a soap or detergent. To be effective as a hygiene measure, this process must be followed by thorough rinsing under running water to remove germs from the surface.
- Using a process or product that inactivates the pathogens in situ. Germ kill is achieved using a "micro-biocidal" product i.e. a disinfectant or antibacterial product or waterless hand sanitizer, or by application of heat.

- In some cases combined germ removal with kill is used, e.g. laundering of clothing and household linens such as towels and bedlinen.

Hand Washing

Hand washing for hand hygiene is the act of cleaning one's hands with or without the use of water or another liquid, or with the use of soap or e.g. ash, for the purpose of removing soil, dirt, and/or microorganisms.

Medical hand hygiene pertains to the hygiene practices related to the administration of medicine and medical care that prevents or minimizes disease and the spreading of disease. The main medical purpose of washing hands is to cleanse the hands of pathogens (including bacteria or viruses) and chemicals which can cause personal harm or disease. This is especially important for people who handle food or work in the medical field, but it is also an important practice for the general public. People can become infected with respiratory illnesses such as influenza or the common cold, for example, if they don't wash their hands before touching their eyes, nose, or mouth. Indeed, the Centres for Disease Control and Prevention (CDC) has stated: "It is well documented that one of the most important measures for preventing the spread of pathogens is effective hand washing." As a general rule, handwashing protects people poorly or not at all from droplet- and airborne diseases, such as measles, chickenpox, influenza, and tuberculosis. It protects best against diseases transmitted through fecal-oral routes (such as many forms of stomach flu) and direct physical contact (such as impetigo).

Symbolic hand washing, using water only to wash hands, is a part of ritual handwashing featured in many religions, including Bahá'í Faith, Hinduism, and tevilah and netilat yadayim in Judaism. Similar to these are the practices of Lavabo in Christianity, Wudu in Islam and Misogi in Shintô.

Substances Used

Soap and Detergents

Removal of microorganisms from skin is enhanced by the addition of soaps or detergents to water. The main action of soaps and detergents is to reduce barriers to solution, and increase solubility. Water is an inefficient skin cleanser because fats and proteins, which are components of organic soil, are not readily dissolved in water. Cleansing is, however, aided by a reasonable flow of water.

Water Temperature

Hot water that is comfortable for washing hands is not hot enough to kill bacteria. Bacteria grow much faster at body temperature (37 C). However, warm, soapy water is more effective than cold, soapy water at removing the natural oils on your hands which hold soils and bacteria. Contrary to popular belief however, scientific studies have shown that using warm water has no effect on reducing the microbial load on hands.

Solid Soap

Solid soap, because of its reusable nature, may hold bacteria acquired from previous uses. Yet, it is unlikely that any bacteria are transferred to users of the soap, as the bacteria are rinsed off with the foam.

Antibacterial Soap

Antibacterial soaps have been heavily promoted to a health-conscious public. To date, there is no evidence that using recommended antiseptics or disinfectants selects for antibiotic-resistant organisms in nature. However, antibacterial soaps contain common antibacterial agents such as Triclosan, which has an extensive list of resistant strains of organisms. So, even if antibiotic resistant strains aren't selected for by antibacterial soaps, they might not be as effective as they are marketed to be.

A comprehensive analysis from the University of Oregon School of Public Health indicated that plain soaps are as effective as consumer-grade anti-bacterial soaps containing triclosan in preventing illness and removing bacteria from the hands.

Hand Antiseptic

A hand sanitizer or hand antiseptic is a non-water-based hand hygiene agent. In the late 1990s and early part of the 21st century, alcohol rub non-water-based hand hygiene agents (also known as alcohol-based hand rubs, antiseptic hand rubs, or hand sanitizers) began to gain popularity. Most are based on isopropyl alcohol or ethanol formulated together with a thickening agent such as Carbomer into a gel, or a humectant such as glycerin into a liquid, or foam for ease of use and to decrease the drying effect of the alcohol.

Hand sanitizers containing a minimum of 60 to 95% alcohol are efficient germ killers. Alcohol rub sanitizers kill bacteria, multi-drug resistant bacteria (MRSA and VRE), tuberculosis, and some viruses (including HIV, herpes, RSV, rhinovirus, vaccinia, influenza, and hepatitis) and fungus. Alcohol rub sanitizers containing 70% alcohol kill 99.97% (3.5 Log reduction, similar to 35 Decibel reduction) of the bacteria on hands 30 seconds after application and 99.99% to 99.999% (4-5 log reduction) of the bacteria on hands 1 minute after application.

Hand sanitizers are most effective against bacteria and less effective against some viruses. Alcohol-based hand sanitizers are almost entirely ineffective against norovirus or Norwalk type viruses, the most common cause of contagious gastroenteritis.

The CDC recommends hand washing over hand sanitizer rubs, particularly when hands are visibly dirty. The increasing use of these agents is based on their ease of use and rapid killing activity against micro-organisms; however, they should not serve as a replacement for proper hand washing unless soap and water are unavailable.

Frequent use of alcohol-based hand sanitizers can cause dry skin unless emollients and/or skin moisturizers are added to the formula. The drying effect of alcohol can be reduced or eliminated by adding glycerin and/or other emollients to the formula. In clinical trials, alcohol-based hand sanitizers containing emollients caused substantially less skin irritation and dryness than soaps or antimicrobial detergents. Allergic contact dermatitis, contact urticaria syndrome or hypersensitivity to alcohol or additives present in alcohol hand rubs rarely occur. The lower tendency to induce irritant contact dermatitis became an attraction as compared to soap and water hand washing. Despite their effectiveness, non-water agents do not cleanse the hands of organic material, but simply disinfect them. It is for this reason that hand sanitizers are not as effective as soap and water at preventing the spread of many pathogens, since the pathogens still remain on the hands.

Alcohol-free hand sanitizer efficacy is heavily dependent on the ingredients and formulation, and historically has significantly under-performed alcohol and alcohol rubs. More recently, formulations that use benzalkonium chloride have been shown to have persistent and cumulative antimicrobial activity after application, unlike alcohol, which has been shown to decrease in efficacy after repeated use, probably due to progressive adverse skin reactions. Purell has been shown to fail to meet the FDA 21 CFR 333.470 performance standards for health-care personnel antiseptic hand washes, not just as a consequence of the decrease in effectiveness with repeated use, but due to a lack of persistence in antimicrobial activity after application and the decrease in effectiveness with heavy soil loads. In the same study, HandClens was shown to meet and exceed the FDA performance standards.

Ash or Mud

Many people in low-income communities cannot afford soap and use ash or soil instead. Ash or soil may be more effective than water alone, but may be less effective than soap. Evidence quality is poor. One concern is that if the soil or ash is contaminated with microorganisms it may increase the spread of disease rather than decrease it. Like soap, ash is also a disinfecting agent (alkaline). WHO recommended ash or sand as alternative to soap when soap is not available.

Techniques

Soap and Water

In overview, one must use soap and if warm running water if possible, and wash all skin and nails thoroughly. However, ash can substitute soap and cold water can also be used.

First one should rinse hands with warm water, keeping hands below wrists and forearms, to prevent contaminated water from moving from the hands to the wrists and arms. The warm water helps to open pores, which helps with the removal of microorganisms, without removing skin oils. One should use five millilitres of liquid soap, to completely cover the hands, and rub wet, soapy hands together, outside the running water, for at least 20 seconds. The most commonly missed areas are the thumb, the wrist, the areas between the fingers, and under fingernails. Artificial nails and chipped nail polish harbour microorganisms.

Then one should rinse thoroughly, from the wrist to the fingertips to ensure that any microorganisms fall off the skin rather than onto skin. One should use a paper towel to turn off the water. Dry hands and arms with a clean towel, disposable or not, and use a paper towel to open the door.

Moisturizing lotion is often recommended to keep the hands from drying out; Dry skin can lead to skin damage which can increase the risk for the transmission of infection.

Various low-cost options can be made to facilitate handwashing where tap-water and/or soap is not available e.g. pouring water from a hanging a jerrycan or gourd with suitable holes and/or using ash if needed in developing countries.

Hand Antiseptics

Enough hand antiseptic or alcohol rub must be used to thoroughly wet or cover both hands. The front and back of both hands and between and the ends of all fingers are rubbed for approximately 30 seconds until the liquid, foam or gel is dry. As well as finger tips must be washed well too rubbing them in both palms alternatively.

Drying

Effective drying of the hands is an essential part of the hand hygiene process, but there is some debate over the most effective form of drying in washrooms. A growing volume of research suggests paper towels are much more hygienic than the electric hand dryers found in many washrooms.

In 2008, a study was conducted by the University of Westminster, London, and sponsored by the paper-towel industry the European Tissue Symposium, to compare the levels of hygiene offered by paper towels, warm-air hand dryers and the more modern jet-air hand dryers. The key findings were:

- after washing and drying hands with the warm-air dryer, the total number of bacteria was found to increase on average on the finger pads by 194% and on the palms by 254%
- drying with the jet-air dryer resulted in an increase on average of the total number of bacteria on the finger pads by 42% and on the palms by 15%
- after washing and drying hands with a paper towel, the total number of bacteria was reduced on average on the finger pads by up to 76% and on the palms by up to 77%.

The scientists also carried out tests to establish whether there was the potential for cross contamination of other washroom users and the washroom environment as a result of each type of drying method. They found that:

- the jet-air dryer, which blows air out of the unit at claimed speeds of 400 mph, was capable of blowing micro-organisms from the hands and the unit and potentially contaminating other washroom users and the washroom environment up to 2 metres away.
- use of a warm-air hand dryer spread micro-organisms up to 0.25 metres from the dryer.
- paper towels showed no significant spread of micro-organisms.

In 2005, in a study conducted by TUV Product and Umwelt, different hand drying methods were evaluated.

The following changes in the bacterial count after drying the hands were observed:

Drying method	*Effect on bacterial count*
Paper towels and roll	Decrease of 24%
Hot-air dryer	Increase of 12%

provides a directory of case studies on hand dryers vs. paper towels provided by major hand dryer manufacturers such as Excel Dryer.

Medical Use

Medical hand-washing is for a minimum of 15 seconds, using generous amounts of soap and water or gel to lather and rub each part of the hands. Hands should be rubbed together with digits interlocking. If there is debris under fingernails, a bristle brush may be used to remove it. Since germs may remain in the water on the hands, it is important to rinse well and wipe dry with a clean towel. After drying, the paper towel should be used to turn off the water (and open any exit door if necessary). This avoids re-contaminating the hands from those surfaces.

The purpose of hand-washing in the health-care setting is to remove pathogenic microorganisms ("germs") and avoid transmitting them. The *New England Journal of Medicine* reports that a lack of hand-washing remains at unacceptable levels in most medical environments, with large numbers of doctors and nurses routinely forgetting to wash their hands before touching patients. One study showed that proper hand-washing and other simple procedures can decrease the rate of catheter-related bloodstream infections by 66 percent.

The World Health Organization has published a sheet demonstrating standard hand-washing and hand-rubbing in health-care sectors. The draft guidance of hand hygiene by the organization can also be found at its website for public comment. A relevant review was conducted by Whitby *et al.* Commercial devices can measure and validate hand hygiene, if demonstration of regulatory compliance is required.

The World Health Organization has "Five Moments" for washing hands

- before patient care
- after environmental contact
- after exposure to blood/body fluids
- before an aseptic task, and
- after patient care.

The addition of antiseptic chemicals to soap ("medicated" or "antimicrobial" soaps) confers killing action to a hand-washing agent. Such killing action may be desired prior to performing surgery or in settings in which antibiotic-resistant organisms are highly prevalent.

To 'scrub' one's hands for a surgical operation, it is necessary to have a tap that can be turned on and off without touching it with the hands, some chlorhexidine or iodine wash, sterile towels for drying the hands after washing, and a sterile brush for scrubbing and another sterile instrument for cleaning under the fingernails. All jewellery should be removed. This procedure requires washing the hands and forearms up to the elbow, usually 2–6 minutes. Long scrub-times (10 minutes) are not necessary. When rinsing, water on the forearms must be prevented from running back to the hands. After hand-washing is completed, the hands are dried with a sterile cloth and a surgical gown is donned.

Medical hand-washing became mandatory long after Hungarian physician Ignaz Semmelweis discovered its effectiveness in preventing disease in a hospital environment. There are electronic devices that provide feedback to remind hospital staff to wash their hands when they forget. One study has found decreased infection rates with their use.

Hand Washing with Wipes

Hand washing using hand sanitizing wipes is also recommended by CDC as a convenient alternative during travelling in the absence of soap and water in certain health care settings.

Effectiveness

This hygienic behavior has been shown to cut the number of child deaths from diarrhea (the second leading cause of child deaths) by almost half and from pneumonia (the leading cause of child deaths) by one-quarter. There are five critical times in washing hands with soap and/or using of a hand antiseptic related to fecal-oral transmission: after using a bathroom (private or public), after changing a diaper, before feeding a child, before eating and before preparing food or handling raw meat, fish, or poultry, or any other situation leading to potential contamination. To reduce the spread of germs, it is also better to wash the hands and/or use a hand antiseptic before and after tending to a sick person.

For control of staphylococcal infections in hospitals, it has been found that the greatest benefit from hand-cleansing came from the first 20% of washing, and that very little additional benefit was gained when hand cleansing frequency was increased beyond 35%. Washing with plain soap results in more than triple the rate of bacterial infectious disease transmitted to food as compared to washing with antibacterial soap. Comparing hand-rubbing with alcohol-based solution with handwashing with antibacterial soap for a median time of 30 seconds each showed that the alcohol hand-rubbing reduced bacterial contamination 26% more than the antibacterial soap. But soap and water is more effective than alcohol-based hand rubs for reducing H1N1 influenza A virus and Clostridium difficile spores from hands.

Religion

In symbolic hand washing using water only to wash hands is a part of ritual handwashing as a feature of many religions, including Bahá'í Faith, Hinduism and tevilah and netilat yadayim in Judaism. Similar to these are the practices of Lavabo in Christianity, Wudu in Islam and Misogi in Shintô.

Hand Washing Behavior

The phrase "washing one's hands of" something, means declaring one's unwillingness to take responsibility for the thing or share complicity in it. In the New Testament book of Matthew, verse 27:24 gives an account of Pontius Pilate washing his hands of the decision to crucify Jesus: "When Pilate saw that he could prevail nothing, but that rather a tumult was made, he took water, and washed his hands before the multitude, saying, 'I am innocent of the blood of this just person'.

In Shakespeare's Macbeth, Lady Macbeth begins to compulsively wash her hands in an attempt to cleanse an imagined stain, representing her guilty conscience regarding crimes she had committed and induced her husband to commit. It has also been found that people, after having recalled or contemplated unethical acts, tend to wash hands more often than others, and tend to value hand washing equipment more. Furthermore, those who are allowed to wash their hands after such a contemplation are less likely to engage in other "cleansing" compensatory actions, such as volunteering.

Excessive hand washing is commonly seen as a symptom of obsessive-compulsive disorder (OCD).

Pros and Cons of Hand Washing Practices

Pros

- helps minimize the spread of influenza
- diarrhea prevention
- avoiding respiratory infections
- a preventive measure for infant deaths at their home-birth-deliveries
- improved handwashing practices have been shown to lead to small improvements in the length growth in children under five years of age

Cons

- prone to skin damage

Respiratory Hygiene

Correct respiratory and hand hygiene when coughing and sneezing reduces the spread of germs particularly during the cold and flu season.

- Carry tissues and use them to catch coughs and sneezes
- Dispose of tissues as soon as possible
- Clean your hands by hand washing or using an alcohol hand sanitizer.

Food Hygiene at Home

Food hygiene is concerned with the hygiene practices that prevent food poisoning. The five key principles of food hygiene, according to WHO, are:

1. Prevent contaminating food with mixing chemicals spreading from people, pets, and pests.
2. Separate raw and cooked foods to prevent contaminating the cooked foods.
3. Cook foods for the appropriate length of time and at the appropriate temperature to kill pathogens.
4. Store food at the proper temperature.
5. Use safe water and raw materials

Household Water Treatment and Safe Storage

Household water treatment and safe storage ensure drinking water is safe for consumption. Drinking water quality remains a significant problem, not only in developing countries but also in developed countries; even in the European region it is estimated that 120 million people do not have access to safe drinking water. Point-of-use water quality interventions can reduce diarrheal disease in communities where water quality is poor, or in emergency situations where there is a breakdown in water supply. Since water can become contaminated during storage at home (e.g. by contact with contaminated hands or using dirty storage vessels), safe storage of water in the home is also important.

Methods for treatment of drinking water, include:

1. Chemical disinfection using chlorine or iodine
2. Boiling
3. Filtration using ceramic filters

4. Solar disinfection - Solar disinfection is an effective method, especially when no chemical disinfectants are available.
5. UV irradiation - community or household UV systems may be batch or flow-though. The lamps can be suspended above the water channel or submerged in the water flow.
6. Combined flocculation/disinfection systems – available as sachets of powder that act by coagulating and flocculating sediments in water followed by release of chlorine.
7. Multibarrier methods – Some systems use two or more of the above treatments in combination or in succession to optimize efficacy.

Hygiene in the Kitchen, Bathroom and Toilet

Routine cleaning of (hand, food and drinking water) sites and surfaces (such as toilet seats and flush handles, door and tap handles, work surfaces, bath and basin surfaces) in the kitchen, bathroom and toilet reduces the risk of spread of germs. The infection risk from the toilet itself is not high, provided it is properly maintained, although some splashing and aerosol formation can occur during flushing, particularly where someone in the family has diarrhea. Germs can survive in the scum or scale left behind on baths and wash basins after washing and bathing.

Water left stagnant in the pipes of showers can be contaminated with germs that become airborne when the shower is turned on. If a shower has not been used for some time, it should be left to run at a hot temperature for a few minutes before use.

Thorough cleaning is important in preventing the spread of fungal infections. Molds can live on wall and floor tiles and on shower curtains. Mold can be responsible for infections, cause allergic responses, deteriorate/damage surfaces and cause unpleasant odours. Primary sites of fungal growth are inanimate surfaces, including carpets and soft furnishings. Air-borne fungi are usually associated with damp conditions, poor ventilation or closed air systems.

Cleaning of toilets and hand wash facilities is important to prevent odours and make them socially acceptable. Social acceptance is an important part of encouraging people to use toilets and wash their hands.

Laundry Hygiene

Laundry hygiene pertains to the practices that prevent or minimize disease and the spreading of disease via soiled clothing and household linens such as towels. Items most likely to be contaminated with pathogens are those that come into direct contact with the body, e.g., underwear, personal towels, facecloths, nappies. Cloths or other fabric items used during food preparation, or for cleaning the toilet or cleaning up material such as faeces or vomit are a particular risk.

Microbiological and epidemiological data indicates that clothing and household linens etc. are a risk factor for infection transmission in home and everyday life settings as well as institutional settings, although the lack of quantitative data directly linking contaminated clothing to infection in the domestic setting makes it difficult to assess the extent of the risk. Although microbiological data indicates that risks from clothing and household linens are somewhat less than those associated with hands, hand contact and food contact surfaces, and cleaning cloths, nevertheless these risks needs to be appropriately managed through effective laundering practices. In the home, this routine should be carried out as part of a multibarrier approach to hygiene which also includes hand, food, respiratory and other hygiene practices.

Infection risks from contaminated clothing etc. can increase significantly under certain conditions. e.g. in healthcare situations in hospitals, care homes and the domestic setting where someone has diarrhoea, vomiting, or a skin or wound infection. It also increases in circumstances where someone has reduced immunity to infection.

Hygiene measures, including laundry hygiene, are an important part of reducing spread of antibiotic resistant strains. In the community, otherwise healthy people can become persistent skin carriers of MRSA, or faecal carriers of enterobacteria strains which can carry multi-antibiotic resistance factors (e.g. NDM-1 or ESBL-producing strains). The risks are not apparent until, for example, they are admitted to hospital, when they can become "self infected" with their own resistant organisms following a surgical procedure. As persistent nasal, skin or bowel carriage in the healthy population spreads "silently" across the world, the risks from resistant strains in both hospitals and the community increases. In particular the data indicates that clothing and household linens are a risk factor for spread of S. aureus (including MRSA and PVL-producing MRSA strains), and that effectiveness of laundry processes may be an important factor in defining the rate of community spread of these strains. Experience in the USA suggests that these strains are transmissible within families, but also in community settings such as prisons, schools and sport teams. Skin-to-skin contact (including unabraded skin) and indirect contact with contaminated objects such as towels, sheets and sports equipment seem to represent the mode of transmission.

During laundering, temperature, together with the action of water and detergent work together to reduce microbial contamination levels on fabrics. During the wash cycle soil and microbes are detached from fabrics and suspended into the wash water. These are then "washed away" during the rinse and spin cycles. In addition to physical removal, micro-organisms can be killed by thermal inactivation which increases as the temperature is increased. Chemical inactivation of microbes by the surfactants and activated oxygen-based bleach used in detergents also contributes to the hygiene effectiveness of laundering. Adding hypochlorite bleach in the washing process also achieves inactivation of microbes. A number of other factors can also contribute including drying and ironing.

Laundry detergents contain a mix of ingredients including surfactants, builders, optical brighteners, etc. Cleaning action arises primarily from the action of the surfactants and other ingredients, which are designed to maximise release and suspension of dirt and microbes into the wash liquid, together with enzymes and/or an activated oxygen-based bleach which digest and remove stains. Although activated oxygen bleach is included in many powder detergents to digest and remove stains, it also produces some chemical inactivation of bacteria, fungi and viruses. As a rule of thumb, powders and tablets normally contain an activated oxygen bleach, but liquids, and all products (liquid or powder) used for "coloureds" do not. Surfactants also exert some chemical inactivation action against certain species although the extent of their action is not known.

In 2013 the International Scientific Forum on Home Hygiene (IFH) reviewed some 30 studies of the hygiene effectiveness of laundering at various temperatures ranging from room temperature to 70 °C, under varying conditions. A key finding was the lack of standardisation and control within studies, and the variability in test conditions between studies such as wash cycle time, number of rinses etc. The consequent variability in the data (i.e. the reduction in contamination on fabrics) obtained, in turn makes it extremely difficult to propose guidelines for laundering with any confidence, based on currently available data. As a result there is significant variability in the recommendations for hygienic laundering of clothing etc. given by different agencies.

Of concern is recent data suggesting that, in reality, modern domestic washing machines do not reach the temperature specified on the machine controls.

Medical Hygiene at Home

Medical hygiene pertains to the hygiene practices that prevents or minimizes disease and the spreading of disease in relation to administering medical care to those who are infected or who are more "at risk" of infection in the home. Across the world, governments are increasingly under pressure to fund the level of healthcare that people expect. Care of increasing numbers of patients in the community, including at home is one answer, but can be fatally undermined by inadequate infection control in the home.

Increasingly, all of these "at-risk" groups are cared for at home by a carer who may be a household member who thus requires a good knowledge of hygiene. People with reduced immunity to infection, who are looked after at home, make up an increasing proportion of the population (currently up to 20%). The largest proportion are the elderly who have co-morbidities, which reduce their immunity to infection. It also includes the very young, patients discharged from hospital, taking immuno-suppressive drugs or using invasive systems, etc. For patients discharged from hospital, or being treated at home special "medical hygiene" procedures may need to be performed for them e.g. catheter or dressing replacement, which puts them at higher risk of infection.

Antiseptics may be applied to cuts, wounds abrasions of the skin to prevent the entry of harmful bacteria that can cause sepsis. Day-to-day hygiene practices, other than special medical hygiene procedures are no different for those at increased risk of infection than for other family members. The difference is that, if hygiene practices are not correctly carried out, the risk of infection is much greater.

Home Hygiene in Low-income Communities

In the developing world, for decades, universal access to water and sanitation has been seen as the essential step in reducing the preventable ID burden, but it is now clear that this is best achieved by programmes that integrate hygiene promotion with improvements in water quality and availability, and sanitation. About 2 million people die every year due to diarrheal diseases, most of them are children less than 5 years of age.

The most affected are the populations in developing countries, living in extreme conditions of poverty, normally peri-urban dwellers or rural inhabitants. Providing access to sufficient quantities of safe water, the provision of facilities for a sanitary disposal of excreta, and introducing sound hygiene behaviours are of capital importance to reduce the burden of disease caused by these risk factors.

Research shows that, if widely practiced, hand washing with soap could reduce diarrhea by almost fifty percent and respiratory infections by nearly twenty-five percent Hand washing with soap also reduces the incidence of skin diseases, eye infections like trachoma and intestinal worms, especially ascariasis and trichuriasis.

Other hygiene practices, such as safe disposal of waste, surface hygiene, and care of domestic animals, are also important in low income communities to break the chain of infection transmission.

Disinfectants and Antibacterials in Home Hygiene

Chemical disinfectants are products that kill germs (harmful bacteria, viruses and fungi). If the product is a disinfectant, the label on the product should say "disinfectant" and/or "kills" germs or bacteria etc. Some commercial products, e.g. bleaches, even though they are technically disinfectants, say that they "kill germs", but are not actually labelled as "disinfectants". Not all disinfectants kill all types of germs. All disinfectants kill bacteria (called bactericidal). Some also kill fungi (fungicidal), bacterial spores (sporicidal) and/or viruses (virucidal).

An antibacterial product is a product that acts against bacteria in some unspecified way. Some products labelled "antibacterial" kill bacteria while others may contain a concentration of active ingredient that only prevent them multiplying. It is, therefore, important to check whether the product label states that it "kills" bacteria." An antibacterial is not necessarily anti-fungal or anti-viral unless this is stated on the label. The term sanitizer has been used to define substances that both clean and disinfect. More recently this term has been applied to alcohol-based products that disinfect the hands (alcohol hand sanitizers). Alcohol hand sanitizers however are not considered to be effective on soiled hands.

The term biocide is a broad term for a substance that kills, inactivates or otherwise controls living organisms. It includes antiseptics and disinfectants, which combat micro-organisms, and also includes pesticides.

Personal Hygiene

Personal hygiene involves those practices performed by an individual to care for one's bodily health and well being, through cleanliness. Motivations for personal hygiene practice include reduction of personal illness, healing from personal illness, optimal health and sense of well being, social acceptance and prevention of spread of illness to others. What is considered proper personal hygiene can be cultural-specific and may change over time. In some cultures removal of body hair is considered proper hygiene. Other practices that are generally considered proper hygiene include bathing regularly, washing hands regularly and especially before handling food, washing scalp hair, keeping hair short or removing hair, wearing clean clothing, brushing one's teeth, cutting finger nails, besides other practices. Some practices are gender-specific, such as by a woman during her menstrual cycle. People tend to develop a routine for attending to their personal hygiene needs. Other personal hygienic practices would include covering one's mouth when coughing, disposal of soiled tissues appropriately, making sure toilets are clean, and making sure food handling areas are clean, besides other practices. Some cultures do not kiss or shake hands to reduce transmission of bacteria by contact.

Personal grooming extends personal hygiene as it pertains to the maintenance of a good personal and public appearance, which need not necessarily be hygienic. It may involve, for example, using deodorants or perfume, shaving, or combing, besides other practices.

Excessive Body Hygiene

Excessive Body Hygiene and Allergies

The hygiene hypothesis was first formulated in 1989 by Strachan who observed that there was an inverse relationship between family size and development of atopic allergic disorders – the more children in a family, the less likely they were to develop these allergies. From this, he hypothesised that lack of exposure to "infections" in early childhood transmitted by contact with older siblings could be a cause of the rapid rise in atopic disorders over the last thirty to forty years. Strachan further proposed that the reason why this exposure no longer occurs is, not only because of the trend towards smaller families, but also "improved household amenities and higher standards of personal cleanliness".

Although there is substantial evidence that some microbial exposures in early childhood can in some way protect against allergies, there is no evidence that we need exposure to harmful microbes (infection) or that we need to suffer a clinical infection. Nor is there evidence that hygiene measures such as hand washing, food hygiene etc. are linked to increased susceptibility to atopic disease. If this is the case, there is no conflict between the goals of preventing infection and minimising allergies. A consensus is now developing among experts that the answer lies in more fundamental changes in lifestyle etc. that have led to decreased exposure to certain microbial or other species, such as helminths, that are important for development of immuno-regulatory mechanisms. There is still much uncertainty as to which lifestyle factors are involved.

Although media coverage of the hygiene hypothesis has declined, a strong 'collective mindset' has become established that dirt is 'healthy' and hygiene somehow 'unnatural'. This has caused concern among health professionals that everyday life hygiene behaviours, which are the foundation of public health, are being undermined.

In response to the need for effective hygiene in home and everyday life settings, the International Scientific Forum on Home Hygiene has developed a "risk-based" or targeted approach to home hygiene that seeks to ensure that hygiene measures are focussed on the places, and at the times most critical for infection transmission. Whilst targeted hygiene was originally developed as an effective approach to hygiene practice, it also seeks, as far as possible, to sustain "normal" levels of exposure to the microbial flora of our environment to the extent that is important to build a balanced immune system.

Excessive Body Hygiene of Internal Ear Canals

Excessive body hygiene of the ear canals can result in infection or irritation. The ear canals require less body hygiene care than other parts of the body, because they are sensitive, and the body system adequately cares for these parts. Most of the time the ear canals are self-cleaning; that is, there is a slow and orderly migration of the skin lining the ear canal from the eardrum to the outer opening of the ear. Old earwax is constantly being transported from the deeper areas of the ear canal out to the opening where it usually dries, flakes, and falls out. Attempts to clean the ear canals through the removal of earwax can actually reduce ear canal cleanliness by pushing debris and foreign material into the ear that the natural movement of ear wax out of the ear would have removed.

Excessive Body Hygiene of Skin

Excessive body hygiene of the skin can result in skin irritation. The skin has a natural layer of oil, which promotes elasticity, and protects the skin from drying. When washing, unless using aqueous creams with compensatory mechanisms, this layer is removed leaving the skin unprotected.

Excessive application of soaps, creams, and ointments can also adversely affect certain of the natural processes of the skin. For examples, soaps and ointments can deplete the skin of natural protective oils and fat-soluble content such as cholecalciferol (vitamin D3), and external substances can be absorbed, to disturb natural hormonal balances.

Culinary (Food) Hygiene

Culinary hygiene pertains to the practices related to food management and cooking to prevent food contamination, prevent food poisoning and minimize the transmission of disease to other foods, humans or animals.

Culinary hygiene practices specify safe ways to handle, store, prepare, serve and eat food.

Culinary practices include:

- Cleaning and disinfection of food-preparation areas and equipment (for example using designated cutting boards for preparing raw meats and vegetables). Cleaning may involve use of chlorine bleach, ethanol, ultraviolet light, etc. for disinfection.
- Careful avoidance of meats contaminated by trichina worms, salmonella, and other pathogens; or thorough cooking of questionable meats.
- Extreme care in preparing raw foods, such as sushi and sashimi.
- Institutional dish sanitizing by washing with soap and clean water.
- Washing of hands thoroughly before touching any food.
- Washing of hands after touching uncooked food when preparing meals.
- Not using the same utensils to prepare different foods.
- Not sharing cutlery when eating.
- Not licking fingers or hands while or after eating.
- Not reusing serving utensils that have been licked.
- Proper storage of food so as to prevent contamination by vermin.
- Refrigeration of foods (and avoidance of specific foods in environments where refrigeration is or was not feasible).
- Labeling food to indicate when it was produced (or, as food manufacturers prefer, to indicate its "best before" date).
- Proper disposal of uneaten food and packaging.

Personal Service Hygiene

Personal service hygiene pertains to the practices related to the care and use of instruments used in the administration of personal care services to people:

Personal hygiene practices include:

- Sterilization of instruments used by service providers including hairdressers, aestheticians, and other service providers.
- Sterilization by autoclave of instruments used in body piercing and tattoo marking.
- Cleaning hands.

History of Hygienic Practices

The earliest written account of Elaborate codes of hygiene can be found in several Hindu texts, such as the Manusmriti and the Vishnu Purana. Bathing is one of the five Nitya karmas (daily duties) in Hinduism, and not performing it leads to sin, according to some scriptures.

Regular bathing was a hallmark of Roman civilization. Elaborate baths were constructed in urban areas to serve the public, who typically demanded the infrastructure to maintain personal cleanliness. The complexes usually consisted of large, swimming pool-like baths, smaller cold and hot pools, saunas, and spa-like facilities where individuals could be depilated, oiled, and massaged. Water was constantly changed by an aqueduct-fed flow. Bathing outside of urban centres involved smaller, less elaborate bathing facilities, or simply the use of clean bodies of water. Roman cities also had large sewers, such as Rome's Cloaca Maxima, into which public and private latrines drained. Romans didn't have demand-flush toilets but did have some toilets with a continuous flow of water under them. (Similar toilets are seen in Acre Prison in the film *Exodus.*)

Until the late 19th Century, only the elite in Western cities typically possessed indoor facilities for relieving bodily functions. The poorer majority used communal facilities built above cesspools in backyards and courtyards. This changed after Dr. John Snow discovered that cholera was transmitted by the fecal contamination of water. Though it took decades for his findings to gain wide acceptance, governments and sanitary reformers were eventually convinced of the health benefits of using sewers to keep human waste from contaminating water. This encouraged the widespread adoption of both the flush toilet and the moral imperative that bathrooms should be indoors and as private as possible.

Islamic Hygienical Jurisprudence

Since the 7th century, Islam has always placed a strong emphasis on hygiene. Other than the need to be ritually clean in time for the daily prayer (Arabic: *Salat*) through Wudu and Ghusl, there are a large number of other hygiene-related rules governing the lives of Muslims. Other issues include the Islamic dietary laws. In general, the Qur'an advises Muslims to uphold high standards of physical hygiene and to be ritually clean whenever possible.

Hygiene in Medieval Europe

Contrary to popular belief and although the Early Christian leaders, such as Boniface I, condemned bathing as unspiritual, bathing and sanitation were not lost in Europe with the collapse of the Roman Empire. Soapmaking first became an established trade during the so-called "Dark Ages". The Romans used scented oils (mostly from Egypt), among other alternatives.

Northern Europeans were not in the habit of bathing: in the ninth century Notker the Stammerer, a Frankish monk of St Gall, related a disapproving anecdote that attributed ill results of personal hygiene to an Italian fashion:

There was a certain deacon who followed the habits of the Italians in that he was perpetually trying to resist nature. He used to take baths, he had his head very closely shaved, he polished his skin, he cleaned his nail, he had his hair cut as short as if it were turned on a lathe, and he wore linen underclothes and a snow-white shirt.

Secular medieval texts constantly refer to the washing of hands before and after meals, but Sone de Nansay, hero of a 13th-century romance, discovers to his chagrin that the Norwegians do not wash up after eating. In the 11th and 12th centuries, bathing was essential to the Western European upper class: the Cluniac monasteries to which they resorted or retired were always provided with bathhouses, and even the monks were required to take full immersion baths twice a year, at the two Christian festivals of renewal, though exhorted not to uncover themselves from under their bathing sheets. In 14th century Tuscany, the newlywed couple's bath together was such a firm convention one such couple, in a large coopered tub, is illustrated in fresco in the town hall of San Gimignano.

Bathing had fallen out of fashion in Northern Europe long before the Renaissance, when the communal public baths of German cities were in their turn a wonder to Italian visitors. Bathing was replaced by the heavy use of sweat-bathing and perfume, as it was thought in Europe that water could carry disease into the body through the skin. Bathing encouraged an erotic atmosphere that was played upon by the writers of romances intended for the upper class; in the tale of Melusine the bath was a crucial element of the plot. "Bathing and grooming were regarded with suspicion by moralists, however, because they unveiled the attractiveness of the body. Bathing was said to be a prelude to sin, and in the penitential of Burchard of Worms we find a full catalogue of the sins that ensued when men and women bathed together." Medieval church authorities believed that public bathing created an environment open to immorality and disease; the 26 public baths of Paris in the late 13th century were strictly overseen by the civil authorities. At a later date Roman Catholic Church officials even banned public bathing in an unsuccessful effort to halt syphilis epidemics from sweeping Europe.

Modern sanitation was not widely adopted until the 19th and 20th centuries. According to medieval historian Lynn Thorndike, people in Medieval Europe probably bathed more than people did in the 19th century. Some time after Louis Pasteur's experiments proved the germ theory of disease and Joseph Lister and others put them into practice in sanitation, hygienic practices came to be regarded as synonymous with health, as they are in modern times.

Industrial Society

A social hygiene movement in the late 19th and early 20th centuries, sometimes including mental hygiene (now mental health), sexual hygiene and racial hygiene movements, was an attempt by Progressive-era reformers to prevent and control disease by changing the public's habits through the use of scientific research methods and modern media techniques. It was also based in part on eugenics, and by the 1930s thousands of forced sterilizations of people deemed undesirable took place in America each year. After 1945 when the Nazis had taken it even further, the movement was largely discredited. The drive for cleanliness persisted, however, particularly cleanliness in children. This showed many benefits such as reduced child mortality rates. It also became increasingly commercialized, however, and may have contributed to environmental pollution, resistance to antibiotics, and even restricting the development of the immune system leading to increased incidence of diseases such as asthma or allergies.

Information Society

In connection with the development of the information society, appeared information pollution, evolving information ecology - associated with information hygiene.

Hygiene Hypothesis

In medicine, the hygiene hypothesis is a hypothesis that states that a lack of early childhood exposure to infectious agents, symbiotic microorganisms (e.g. gut flora or probiotics), and parasites increases susceptibility to allergic diseases by suppressing the natural development of the immune system. In particular, the lack of exposure is thought to lead to defects in the establishment of immune tolerance.

The hygiene hypothesis has also been called the "biome depletion theory" and the "lost friends theory".

Overview

The original formulation of the hygiene hypothesis dates from 1989 when Strachan proposed that lower incidence of infection in early childhood could be an explanation for the rapid 20th century rise in allergic diseases such as asthma and hay fever. It is now also recognised that the "reduced microbial exposure" concept applies to a much broader range of chronic inflammatory diseases than asthma and hay fever, which includes diseases such as type 1 diabetes and multiple sclerosis, and also some types of depression and cancer.

In 2003 Graham Rook proposed the "old friends hypothesis" which seems to offer a more rational explanation for the link between microbial exposure and inflammatory disorders. He argues that the vital microbial exposures are not colds, influenza, measles and other common childhood infections which have evolved relatively recently over the last 10,000 years, but rather the microbes already present during mammalian and human evolution, that could persist in small hunter gatherer groups as microbiota, tolerated latent infections or carrier states. He proposes that we have become so dependent on these "old friends" that our immune systems neither develop properly nor function properly without them.

Strachan's original formulation of the hygiene hypothesis also centred around the idea that smaller families provided insufficient microbial exposure partly because of less person to person spread of infections, but also because of "improved household amenities and higher standards of personal cleanliness". It seems likely that this was the reason he named it the "hygiene" hypothesis". Although the "hygiene revolution" of the nineteenth and twentieth centuries may have been a major factor, it now seems more likely that, although public health measures such as sanitation, potable water and garbage collection were instrumental in reducing our exposure to cholera, typhoid and so on, they also deprived us of our exposure to the "old friends" that occupy the same environmental habitats.

The rise of autoimmune diseases and acute lymphoblastic leukemia in young people in the developed world was linked to the hygiene hypothesis.

Some evidence indicates that autism is correlated to factors (such as certain cytokines) that are indicative of an immune disease. One publication speculated that the lack of early childhood exposure could be a cause of autism.

The risk of chronic inflammatory diseases also depends on factors such as diet, pollution, physical activity, obesity, socio-economic factors and stress. Genetic predisposition is also a factor.

History

Hygiene: Although the idea that exposure to certain infections may decrease the risk of allergy is not new, Strachan was one of the first to formally propose it, in an article published in the *British Medical Journal* (now the *BMJ*), in 1989. This article proposed to explain the observation that hay fever and eczema, both allergic diseases, were less common in children from larger families, which were presumably exposed to more infectious agents through their siblings, than in children from families with only one child.

The hypothesis was extensively investigated by immunologists and epidemiologists and has become an important theoretical framework for the study of chronic inflammatory disorders. It explains the increase in allergic diseases that has been seen since industrialization and the higher incidence of allergic diseases in more developed countries. Epidemiological studies continue to confirm the protective effect of large family size and of growing up on a farm. However, exposure to common childhood infections such as chickenpox or measles is not thought to be protective.

Old Friends

The "old friends hypothesis" proposed in 2003 may offer a better explanation for the link between microbial exposure and inflammatory diseases. This hypothesis argues that the vital exposures are not common childhood and other recently evolved infections, over the last 10,000 years, but rather microbes already present in hunter-gatherer times when the human immune system was evolving. Conventional childhood infections are mostly "crowd infections" that kill or immunise and thus cannot persist in isolated hunter-gatherer groups. Crowd infections started to appear after the neolithic agricultural revolution, when human populations increased in size and proximity. The microbes that co-evolved with mammalian immune systems are much more ancient. Humans became so dependent on them that their immune systems can neither develop nor function properly without them.

Rook proposed that these microbes most likely include:

- Ambient species that exist in the same environments as humans
- Species that inhabit human skin, gut and respiratory tract, and that of the animals we live with
- Organisms such as viruses and helminths (worms) that establish chronic infections or carrier states that humans can tolerate and so could co-evolve a specific immunoregulatory relationship with the immune system.

The modified hypothesis later expanded to include exposure to symbiotic bacteria and parasites.

"Evolution turns the inevitable into a necessity," this means that the majority of mammalian evolution took place in mud and rotting vegetation and more than 90 percent of human evolution took place in isolated hunter-gatherer communities and farming communities. Therefore, the human immune systems have evolved to anticipate certain types of microbial input, making the inevitable exposure into a necessity. The organisms that are implicated in the hygiene hypothesis are not proven to cause the disease prevalence, however there are sufficient data on lactobacilli, saprophytic environment mycobacteria, and helminthes and their association. These bacteria and parasites have commonly been found in vegetation, mud, and water throughout evolution.

Microbial Diversity

The "microbial diversity" hypothesis, proposed by Paolo Matricardi and developed by von Hertzen, holds that diversity and turnover of bacterial species in the gut mucosa and other sites is a key factor for priming and regulating the immune system, rather than stable colonisation with a particular species. It is not clear whether diversity per se, or that a diverse population will include certain organisms without which the immune system fails to develop. Rook likened the embryonic immune system to a computer that contains programmes but little data. During gestation and infancy exposure to diverse organisms builds a "database" that allows the immune system to identify and respond to harmful agents and normalize once the danger is eliminated.

For allergic disease, the most important times for exposure are: early in development; later during pregnancy; and the first few days or months of infancy. Exposure needs to be maintained over a significant period. This fits with evidence that delivery by Caesarean section may be associated with increased allergies, whilst breastfeeding can be protective. The extent to which exposures need to be maintained after infancy and whether these conditions could be managed by on-going exposure is as yet unknown.

Biological Basis

Allergic conditions are caused by inappropriate immunological responses to harmless antigens driven by a T_H2-mediated immune response. Many bacteria and viruses elicit a T_H1-mediated immune response, which down-regulates T_H2 responses. The mechanism of action of the hygiene hypothesis was insufficient stimulation of the T_H1 arm, stimulating the cell defence of the immune system and leading to an overactive mother T_H2 arm, stimulating the antibody-mediated immunity of the immune systems, which in turn led to allergic disease.

This explanation however, cannot explain the rise in incidence (similar to the rise of allergic diseases) of several T_H1-mediated autoimmune diseases, including inflammatory bowel disease, multiple sclerosis and type I diabetes.

An alternative explanation is that the developing immune system must receive stimuli (from infectious agents, symbiotic bacteria, or parasites) to adequately develop regulatory T cells. Without that stimuli it becomes more susceptible to autoimmune diseases and allergic diseases, because of insufficiently repressed T_H1 and T_H2 responses, respectively. For example, all chronic inflammatory disorders show evidence of failed immunoregulation. Secondly, helminths, non-pathogenic ambient pseudocommensal bacteria or certain gut commensals and probiotics) drive immunoregulation. They block or treat models of all chronic inflammatory conditions. Thirdly, some such organisms (or molecules that they secrete), specifically expand populations of regulatory T cells (Treg), or cause dendritic cells to switch to regulatory forms that preferentially drive immunoregulation. Finally, when multiple sclerosis patients become infected with helminths, the disease stops progressing and circulating myelin-recognising regulatory T cells appear in the peripheral blood. This indicates that helminths act as adjuvants for regulatory T cells. This observation led to clinical trials.

Epidemiological Evidence

The hygiene hypothesis is supported by epidemiological data. Studies have shown that various immunological and autoimmune diseases are much less common in the developing world than the industrialized world and that immigrants to the industrialized world from the developing world increasingly develop immunological disorders in relation to the length of time since arrival in the industrialized world. This is true for asthma and other chronic inflammatory disorders.

Recently, *Opisthorchis felineus* chronic helminthic infection in the endemic region of Russia was found to be associated with lower total serum cholesterol levels and a significant attenuation of atherosclerosis in humans.

Mouse studies have shown that exposure of young mice to viruses can result in a decreased incidence of type I diabetes. However timing is crucial, and coxsackieviruses, rotaviruses and lymphocytic choriomeningitis virus that can be protective when given very early and can provoke autoimmunity when given late (for instance at weaning). Rook also reviewed this issue.

In developed countries where childhood diseases were eliminated, the asthma rate for youth is approximately 10%. In the 19th century, hay-fever, an easily recognisable allergy, was a very rare condition.

Longitudinal studies in Ghana demonstrate an increase in immunological disorders as it grew more affluent and presumably cleaner. The use of antibiotics in the first year of life has been linked to asthma and other allergic diseases. The use of antibacterial cleaning products has also been associated with higher incidence of asthma. Increased asthma rates are associated with birth by Caesarean section. The data supporting links to antibiotic use and caesarean section (but not to antibacterial use) are rapidly strengthening.

Antibiotic usage, which reduces the diversity of gut microbiota, is another cited factor. Although several studies have shown associations between antibiotic use and later development of asthma or allergy, other studies suggest that the effect is due to more frequent antibiotic use in asthmatic children. Trends in vaccine use may also be relevant, but epidemiological studies provide no consistent support for a detrimental effect of vaccination/immunisation on atopy rates.

Experimental Evidence

King et al. 2004 showed that when short lived T cells were replaced during a state of too few long lived T-cells (memory T cell), because of lack of infections, the risk of developing autoimmune diseases increases. They showed that in a state of too few long lived T-cells, because of lack of infections, not enough short lived T cells could be produced by long lived T cells during homeostatic expansion. Therefore, more auto reactive T cells divide in such a state, causing multiplying auto reactive T cells with a greater risk of causing autoimmune diseases like type I diabetes or multiple sclerosis.

Cooke showed that NOD mice (which spontaneously develop type 1 diabetes) had significantly reduced incidence of this disease when infected with the helminth parasite *Schistosoma mansoni*. Other animal models also showed that helminth infections block or treat various chronic inflammatory disorders were comprehensively reviewed recently.

In November 2009 showed that Staphylococci helped reduce inflammation.

Early life exposure to specific microbe-enriched environments decreases susceptibility to diseases such as inflammatory bowel disease and asthma, whereas its absence, as in antibiotic treatment during childhood, may have the opposite effect. Olszak and colleagues, compared germ-free mice and specific-pathogen-free mice, challenged with aerosol ovoalbumin to promote allergen-induced airway inflammation. They found that early exposure to conventional microbiota protected animals from developing asthma.

Public Health Trends

Since allergies and other chronic inflammatory diseases are largely diseases of the last 100 years or so, the "hygiene" revolution of the last 200 years came under scrutiny as a possible cause. During the 1800s radical improvements to sanitation and water quality occurred in Europe and North America. The introduction of toilets and sewer systems and the cleanup of city streets, and cleaner food were part of this programme. This in turn led to a rapid decline in infectious diseases, particularly during the period 1900-1950, through reduced exposure to infectious agents.

Public health activities have also played a part in affecting diet and lifestyle, such as physical activity levels and locations.

Treatment

While no hygiene-related treatments are part of the standard of care, various approaches are under investigation. Helminth therapy is one alternative. Probiotics (drinks or foods) have never been shown to reintroduce microbes to the gut. As yet, therapeutically relevant microbes have not been specifically identified.

Lifestyle changes could increase microbial exposure, but whether this on balance improves the balance of risks remains the subject of research. Proposals include natural childbirth, sustained breast feeding and physical interaction between siblings, and encouraging children to spend more time in "uncleaned" outdoor environments.

Should these therapies become accepted, public policy implications include providing green spaces in urban areas or even providing access to agricultural environments for children.

Helminthic Therapy

Helminthic therapy is the treatment of autoimmune diseases and immune disorders by means of deliberate infestation with a helminth larva or ova. Helminthic therapy is currently being studied as a promising treatment for several (non-viral) autoimmune diseases including Crohn's disease, multiple sclerosis, asthma, and ulcerative colitis. Autoimmune liver disease can be modulated by active helminth infections. The anti-inflammatory effects of helminth infection are prompting interest and research into diseases that involve inflammation but that are not currently considered to include autoimmunity or immune dysregulation as a causative factor. Heart disease and arteriosclerosis both have similar epidemiological profiles as autoimmune diseases and both involve inflammation. Their increased incidence cannot be solely attributed to environmental factors. Recent research explored the eradication of helminths as contributing to this discrepancy.

Helminthic therapy emerged from the search for reasons why the incidence of immunological disorders and autoimmune diseases correlates with the level of industrial development.

Related therapies include use other types of infectious organisms, such as protozoa.

Cleanliness

No evidence supports the idea that reducing modern practices of cleanliness and hygiene would have any impact on rates of chronic inflammatory and allergic disorders, but a significant amount of evidence that it would increase the risks of infectious diseases. If home and personal cleanliness contributes to reduced exposure to vital microbes, its role is likely to be small. The idea that homes can be made "sterile" through excessive cleanliness is implausible. The evidence shows that, as fast as they are removed by cleaning, microbes are replaced, via dust and air from outdoors, by shedding from the body and other living things as well as from food. The key point may be that the microbial content of urban housing has altered, not because of home and personal hygiene habits, but because they are part of urban environments. Diet and lifestyle changes also affects the gut, skin and respiratory microbiota.

At the same time that concerns about allergies and other chronic inflammatory diseases have been increasing, so also have concerns about infectious disease. Infectious diseases continue to exert a heavy health toll. Preventing pandemics and reducing antibiotic resistance are global priorities. Hygiene is a cornerstone of containing these threats.

Infection Risk Management

The International Scientific Forum on Home Hygiene has developed a risk management approach to reducing home infection risks. This approach uses microbiological and epidemiological evidence to identify the key routes of infection transmission in the home. These data indicate that the critical routes involve the hands, hand and food contact surfaces and cleaning utensils. Clothing and household linens involve somewhat lower risks. Surfaces that contact the body, such as baths and hand basins, can act as infection vehicles, as can surfaces associated with toilets. Airborne transmission can be important for some pathogens. A key aspect of this approach is that it maximises protection against pathogens and infection, but is more relaxed about visible cleanliness in order to sustain normal exposure to other human, animal and environmental microbes.

Alternative Hypotheses

There are other hypotheses that try to explain the increase in allergies in developed nations. Major areas of focus include infant feeding, over-exposure and exposure to certain pollutants.

Infant feeding topics includes breastfeeding, when babies begin to eat solid foods and the type of these foods, cow's milk vs other milks and variations in milk processing.

Over-exposure to allergens in occupational situations can cause allergic responses, such as Laboratory animal allergy, bird lung, farmer's lung and bakers lung.

Another theory suggests that pollution (such as diesel exhaust) might be responsible; however, improvements in air quality since the 1970s do not self-evidently support such claims. The pool chlorine hypothesis was proposed by Albert Bernard and his colleagues as an alternative hypothesis based on epidemiological evidence in 2003.

Extensions

The rising incidence of metabolic disease, including obesity, diabetes and hypertension has been hypothesized to be exacerbated by the absence of certain infections. Inflammation has long been recognized as a major etiological factor for metabolic diseases. Chronic inflammation leading to insulin resistance is a major etiological factor for metabolic conditions apart from obesity and type-2 diabetes. Insulin resistance typically starts as an organ-specific inflammation affecting the major organs of insulin action namely adipose tissue, skeletal muscles and liver. With disease progression, the inflammation becomes more systemic and starts affecting blood vessels leading to endothelial dysfunction, a pre-stage for vasculopathies. In fact the inflammation associated with macrovasculopathies like cardio-vascular disease, cerebro-vascular disease and perivascular disease seems to be very different from microvascular complications like diabetic retinopathy, nephropathy and neuropathy. The exact cause of inflammation in IR is not known even though dietary, genetic and a variety of environmental factors have been implicated.

The reduced prevalence of lymphatic filariasis among diabetic subjects compared to non-diabetic and pre-diabetic subjects was noted, and supported the influence of childhood helminth infestations. Within the diabetic subjects, those who were filarial positive had reduced levels of pro-inflammatory markers compared to those who were filarial negative.

In mice, animals infected with helminths had lesser disease severity compared to uninfected subjects in a diet-induced obesity mice model that is well-recognized for metabolic diseases. In light of these findings, the decreasing incidence of filarial infection due to mass drug administration could potentially have an unexpected adverse impact on the prevalence of diabetes in developing countries. Infections serve as an important source of inflammation and inflammation itself can serve as a link between infections and metabolic diseases. In general, infections that promote inflammation are thought to augment metabolic diseases while those that dampen inflammation by immunomodulation can confer protection against metabolic diseases. A much higher level of complexity is brought about by the recently identified helminth induced immunomodulation in conferring protection against inflammation and insulin resistance.

Hygiene Programme

Hygiene programmes are ways of providing basic hygiene facilities to homeless people. Some are stand-alone hygiene centres, while others are at locations that also provide other services to the homeless. They are one of the more modern responses to providing services for the homeless, especially compared to things like basic homeless shelters that just provide a bed and toilet for the night, or soup kitchens, which traditionally have not even had places for patrons to wash their hands.

At a minimum, they have a toilet, wash basin, and a shower. But many have other amenities, such as a mirror to assist with shaving and applying makeup, a diaper-changing station, electric outlets for appliances such as irons, private dressing stalls, hygiene supplies such as soap and toothpaste, tampons, pads, condoms, and/or laundry facilities. Public support of hygiene programmes has been growing, due in part to the realization that, besides basic humanitarian reasons, such facilities offer homeless people an alternative to using restrooms in libraries and other public buildings.

Infection Control

Infection control is the discipline concerned with preventing nosocomial or healthcare-associated infection, a practical (rather than academic) sub-discipline of epidemiology. It is an essential, though often underrecognized and undersupported, part of the infrastructure of health care. Infection control and hospital epidemiology are akin to public health practice, practiced within the confines of a particular health-care delivery system rather than directed at society as a whole.

Infection control addresses factors related to the spread of infections within the healthcare setting (whether patient-to-patient, from patients to staff and from staff to patients, or among-staff), including prevention (via hand hygiene/hand washing, cleaning/ disinfection/sterilization, vaccination, surveillance), monitoring/ investigation of demonstrated or suspected spread of infection within a particular health-care setting (surveillance and outbreak investigation), and management (interruption of outbreaks). It is on this basis that the common title being adopted within health care is "Infection Prevention & Control."

Infection Control in Healthcare Facilities

Aseptic technique is a key component of all invasive medical procedures. Similarly, infection control measures are most effective when Standard Precautions (health care) are applied because undiagnosed infection is common.

Sterilization

Sterilization is a process intended to kill all microorganisms and is the highest level of microbial kill that is possible. Sterilizers may be heat only, steam, or liquid chemical. Effectivness of the sterilizer (e.g., a steam autoclave) is determined in three ways. First, mechanical indicators and gauges on the machine itself indicate proper operation of the machine. Second heat sensitive indicators or tape on the sterilizing bags change colour which indicate proper levels of heat or steam. And, third (most importantly) is biological testing in which a microorganism that is highly heat and chemical resistant (often the bacterial endospore) is selected as the standard challenge. If the process kills this microorganism, the sterilizer is considered to be effective. It should be noted that in order to be effective, instruments must be cleaned, otherwise the debris may form a protective barrier, shielding the microbes from the lethal process. Similarly care must be taken after sterilization to ensure sterile instruments do not become contaminated prior to use.

Sterilization, if performed properly, is an effective way of preventing bacteria from spreading. It should be used for the cleaning of the medical instruments or gloves, and basically any type of medical item that comes into contact with the blood stream and sterile tissues.

There are four main ways in which such items can be sterilized: autoclave (by using high-pressure steam), dry heat (in an oven), by using chemical sterilants such as glutaraldehydes or formaldehyde solutions or by radiation (with the help of physical agents). The first two are the most used methods of sterilizations mainly because of their accessibility and availability. Steam sterilization is one of the most effective types of sterilizations, if done correctly which is often hard to achieve. Instruments that are used in health care facilities are usually sterilized with this method.

The general rule in this case is that in order to perform an effective sterilization, the steam must get into contact with all the surfaces that are meant to be disinfected. On the other hand, dry heat sterilization, which is performed with the help of an oven, is also an accessible type of sterilization, although it can only be used to disinfect instruments that are made of metal or glass. The very high temperatures needed to perform sterilization in this way are able to melt the instruments that are not made of glass or metal.

Steam sterilization is done at a temperature of 121 C (250 F) with a pressure of 106 kPa (15 lbs/in2). In these conditions, unwrapped items must be sterilized for 20 minutes, and wrapped items for 30 minutes. The time is counted once the temperature that is needed has been reached. Steam sterilization requires four conditions in order to be efficient: adequate contact, sufficiently high temperature, correct time and sufficient moisture. Sterilization using steam can also be done at a temperature of 132 C (270 F), at a double pressure. Dry heat sterilization is performed at 170 C (340 F) for one hour or two hours at a temperature of 160 C (320 F). Dry heat sterilization can also be performed at 121 C, for at least 16 hours.

Chemical sterilization, also referred to as cold sterilization, can be used to sterilize instruments that cannot normally be disinfected through the other two processes described above. The items sterilized with cold sterilization are usually those that can be damaged by regular sterilization. Commonly, glutaraldehydes and formaldehyde are used in this process, but in different ways. When using the first type of disinfectant, the instruments are soaked in a 2-4% solution for at least 10 hours while a solution of 8% formaldehyde will sterilize the items in 24 hours or more. Chemical sterilization is generally more expensive than steam sterilization and therefore it is used for instruments that cannot be disinfected otherwise.

After the instruments have been soaked in the chemical solutions, they are mandatory to be rinsed with sterile water which will remove the residues from the disinfectants. This is the reason why needles and syringes are not sterilized in this way, as the residues left by the chemical solution that has been used to disinfect them cannot be washed off with water and they may interfere with the administered treatment. Although formaldehyde is less expensive than glutaraldehydes, it is also more irritating to the eyes, skin and respiratory tract and is classified as a potential carcinogen.

Other sterilization methods exist, though their efficiency is still controversial. These methods include gas, UV, gas plasma, and chemical sterilization with agents such as peroxyacetic acid or paraformaldehyde.

Cleaning

Infections can be prevented from occurring in homes as well. In order to reduce their chances to contract an infection, individuals are recommended to maintain a good hygiene by washing their hands after every contact with questionable areas or bodily fluids and by disposing of garbage at regular intervals to prevent germs from growing.

Disinfection

Disinfection uses liquid chemicals on surfaces and at room temperature to kill disease causing microorganisms. Ultraviolet light has also been used to disinfect the rooms of patients infected with *Clostridium difficile* after discharge. Disinfection is less effective than sterilization because it does not kill bacterial endospores.

Personal Protective Equipment

Personal protective equipment (PPE) is specialized clothing or equipment worn by a worker for protection against a hazard. The hazard in a health care setting is exposure to blood, saliva, or other bodily fluids or aerosols that may carry infectious materials such as Hepatitis C, HIV, or other blood borne or bodily fluid pathogen.

PPE prevents contact with a potentially infectious material by creating a physical barrier between the potential infectious material and the healthcare worker.

The United States Occupational Safety and Health Administration (OSHA) requires the use of Personal protective equipment (PPE) by workers to guard against blood borne pathogens if there is a reasonably anticipated exposure to blood or other potentially infectious materials.

Components of PPE include gloves, gowns, bonnets, shoe covers, face shields, CPR masks, goggles, surgical masks, and respirators. How many components are used and how the components are used is often determined by regulations or the infection control protocol of the facility in question. Many or most of these items are disposable to avoid carrying infectious materials from one patient to another patient and to avoid difficult or costly disinfection. In the US, OSHA requires the immediate removal and disinfection or disposal of a worker's PPE prior to leaving the work area where exposure to infectious material took place.

Antimicrobial Surfaces

Microorganisms are known to survive on non-antimicrobial in animate 'touch' surfaces (e.g., bedrails, over-the-bed trays, call buttons, bathroom hardware, etc.) for extended periods of time. This can be especially troublesome in hospital environments where patients with immunodeficiencies are at enhanced risk for contracting nosocomial infections.

Products made with antimicrobial copper alloy (brasses, bronzes, cupronickel, copper-nickel-zinc, and others) surfaces destroy a wide range of microorganisms in a short period of time.

The United States Environmental Protection Agency has approved the registration of 355 different antimicrobial copper alloys and one synthetic copper-infused hard surface that kill *E. coli* O157:H7, methicillin-resistant *Staphylococcus aureus* (MRSA), *Staphylococcus, Enterobacter aerogenes,* and *Pseudomonas aeruginosa* in less than 2 hours of contact.

Other investigations have demonstrated the efficacy of antimicrobial copper alloys to destroy *Clostridium difficile*, influenza A virus, adenovirus, and fungi. As a public hygienic measure in addition to regular cleaning, antimicrobial copper alloys are being installed in healthcare facilities in the U.K., Ireland, Japan, Korea, France, Denmark, and Brazil. The synthetic hard surface is being installed in the United States as well as in Israel.

Vaccination of Health Care Workers

Health care workers may be exposed to certain infections in the course of their work. Vaccines are available to provide some protection to workers in a healthcare setting. Depending on regulation, recommendation, the specific work function, or personal preference, healthcare workers or first responders may receive vaccinations for hepatitis B; influenza; measles, mumps and rubella; Tetanus, diphtheria, pertussis; N. meningitidis; and varicella. In general, vaccines do not guarantee complete protection from disease, and there is potential for adverse effects from receiving the vaccine.

Post Exposure Prophylaxis

In some cases where vaccines do not exist Post Exposure prophylaxis is another method of protecting the health care worker exposed to a life-threatening infectious disease. For example, the viral particles for HIV-AIDS can be precipitated out of the blood through the use of an antibody injection if given within 4 hours of a significant exposure.

Surveillance for Infections

Surveillance is the act of infection investigation using the CDC definitions. Determining the presence of a hospital acquired infection requires an infection control practitioner (ICP) to review a patient's chart and see if the patient had the signs and symptom of an infection. Surveillance definitions exist for infections of the bloodstream, urinary tract, pneumonia, surgical sites and gastroenteritis.

Surveillance traditionally involved significant manual data assessment and entry in order to assess preventative actions such as isolation of patients with an infectious disease. Increasingly, computerized software solutions are becoming available that assess incoming risk messages from microbiology and other online sources. By reducing the need for data entry, software can reduce the data workload of ICPs, freeing them to concentrate on clinical surveillance.

As of 1998, approximately one third of healthcare acquired infections were preventable. Surveillance and preventative activities are increasingly a priority for hospital staff. The *Study on the Efficacy of Nosocomial Infection Control* (SENIC) project by the U.S. CDC found in the 1970s that hospitals reduced their nosocomial infection rates by approximately 32 per cent by focusing on surveillance activities and prevention efforts.

Isolation

In the health care context, isolation refers to various physical measures taken to interrupt nosocomial spread of contagious diseases. Various forms of isolation exist, and are applied depending on the type of infection and agent involved, to address the likelihood of spread via airborne particles or droplets, by direct skin contact, or via contact with body fluid

Outbreak Investigation

When an unusual cluster of illness is noted, infection control teams undertake an investigation to determine whether there is a true outbreak, a pseudo-outbreak (a result of contamination within the diagnostic testing process), or just random fluctuation in the frequency of illness. If a true outbreak is discovered, infection control practitioners try to determine what permitted the outbreak to occur, and to rearrange the conditions to prevent ongoing propagation of the infection. Often, breaches in good practice are responsible, although sometimes other factors (such as construction) may be the source of the problem.

Outbreaks investigations have more than a single purpose. These investigations are carried out in order to prevent additional cases in the current outbreak, prevent future outbreaks, learn about a new disease or learn something new about an old disease. Reassuring the public, minimizing the economic and social disruption as well as teaching epidemiology are some other obvious objectives of outbreak investigations.

According to the WHO, outbreak investigations are meant to detect what is causing the outbreak, how the pathogenic agent is transmitted, where it all started from, what is the carrier, what is the population at risk of getting infected and what are the risk factors.

The results of outbreak investigations are always made public in the means of a report in which the findings are communicated to the authorities, media, scientific community and so on. These reports are commonly used as pedagogical tools.

Training in Infection Control and Health Care Epidemiology

Practitioners can come from several different educational streams. Many begin as nurses, some as medical technologists (particularly in clinical microbiology), and some as physicians (typically infectious disease specialists). Specialized training in infection control and health care epidemiology are offered by the professional organizations described below. Physicians who desire to become infection control practitioners often are trained in the context of an infectious disease fellowship.

In the United States, Certification Board of Infection Control and Epidemiology is a private company that certifies infection control practitioners based on their educational background and professional experience, in conjunction with testing their knowledge base with standardized exams. The credential awarded is CIC, Certification in Infection Control and Epidemiology. It is recommended that one has 2 years of Infection Control experience before applying for the exam. Certification must be renewed every five years.

A course in hospital epidemiology (infection control in the hospital setting) is offered jointly each year by the Centres for Disease Control and Prevention (CDC) and the Society for Healthcare Epidemiology of America.

The Association for Professionals in Infection Control and Epidemiology (APIC) offers training and courses in infection control.

Chapter 3

Standardization

Australia

In 2002, the Royal Australian College of General Practitioners published a revised standard for office-based infection control which covers the sections of managing immunisation, sterilisation and disease surveillance. However, the document on the personal hygiene of health workers is only limited to hand hygiene, waste and linen management, which may not be sufficient since some of the pathogens are air-born and could be spread through air flow.

United States

Currently, the federal regulation that describes infection control standards is found at 29 CFR Part 1910.1030 Bloodborne pathogens.

Oral Hygiene

Oral hygiene is the practice of keeping the mouth and teeth clean to prevent dental problems, most commonly, dental cavities, gingivitis, and bad breath. There are also oral pathologic conditions in which good oral hygiene is required for healing and regeneration of the oral tissues. These conditions included gingivitis, periodontitis, and dental trauma, such as subluxation, oral cysts, and following wisdom tooth extraction.

Cleaning

Cleaning of Teeth: Teeth cleaning is the removal of dental plaque and tartar from teeth to prevent cavities, gingivitis, gum disease, and tooth decay. Severe gum disease causes at least one-third of adult tooth loss. Tooth decay is the most common global disease. Over 80% of cavities occur inside pits and fissures on chewing surfaces where brushing cannot reach food left trapped after every meal or snack, and saliva or fluoride have no access to neutralise acid and remineralise demineralised teeth, unlike easy-to-reach surfaces, where fewer cavities occur.

Dental sealants, which are applied by dentists, cover and protect fissures and grooves in the chewing surfaces of back teeth, preventing food from becoming trapped thus halting the decaying process. An elastomer strip has been shown to force sealant deeper inside opposing chewing surfaces and can also force fluoride toothpaste inside chewing surfaces to aid in remineralising demineralised teeth.

Since before recorded history, a variety of oral hygiene measures have been used for teeth cleaning. This has been verified by various excavations done throughout the world, in which chew sticks, tree twigs, bird feathers, animal bones and porcupine quills were recovered. Many people used different forms of teeth cleaning tools. Indian medicine (Ayurveda) has used the neem tree, or *daatun,* and its products to create teeth cleaning twigs and similar products; a person chews one end of the neem twig until it somewhat resembles the bristles of a toothbrush, and then uses it to brush the teeth. In the Muslim world, the miswak, or *siwak,* made from a twig or root, has antiseptic properties and has been widely used since the Islamic Golden Age. Rubbing baking soda or chalk against the teeth was also common.

Generally, dentists recommend that teeth be cleaned professionally at least twice per year. Professional cleaning includes tooth scaling, tooth polishing, and, if tartar has accumulated, debridement; this is usually followed by a fluoride treatment. However, the American Dental Hygienists' Association (ADHA) publicly stated in 1998 that there is an absence of evidence that scaling and polishing provides therapeutic value. The Cochrane Oral Health Group reviewed nine studies but found them to be of insufficient quality and not enough evidence to support the claims of the benefits of regular tooth scaling or tooth polishing. Between cleanings by a dental hygienist, good oral hygiene is essential for preventing tartar build-up which causes the problems mentioned above. This is done through careful, frequent brushing with a toothbrush, combined with the use of dental floss to prevent accumulation of plaque on the teeth.

Removing Plaque

Plaque is a yellow sticky film that forms on the teeth and gums and can be seen at gum margins of teeth with a food dye. The bacteria in plaque convert carbohydrates in food (such as sugar) into acid that demineralises teeth, eventually causing cavities. Daily brushing and flossing removes plaque and can prevent tartar from forming on the teeth.

Plaque can also cause inflammation of the gum (gingivitis), making it red, tender and can easily bleed when flossing or brushing your teeth. If this is not treated, bones around the teeth can be affected by the various inflammatory factors, eventually leading to bone resorption. This condition is called periodontitis, which is mostly seen in the adult population. If not treated, the loss of bone structure may cause teeth to become mobile.

The treatment is to remove plaque inside the deep pockets between the tooth surface and the soft tissues using specialized dental equipment. If the treatment is successful, the gum will pull away from the teeth (receding gums) as a result of the cessation of the inflammatory swelling. Eating a balanced diet and limiting snacks can prevent tooth decay and periodontal disease. The *Fédération dentaire internationale* (FDI World Dental Federation) has promoted foods such as raw vegetables, plain yogurt, cheese, or fruit as dentally beneficial—this has been echoed by the American Dental Association (ADA).

Flossing

The use of dental floss is an important element of oral hygiene, since it removes plaque and decaying food remaining stuck between the teeth. This food decay and plaque cause irritation to the gums, allowing the gum tissue to bleed more easily. Acidic foods left on the teeth can also demineralise teeth, eventually causing cavities.

Flossing for a proper inter-dental cleaning is recommended at least once per day, preferably before brushing so fluoride toothpaste has better access between teeth to help remineralise teeth, prevent receding gums, gum disease, and cavities on the surfaces between the teeth.

It is recommended to use enough floss to enable easy use, usually ten or more inches with three to four inches of taut floss to put between teeth. Floss is then wrapped around the middle finger and/or index finger, and supported with the thumb on each hand. It is then held tightly to make taut, and then gently moved up and down between each tooth. It is important to floss under visible areas by curving the floss around each tooth instead of moving up and down on gums, which are much more sensitive than teeth.

However, bleeding gums are normal upon first usage of floss, and will harden with use. One should use an unused section of the floss when moving around different teeth. Removing floss from between teeth requires using the same back-and-forth motion as flossing, but gently bringing the floss up and out of gaps between teeth.

Interdental Brushes

An interdental brush, also called an interproximal brush or a proxy brush, is a small brush, typically disposable, either supplied with a reusable angled plastic handle or an integral handle, used for cleaning between teeth and between the wire of dental braces and the teeth. Brushes are available in a range of widths, colour coded as per ISO 16409. Interdental brushes are classified according to ISO standard 16409:2006. The ISO brush sizes range from 1 to 7. The ISO brush size is determined by the PHD or Passage Hole Diameter in mm. This PHD is the minimum diameter of a hole that the interdental brush will pass through without deforming the brush wire stem. A peer-reviewed clinical study has found that using a toothbrush and an interdental brush more effectively removes plaque than using a toothbrush and dental floss.

Tongue Cleaning

Cleaning the tongue as part of daily oral hygiene is essential, since it removes the white/yellow bad-breath-generating coating of bacteria, decaying food particles, fungi (such as *Candida*), and dead cells from the dorsal area of the tongue. Tongue cleaning also removes some of the bacteria species which generate tooth decay and gum problems.

Gum Care

Massaging the gums with toothbrush bristles is generally recommended for good oral health.

Oral Irrigation

Some dental professionals recommend oral irrigation as a way to clean teeth and gums.

Oral irrigators reach 3–4 mm under the gum line. Oral irrigators use a pressured, directed stream of water to disrupt plaque and bacteria.

Food and Drink

Foods that help muscles and bones also help teeth and gums. Breads and cereals are rich in vitamin B while fruits and vegetables contain vitamin C, both of which contribute to healthy gum tissue. Lean meat, fish, and poultry provide magnesium and zinc for teeth. For some people, flossing might be recommended after every meal.

Beneficial Foods

Some foods may protect against cavities by naturally containing fluorine, from which fluoride is derived. Fluoride is naturally present in all water. Community water fluoridation is the addition of fluoride to adjust the natural fluoride concentration of a community's water supply to the level recommended for optimal dental health, approximately 1.0 ppm (parts per million). One ppm is the equivalent of 1 mg/L, or 1 inch in 16 miles. Fluoride is a primary protector against dental cavities. Fluoride makes the surface of teeth more resistant to acids during the process of remineralisation. Drinking fluoridated water is recommended by some dental professionals while others say that using toothpaste alone is enough.

Milk and cheese are also rich in calcium and phosphate, and may also encourage remineralisation. All foods increase saliva production, and since saliva contains buffer chemicals this helps to stabilize the pH to near 7 (neutral) in the mouth. Foods high in fibre may also help to increase the flow of saliva and a bolus of fibre like celery string can force saliva into trapped food inside pits and fissures on chewing surfaces where over 80% of cavities occur, to dilute carbohydrate like sugar, neutralise acid and remineralise tooth like on easy to reach surfaces. Sugar-free chewing gum stimulates saliva production, and helps to clean the surface of the teeth.

According to World Dental, these are the top ten beneficial foods for teeth.

1. Green tea contains polyphenol antioxidant plant compounds that reduce plaque, cavities, and gum disease. Green tea may also reduce bad breath and strengthen the tooth enamel because of its high fluoride content.
2. Dairy foods are beneficial because of their low acidity, which reduces wear and tear on teeth. Additionally, dairy foods are high in calcium, the main component of teeth.
3. Cheese contains calcium and phosphate, which help balance pH in the mouth, preserves (and rebuilds) tooth enamel, produces saliva, and kills bacteria that cause cavities and disease.
4. Fruits such as apples, strawberries and kiwis contain Vitamin C. This vitamin helps holding the cells together. If this vitamin is neglected, gum cells can break down, making gums tender and susceptible to disease.
5. Vegetables: Vitamin A, found in pumpkins, carrots, sweet potatoes and broccoli, is necessary for the formation of tooth enamel. Crunchy vegetables may also help clean gums.
6. Onions contain antibacterial sulphur compounds. Tests show that onions kill various types of bacteria, especially when eaten raw.

7. Celery protects teeth by producing saliva which neutralizes acid that causes demineralisation and cavities. It also massages the teeth and gums.
8. Sesame seeds reduce plaque and help build tooth enamel. They are also very high in calcium.
9. Animal food: beef, chicken, turkey, and eggs contain phosphorus which, with calcium, is one of the two most vital minerals of teeth and bone.
10. Water cleans the mouth and produces saliva that deposits essential minerals into the teeth. It keeps gums hydrated and washes away particles from the teeth.

Harmful Foods

Sugars are commonly associated with dental cavities. Other carbohydrates, especially cooked starches, e.g. crisps/potato chips, may also damage teeth, although to a lesser degree (and indirectly) since starch has to be converted to sugars by salivary amylase (an enzyme in the saliva) first. Sugars that are higher in the stickiness index, such as toffee, are likely to cause more damage to teeth than those that are lower in the stickiness index, such as certain forms of chocolate or most fruits.

Sucrose (table sugar) is most commonly associated with cavities. The amount of sugar consumed at any one time is less important than how often food and drinks that contain sugar are consumed. The more frequently sugars are consumed, the greater the time during which the tooth is exposed to low pH levels, at which point demineralisation occurs (below 5.5 for most people). It is important therefore to try to encourage infrequent consumption of food and drinks containing sugar so that teeth have a chance to be repaired by remineralisation and fluoride. Limiting sugar-containing foods and drinks to meal times is one way to reduce the incidence of cavities. Sugars from fruit and fruit juices, e.g., glucose, fructose, and maltose seem equally likely to cause cavities.

Acids contained in fruit juice, vinegar and soft drinks lower the pH level of the oral cavity which causes the enamel to demineralize. Drinking drinks such as orange juice or cola throughout the day raises the risk of dental cavities tremendously.

Another factor which affects the risk of developing cavities is the stickiness of foods. Some foods or sweets may stick to the teeth and so reduce the pH in the mouth for an extended time, particularly if they are sugary. It is important that teeth be cleaned at least twice a day, preferably with a toothbrush and fluoride toothpaste, to remove any food sticking to the teeth. Regular brushing and the use of dental floss also removes the dental plaque coating the tooth surface.

Chewing gum assists oral irrigation between and around the teeth, cleaning and removing particles, but for teeth in poor condition it may damage or remove loose fillings as well. Chewing sugar free chewing gum that contains xylitol may be good for teeth.

Other

Smoking and chewing tobacco are both strongly linked with multiple dental diseases. Regular vomiting, as seen in bulimia nervosa, also causes significant damage.

Caffeine products are known to cause teeth to stain, though this can usually be cleaned by drinking fresh water after a caffeinated drink and also at the dentist by surface cleaning.

Mouthwash or mouth rinse with saline (salty water), fluoridated solution or the antiseptic chlorhexidine gluconate solution improve oral hygiene. Dental chewing gums claim to improve dental health.

Retainers can be cleaned in mouthwash or denture cleaning fluid. Dental braces may be recommended by a dentist for best oral hygiene and health. Dentures, retainers, and other appliances must be kept extremely clean. This includes regular brushing and may include soaking them in a cleansing solution such as a denture cleaner.

Oral Hygiene and Systemic Diseases

Several recent clinical studies suggest oral disease and inflammation (oral bacteria & oral infections) may be a potential risk factor for serious systemic diseases, such as:

- Cardiovascular Disease (Heart attack and Stroke)
- Bacterial Pneumonia
- Low Birth Weight/Extreme High Birth Weight
- Diabetes complications
- Osteoporosis

Injury Prevention

Injury prevention is an effort to prevent or reduce the severity of bodily injuries caused by external mechanisms, such as accidents, before they occur. Injury prevention is a component of safety and public health, and its goal is to improve the health of the population by preventing injuries and hence improving quality of life. Among laypersons, the term "accidental injury" is often used. However, "accidental" implies the causes of injuries are random in nature.. Researchers use the term "unintentional injury" to refer to injuries that are nonvolitional but preventable. Within the field of public health, efforts are also made to prevent or reduce "intentional injury."

Data from the U.S. Centres for Disease Control, for example, show unintentional injuries are the leading cause of death from early childhood until middle adulthood. During these years, unintentional injuries account for more deaths than the next nine leading causes of death combined.

Injury prevention strategies cover a variety of approaches, many of which are classified as falling under the "3 E's" of injury prevention: education, engineering modifications, and enforcement/enactment. Some organizations, such as Safe Kids Worldwide, have expanded the list to six E's adding: evaluation, economic incentives and empowerment.

Measuring Effectiveness

Research in is challenging, because the usual outcome of interest is deaths or injuries prevented, and it is nearly impossible to measure how many people *did not* get hurt who otherwise would have. Education efforts can be measured by changes in knowledge, attitudes, beliefs and behaviours, before and after the intervention, however tying these changes back into reductions in morbidity and mortality is often problematic.

Examining trends in morbidity and mortality in the population is usually not difficult and may provide some indication of the effectiveness of injury prevention interventions. However, this approach suffers from the potential of ecological fallacy, where the data shows an association between an intervention and a change in the outcome, but there is actually no causal relationship.

Common Types of Injury Prevention

Traffic and Automobile Safety

Traffic safety and automobile safety are a major component of injury prevention because it is the leading cause of death for children and young adults into their mid 30's. Injury prevention efforts began in the early 1960s when activist Ralph Nader, exposed the automobiles as being more dangerous than necessary with his book Unsafe at Any Speed. This led to engineering changes in the way cars are designed to allow for more crush space between the vehicle and the occupant.

Engineering: vehicle crash worthiness, seat belts, airbags, locking seat belts for child seats.

Education: promote seat belt use, discourage impaired driving, promote child safety seats.

Enforcement and enactment: passage and enforcement of primary seat belt laws, speed limits, impaired driving enforcement.

Pedestrian Safety

Pedestrian safety is the focus of both epidemiological and psychological injury prevention research. Epidemiological studies typically focus on causes external to the individual such as traffic density, access to safe walking areas, socioeconomic status, injury rates, legislation for safety (e.g., traffic fines), or even the shape of vehicles which affects the severity of injuries resulting from a collision. Epidemiological data show children aged 1–4 are at greatest risk for injury in driveway and sidewalks. Children aged 5–14 are at greatest risk while attempting to cross streets.

The body of psychological research on pedestrian safety is currently much smaller than that in the epidemiological field, but is rapidly growing. Psychological pedestrian safety studies extend as far back as the mid-1980s when researchers began examining behavioural variables in children. Behavioural variables of interest include selection of crossing gaps in traffic, attention to traffic, the number of near hits or actual hits, or the routes children chose when crossing multiple streets such as while walking to school. Behavioural studies often collect such variables which imply risk of injury; e.g., children engaging in risky behaviours may be assumed to be at greater risk if actually crossing a street alone. The most common technique used in behavioural pedestrian research is the pretend road, in which a child stands some distance from the curb and watches traffic on the real road. The child then walks to the edge of the street when a crossing opportunity is chosen. Research is gradually shifting to more ecologically valid virtual reality techniques. Leading scientists in psychological pedestrian safety research are Dr. Benjamin Barton, Dr. David Schwebel and Dr. James Thomson.

Other

The following is an abbreviated topic list of some common focus areas of injury prevention efforts:

- Bicycle safety
- Boat and water safety

- Child passenger safety
- Consumer product safety
- Firearm safety
- Fire and burn safety
- Home safety
- Impaired driving
- Pedestrian safety
- Poison control
- Toy safety
- Traffic safety
- Sports injury safety
- Occupational safety and health

Patient Safety

Patient safety is a new healthcare discipline that emphasizes the reporting, analysis, and prevention of medical error that often leads to adverse healthcare events. The frequency and magnitude of avoidable adverse patient events was not well known until the 1990s, when multiple countries reported staggering numbers of patients harmed and killed by medical errors. Recognizing that healthcare errors impact 1 in every 10 patients around the world, the World Health Organization calls patient safety an endemic concern. Indeed, patient safety has emerged as a distinct healthcare discipline supported by an immature yet developing scientific framework. There is a significant transdisciplinary body of theoretical and research literature that informs the science of patient safety. The resulting patient safety knowledge continually informs improvement efforts such as: applying lessons learned from business and industry, adopting innovative technologies, educating providers and consumers, enhancing error reporting systems, and developing new economic incentives.

Prevalence of Adverse Events

Millennia ago, Hippocrates recognized the potential for injuries that arise from the well-intentioned actions of healers. Greek healers in the 4th century BC drafted the Hippocratic Oath and pledged to "prescribe regimens for the good of my patients according to my ability and my judgement and never do harm to anyone." Since then, the directive *primum non nocere* ("first do no harm) has become a central tenet for contemporary medicine. However, despite an increasing emphasis on the scientific basis of medical practice in Europe and the

United States in the late 19th Century, data on adverse outcomes were hard to come by and the various studies commissioned collected mostly anecdotal events.

In the United States, the public and the medical speciality of anesthesia were shocked in April 1982 by the ABC television programme 20/20 entitled *The Deep Sleep*. Presenting accounts of anesthetic accidents, the producers stated that, every year, 6,000 Americans die or suffer brain damage related to these mishaps. In 1983, the British Royal Society of Medicine and the Harvard Medical School jointly sponsored a symposium on anesthesia deaths and injuries, resulting in an agreement to share statistics and to conduct studies. By 1984 the American Society of Anesthesiologists (ASA) had established the Anesthesia Patient Safety Foundation (APSF). The APSF marked the first use of the term "patient safety" in the name of professional reviewing organization. Although anesthesiologists comprise only about 5% of physicians in the United States, anesthesiology became the leading medical speciality addressing issues of patient safety. Likewise in Australia, the Australian Patient Safety Foundation was founded in 1989 for anesthesia error monitoring. Both organizations were soon expanded as the magnitude of the medical error crisis became known.

To Err is Human

In the United States, the full magnitude and impact of errors in health care was not appreciated until the 1990s, when several reports brought attention to this issue. In 1999, the Institute of Medicine (IOM) of the National Academy of Sciences released a report, *To Err is Human: Building a Safer Health System*. The IOM called for a broad national effort to include establishment of a Centre for Patient Safety, expanded reporting of adverse events, development of safety programmes in health care organizations, and attention by regulators, health care purchasers, and professional societies. The majority of media attention, however, focused on the staggering statistics: from 44,000 to 98,000 preventable deaths annually due to medical error in hospitals, 7,000 preventable deaths related to medication errors alone. Within 2 weeks of the report's release, Congress began hearings and President Clinton ordered a government-wide study of the feasibility of implementing the report's recommendations. Initial criticisms of the methodology in the IOM estimates focused on the statistical methods of amplifying low numbers of incidents in the pilot studies to the general population. However, subsequent reports emphasized the striking prevalence and consequences of medical error.

The experience has been similar in other countries.

- Ten years after a groundbreaking Australian study revealed 18,000 annual deaths from medical errors, Professor Bill Runciman, one of the study's authors and president of the Australian Patient Safety Foundation since its inception in 1989, reported himself a victim of a medical dosing error.
- The Department of Health Expert Group in June 2000 estimated that over 850,000 incidents harm National Health Service hospital patients in the United Kingdom each year. On average forty incidents a year contribute to patient deaths in each NHS institution.
- In 2004, the Canadian Adverse Events Study found that adverse events occurred in more than 7% of hospital admissions, and estimated that 9,000 to 24,000 Canadians die annually after an avoidable medical error.
- These and other reports from New Zealand, Denmark and developing countries have led the World Health Organization to estimate that one in ten persons receiving health care will suffer preventable harm.

Communication

Effective communication is essential for ensuring patient safety.

Effective and Ineffective Communication

The use of effective communication among patients and healthcare professionals is critical for achieving a patient's optimal health outcome. However, ineffective communication has the opposite effect as it can lead to patient harm. Communication with regards to patient safety can be classified into two categories: prevention of adverse events and responding to adverse events. Use of effective communication can aid in the prevention of adverse events, whereas ineffective communication can contribute to these incidences. If ineffective communication contributes to an adverse event, then better and more effective communication skills must be applied in response to achieve optimal outcomes for the patient's safety. There are different modes in which healthcare professionals can work to optimize the safety of patients which include both verbal and nonverbal communication, as well as the effective use of appropriate communication technologies.

Methods of effective verbal and nonverbal communication include treating patients with respect and showing empathy, clearly communicating with patients in a way that best fits their needs, practicing active listening skills, being sensitive with regards to cultural diversity and respecting the privacy and confidentiality rights of the patient. To use appropriate communication technology, healthcare professionals must choose which channel of communication is best suited to benefit the patient.

Some channels are more likely to result in communication errors than others, such as communicating through telephone or email (missing nonverbal messages which are an important element of understanding the situation).

It is also the responsibility of the provider to know the advantages and limitations of using electronic health records, as they do not convey all information necessary to understanding patient needs. If a health care professional is not practicing these skills, they are not being an effective communicator which may affect patient outcome.

The goal of a healthcare professional is to aid a patient in achieving their optimal health outcome, which entails that the patient's safety is not at risk. Practice of effective communication plays a large role in promoting and protecting patient safety.

Teamwork and Communication

During complex situations, communication between health professionals must be at its best. There are several techniques, tools, and strategies used to improve communication. First and foremost, the team must have a clear purpose and each member should be aware of their role and be involved accordingly.

To increase the quality of communication between members, regular feedback should be provided. Strategies such as briefings allow the team to be set on their purpose and ensure that members not only share the goal but also the process they will follow to achieve it. Briefings reduce interruptions, prevent delays and build stronger relationships, resulting in a strong patient safety environment.

Debriefing is another useful strategy. Healthcare providers meet to discuss a situation, record what they learned and discuss how it might be better handled. Closed loop communication is another important technique used to ensure that the message that was sent is received and interpreted by the receiver. SBAR is a structured system designed to help team members communicate about the patient in the most convenient form possible. Communication between healthcare professionals not only helps achieve the best results for the patient but also prevents any unseen incidents.

Safety Culture

As is the case in other industries, when there is a mistake or error made people look for someone to blame. This may seem natural, but it creates a blame culture where *who* is more important than *why* or *how*. A *just culture*, also sometimes known as *no blame* or *no fault*, seeks to understand the root causes of an incident rather than just who was involved.

In health care, there is a move towards a patient safety culture. This applies the lessons learned from other industries, such as aviation, marine, and industrial, to a health care setting.

When assessing and analysing an incident, individuals involved are much more likely to be forthcoming with their own mistakes if they know that their job is not at risk. This allows a much more complete and clear picture to be formed of the facts of an event. From there, root cause analysis can occur. There are often multiple causative factors involved in an adverse or near miss event. It is only after all contributing factors have been identified that effective changes can be made that will prevent a similar incident from occurring.

Disclosure of an Incident

After an adverse event, healthcare providers need to know how to respond. Every country has its own way of dealing with an incident. In Canada, a quality improvement review is primarily used. A quality improvement review is an evaluation that is completed after an adverse event occurs with the intention to both fix the problem, as well as preventing it from happening again. The individual provinces and territories have laws on whether it is required to disclose the quality improvement review to the patient. Healthcare providers have an obligation to disclose any adverse event to their patients because of ethical and professional guidelines. If more providers participate in the quality improvement review, it can increase interdisciplinary collaboration and can sustain relationships between departments and staff. In the US, clinical peer review is used: uninvolved medical staff review the event and work toward preventing further incidents.

The disclosure of adverse events is important in maintaining trust in the relationship between healthcare provider and patient. It is also important in learning how to avoid these mistakes in the future by conducting quality improvement reviews, or clinical peer review. If the provider accurately handles the event, and disclose it to the patient and their family, he/she can avoid getting punished, which includes lawsuits, fines and suspension.

Causes of Healthcare Error

The simplest definition of a health care error is a preventable adverse effect of care, whether or not it is evident or harmful to the patient. Errors have been, in part, attributed to:

Human Factors

- Variations in healthcare provider training & experience, fatigue, depression and burnout.
- Diverse patients, unfamiliar settings, time pressures.
- Failure to acknowledge the prevalence and seriousness of medical errors.

Medical Complexity

- Complicated technologies, powerful drugs.
- Intensive care, prolonged hospital stay.

System Failures

- Poor communication, unclear lines of authority of physicians, nurses, and other care providers.
- Complications increase as patient to nurse staffing ratio increases.
- Disconnected reporting systems within a hospital: fragmented systems in which numerous hand-offs of patients results in lack of coordination and errors.
- Drug names that look alike or sound alike.
- The impression that action is being taken by other groups within the institution.
- Reliance on automated systems to prevent error.
- Inadequate systems to share information about errors hamper analysis of contributory causes and improvement strategies.
- Cost-cutting measures by hospitals in response to reimbursement cutbacks.
- Environment and design factors. In emergencies, patient care may be rendered in areas poorly suited for safe monitoring. The American Institute of Architects has identified concerns for the safe design and construction of health care facilities.
- Infrastructure failure. According to the WHO, 50% of medical equipment in developing countries is only partly usable due to lack of skilled operators or parts.

As a result, diagnostic procedures or treatments cannot be performed, leading to substandard treatment.

The Joint Commission's Annual Report on Quality and Safety 2007 found that inadequate communication between healthcare providers, or between providers and the patient and family members, was the root cause of over half the serious adverse events in accredited hospitals. Other leading causes included inadequate assessment of the patient's condition, and poor leadership or training.

Common misconceptions about adverse events are:

- "'Bad apples' or incompetent health care providers are a common cause." Many of the errors are normal human slips or lapses, and not the result of poor judgement or recklessness.
- "High risk procedures or medical specialties are responsible for most *avoidable* adverse events". Although some mistakes, such as in surgery, are easier to notice, errors occur in all levels of care. Even though complex procedures entail more risk, adverse outcomes are not usually due to error, but to the severity of the condition being treated. However, USP has reported that medication errors during the course of a surgical procedure are three times more likely to cause harm to a patient than those occurring in other types of hospital care.
- "If a patient experiences an adverse event during the process of care, an error has occurred". Most medical care entails some level of risk, and there can be complications or side effects, even unforeseen ones, from the underlying condition or from the treatment itself.

Safety Programmes in Industry

Aviation Safety: In the United States, two organizations contribute to one of the world's lowest aviation accident rates. Mandatory accident investigation is carried out by the National Transportation Safety Board, while the Aviation Safety Reporting System receives voluntary reports to identify deficiencies and provide data for planning improvements. The latter system is confidential and provides reports back to stakeholders without regulatory action. Similarities and contrasts have been noted between the "cultures of safety" in medicine and aviation. Pilots and medical personnel operate in complex environments, interact with technology, and are subject to fatigue, stress, danger, and loss of life and prestige as a consequence of error. Given the enviable record of aviation in accident prevention, a similar medical adverse event system would include both mandatory (for severe incidents) and voluntary non-punitive reporting, teamwork training, feedback on performance and an institutional commitment to data collection and analysis. The Patient Safety Reporting System (PSRS) is a programme modelled upon the Aviation Safety Reporting System and developed by the Department of Veterans Affairs (VA) and the National Aeronautics and Space Administration (NASA) to monitor patient safety through voluntary, confidential reports. Required training in crew resource management (CRM), which focused on team dynamics both inside the cockpit and outside was introduced in the early 1980's after the tragic mishap of United Airlines 173. CRM is considered an effective means of improving safety in aviation and is utilized by the DoD, NASA, and almost all commercial airlines. Many of the tenets of this training have been incorporated into medicine under the guise of Team Stepps, which was introduced by the Agency for Healthcare Research and Quality (AHRQ). The AHRQ calls this programme "an evidence-based teamwork system to improve communication and teamwork skills among health care professionals."

Near-miss Reporting: A near miss is an unplanned event that did not result in injury, illness, or damage - but had the potential to do so. Reporting of near misses by observers is an established error reduction technique in aviation, and has been extended to private industry, traffic safety and fire-rescue services with reductions in accidents and injury. AORN, a US-based professional organization of perioperative registered nurses, has put in effect a voluntary near miss reporting system (SafetyNet), covering medication or transfusion reactions, communication or consent issues, wrong patient or procedures, communication breakdown or technology malfunctions. An analysis of incidents allows safety alerts to be issued to AORN members. AlmostME is another commercially offered solution for near-miss reporting in healthcare.

Limits of the Industrial Safety Model: Unintended consequences may occur as improvements in safety are undertaken. It may not be possible to attain maximum safety goals in healthcare without adversely affecting patient care in other ways. An example is blood transfusion; in recent years, to reduce the risk of transmissible infection in the blood supply, donors with only a small probability of infection have been excluded. The result has been a critical shortage of blood for other lifesaving purposes, with a broad impact on patient care. Application of high-reliability theory and normal accident theory can help predict the organizational consequences of implementing safety measures.

Technology in Healthcare

Overview

According to a study by RAND Health, the U.S. healthcare system could save more than $81 billion annually, reduce adverse healthcare events, and improve the quality of care if health information technology (HIT) is widely adopted. The most immediate barrier to widespread adoption of technology is cost despite the patient benefit from better health, and payer benefit from lower costs. However, hospitals pay in both higher costs for implementation and potentially lower revenues (depending on reimbursement scheme) due to reduced patient length of stay. The benefits provided by technological innovations also give rise to serious issues with the introduction of new and previously unseen error types.

Types of Healthcare Technology

Handwritten reports or notes, manual order entry, non-standard abbreviations and poor legibility lead to substantial errors and injuries, according to the IOM (2000) report. The follow-up IOM report, *Crossing the Quality Chasm: A New Health System for the 21st Century*, advised rapid adoption of electronic patient records, electronic medication ordering, with computer- and internet-based information systems to support clinical decisions. This section contains only the patient safety related aspects of HIT.

Electronic Health Record (EHR)

The Electronic health record (EHR), previously known as the Electronic medical record (EMR), reduces several types of errors, including those related to prescription drugs, to emergent and preventive care, and to tests and procedures. Important features of modern EHR include automated drug-drug/drug-food interaction checks and allergy checks, standard drug dosages and patient education information. Drug Information at the point-of-care and drug dispensing points help in reducing errors. Example: India, MedCLIK. Also, these systems provide recurring alerts to remind clinicians of intervals for preventive care and to track referrals and test results. Clinical guidelines for disease management have a demonstrated benefit when accessible within the electronic record during the process of treating the patient. Advances in health informatics and widespread adoption of interoperable electronic health records promise access to a patient's records at any health care site. Still, there may be a weak link because of physicians' deficiencies in understanding the patient safety features of e.g. government approved software. Errors associated with patient misidentification may be exacerbated by EHR use, but inclusion of a prominently displayed patient photograph in the EHR can reduce errors and near misses. Portable offline emergency medical record devices have been developed to provide access to health records during widespread or extended infrastructure failure, such as in natural disasters or regional conflicts.

Active RFID Platform

These systems' basic security measures are based on sound identifying electronic tags, in order that the patient details provided in different situations are always reliable. These systems offer three differently qualified options:

- Identification upon request of health care personnel, using scanners (similar to readers for passive RFID tags or scanners for barcode labels) to identify patient semi-automatically upon presentation of patient with tag to staff
- Automatic identification upon entry of patient. An automatic identification check is carried out on each person with tags (primarily patients) entering the area to determine the presented patient in contrast to other patient earlier entered into reach of the used reader.
- Automatic identification and range estimation upon approach to most proximate patient, excluding reads from more distant tags of other patients in the same area

Any of these options may be applied whenever and wherever patient details are required in electronic form Such identifying is essential when the information concerned is critical. There are increasing numbers of hospitals that have an RFID system to identify patients, for instance: Hospital La Fe in Valencia(Spain); Wayne Memorial Hospital (USA); Royal Alexandria Hospital (UK).

Computerized Provider Order Entry (CPOE)

Prescribing errors are the largest identified source of preventable errors in hospitals (IOM, 2000; 2007). The IOM (2006) estimates that each hospitalized patient, on average, is exposed to one medication error each day.

Computerized provider order entry (CPOE), formerly called computer physician order entry, can reduce medication errors by 80% overall but more importantly decrease harm to patients by 55%. A Leapfrog (2004) survey found that 16% of US clinics, hospitals, and medical practices are expected to utilize CPOE within 2 years.

Complete Safety Medication System

A standardized bar code system for dispensing drugs might prevent 25% of drug errors. Despite ample evidence to reduce medication errors, compete medication delivery systems (barcoding and Electronic prescribing) have slow adoption by doctors and hospitals in the United States, due to concern with interoperability and compliance with future national standards. Such concerns are not inconsequential; standards for electronic prescribing for Medicare Part D conflict with regulations in many US states.

Technological Iatrogenesis

Technology induced errors are significant and increasingly more evident in care delivery systems. This idiosyncratic and potentially serious problems associated with HIT implementation has recently become a tangible concern for healthcare and information technology professionals. As such, the term technological iatrogenesis describes this new category of adverse events that are an emergent property resulting from technological innovation creating system and microsystem disturbances.

Healthcare systems are complex and adaptive, meaning there are many networks and connections working simultaneously to produce certain outcomes. When these systems are under the increased stresses caused by the diffusion of new technology, unfamiliar and new process errors often result. If not recognized, over time these new errors can collectively lead to catastrophic system failures. The term "e-iatrogenesis" can be used to describe the local error manifestation. The sources for these errors include:

- Prescriber and staff inexperience may lead to a false sense of security; that when technology suggests a course of action, errors are avoided.
- Shortcut or default selections can override non-standard medication regimens for elderly or underweight patients, resulting in toxic doses.
- CPOE and automated drug dispensing was identified as a cause of error by 84% of over 500 health care facilities participating in a surveillance system by the United States Pharmacopoeia.
- Irrelevant or frequent warnings can interrupt work flow.

Solutions include ongoing changes in design to cope with unique medical settings, supervising overrides from automatic systems, and training (and re-training) all users.

Evidence-based Medicine

Evidence-based medicine integrates an individual doctor's exam and diagnostic skills for a specific patient, with the best available evidence from medical research. The doctor's expertise includes both diagnostic skills and consideration of individual patient's rights and preferences in making decisions about his or her care. The clinician uses pertinent clinical research on the accuracy of diagnostic tests and the efficacy and safety of therapy, rehabilitation, and prevention to develop an individual plan of care. The development of evidence-based recommendations for specific medical conditions, termed clinical practice guidelines or "best practices", has accelerated in the past few years. In the United States, over 1,700 guidelines have been developed as a resource for physicians to apply to specific patient presentations. The National Institute for Health and Clinical Excellence (NICE) in the United Kingdom provides detailed "clinical guidance" for both health care professionals and the public about specific medical conditions. National Guideline Agencies from all continents collaborate in the Guidelines International Network, which entertains the largest guideline library worldwide.

Advantages:

1. Evidence-based medicine may reduce adverse events, especially those involving incorrect diagnosis, outdated or risky tests or procedures, or medication overuse.
2. Clinical guidelines provide a common framework for improving communication among clinicians, patients and non-medical purchasers of health care.
3. Errors related to changing shifts or multiple specialists are reduced by a consistent plan of care.
4. Information on the clinical effectiveness of treatments and services can help providers, consumers and purchasers of health care make better use of limited resources.
5. As medical advances become available, doctors and nurses can keep up with new tests and treatments as guidelines are improved.

Drawbacks:

1. Managed care plans may attempt limit "unnecessary" services to cut the costs of health care, despite evidence that guidelines are not designed for general screening, rather as decision-making tools when an individual practitioner evaluates a specific patient.

2. The medical literature is evolving and often controversial; development of guidelines requires consensus.
3. Implementing guidelines and educating the entire health care team within a facility costs time and resources (which may be recovered by future efficiency and error reduction).
4. Clinicians may resist evidence-based medicine as a threat to traditional relationships between patients, doctors and other health professionals, since any participant can influence decisions.
5. Failing to follow guidelines might increase the risk of liability or disciplinary action by regulators.

Quality and Safety Initiatives in Community Pharmacy Practice

Community pharmacy practice is making important advances in the quality and safety movement despite the limited number of federal and state regulations that exist and in the absence of national accreditation organizations such as the Joint Commission - a driving force for performance improvement in health care systems. Community pharmacies are using automated drug dispensing devices (robots), computerized drug utilization review tools, and most recently, the ability to receive electronic prescriptions from prescribers to decrease the risk for error and increase the likelihood of delivering high quality of care.

Quality Assurance (QA) in community practice is a relatively new concept. As of 2006, only 16 states have some form of legislation that regulates QA in community pharmacy practice. While most state QA legislation focuses on error reduction, North Carolina has recently approved legislation that requires the pharmacy QA programme to include error reduction strategies and assessments of the quality of their pharmaceutical care outcomes and pharmacy services.

Quality Improvement and Safety Initiatives in Pediatrics

Quality improvement and patient safety is a major concern in the pediatric world of health care. This next section will focus on quality improvement and patient safety initiatives in inpatient settings.

Over the last several years, pediatric groups have partnered to improve general understanding, reporting, process improvement methodologies, and quality of pediatric inpatient care. These collaborations have created a robust programme of projects, benchmarking efforts, and research. Much of the research and focus on adverse events has been on medication errors–the most frequently reported adverse event for both adult and pediatric patients. It is also of interest to note that medication errors are also the most preventable type of harm that can occur within the pediatric population. It has been reported that when pediatric medication errors occur, these patients have a higher rate of death associated with the error than adult patients. A more recent review of potential pediatric safety issues conducted by Miller, Elixhauser, and Zhan found that hospitalized children who experienced a patient safety incident, compared with those who did not, had

- 1) Length of stay 2- to 6-fold longer
- 2) Hospital mortality 2- to 18-fold greater
- 3) Hospital charges 2- to 20-fold higher

In order to reduce these errors the attention on safety needs to revolve around designing safe systems and processes. Slonim and Pollack point out that safety is critical to reduce medical errors and adverse events. These problems can range from diagnostic and treatment errors to hospital-acquired infections, procedural complications, and failure to prevent problems such as pressure ulcers. In addition to addressing quality and safety issues found in adult patients there are a few characteristics that are unique to the pediatric population.

- Development: As children mature both cognitively and physically, their needs as consumers of health care goods and services change. Therefore, planning a unified approach to pediatric safety and quality is affected by the fluid nature of childhood development.
- Dependency: Hospitalized children, especially those who are very young and/or nonverbal, are dependent on caregivers, parents, or other surrogates to convey key information associated with patient encounters. Even when children can accurately express their needs, they are unlikely to receive the same acknowledgment accorded adult patients. In addition, because children are dependent on their caregivers, their care must be approved by parents or surrogates during all encounters.
- Different epidemiology: Most hospitalized children require acute episodic care, not care for chronic conditions as with adult patients. Planning safety and quality initiatives within a framework of "wellness, interrupted by acute conditions or exacerbations," presents distinct challenges and requires a new way of thinking.

- Demographics: Children are more likely than other groups to live in poverty and experience racial and ethnic disparities in health care. Children are more dependent on public insurance, such as State Children's Health Insurance Programme (SCHIP) and Medicaid.

One of the main challenges faced by pediatric safety and quality efforts is that most of the work on patient safety to date has focused on adult patients. In addition, there is no standard nomenclature for pediatric patient safety that is widely used. However, a standard framework for classifying pediatric adverse events that offers flexibility has been introduced. Standardization provides consistency between interdisciplinary teams and can facilitate multisite studies. If these large-scale studies are conducted, the findings could generate large-scale intervention studies conducted with a faster life cycle.

Leaders in Pediatric Safety and Quality

The Agency for Healthcare Research and Quality (AHRQ) is the Federal authority for patient safety and quality of care and has been a leader in pediatric quality and safety. AHRQ has developed Pediatric Quality Indicators (PedQIs) with the goal to highlight areas of quality concern and to target areas for further analysis. Eighteen pediatric quality indicators are included in the AHRQ quality measure modules; based on expert input, risk adjustment, and other considerations. Thirteen inpatient indicators are recommended for use at the hospital level, and five are designated area indicators. Inpatient indicators are treatments or conditions with the greatest potential of an adverse event for hospitalized children.

Pediatric Quality & Provider-Level Indicators	*Area-Level Indicators*
Accidental puncture or laceration	Asthma admission rate
Decubitus ulcer	Diabetes short-term complication rate
Foreign body left during procedure	Gastroenteritis admission rate
Iatrogenic pneumothorax in neonates at risk	Perforated appendix admission rate
Iatrogenic pneumothorax in nonneonates	Urinary tract admission rate
Pediatric heart surgery mortality	
Pediatric heart surgery volume	
Postoperative hemorrhage or hematoma	
Postoperative respiratory failure	
Postoperative sepsis	
Postoperative wound dehiscence	
Selected infections due to medical care	

Possible additions to the dataset will address the patient's condition on admission and increase the understanding of how laboratory and pharmacy utilization impact patient outcomes. The goal of AHRQ is to refine the area-level indicators to improve outcomes for children receiving outpatient care and reduce the incidence of hospitalization for those defined conditions.

Collaborations for Pediatric Safety and Quality

Numerous groups are engaged in improving pediatric care, quality and safety. Each of these groups has a unique mission and membership. The following table details these groups' missions and websites.

Organization	*Mission*	*Web Site*
The National Association of Children's Hospitals & Related Institutions	Clinical care, research, training, and advocacy	www.childrenshospitals.net
Child Health Corporation of America	Business strategies, safety & quality	www.chca.com
National Initiative for Children's Healthcare Quality	Education and research	www.nichq.org
Neonatal Intensive Care/Quality & Vermont Oxford Network	Quality improvement, safety & cost effectiveness for newborns & families	www.nicq.org
Children's Oncology Group	Cures for childhood cancers, family support	www.childrensoncologygroup.org
Initiative for Pediatric Palliative Care	Education, research & quality improvement	www.ippcweb.org
End-of-Life Nursing Education Consortium	End-of-life education & support	www.aacn.nche.edu/elnec

Nurse Staffing and Pediatric Outcomes

While the number of nurses providing patient care is recognized as an inadequate measure of nursing care quality, there is hard evidence that nurse staffing is directly related to patient outcomes. Studies by Aiken and Needleman have demonstrated that patient death, nosocomial infections, cardiac arrest, and pressure ulcers are linked to inadequate nurse-to-patient ratios. The presence or absence of registered nurses (RNs) impacts the outcome for pediatric patients requiring pain management and/or peripheral administration of intravenous fluids and/or medications. These two indicators of pediatric nursing care quality are sensitive measures of nursing care. Professional nurses play a key role in successful pain management, especially among pediatric patients unable to verbally describe pain. Astute assessment skills are required to intervene successfully and relieve discomfort.33 Maintenance of a patient's intravenous access is a clear nursing responsibility. Pediatric patients are at increased risk for intravenous infiltration and for significant complications of infiltration, should it occur.

The characteristics of effective indicators of pediatric nursing care quality include the following:

- Scalable: The indicators are applicable to pediatric patients across a broad range of units and hospitals, in both intensive care and general care settings.
- Feasible: Data collection does not pose undue burden on staff of participating units as the data is available from existing sources, such as the medical record or a quality improvement database, and can be collected in real time.
- Valid and reliable: Indicator measurement within and across participating sites is accurate and consistent over time.

Conclusions

Pediatric care is complex due to developmental and dependency issues associated with children. How these factors impact the specific processes of care is an area of science in which little is known. Throughout health care providing safe and high quality patient care continues to provide significant challenges. Efforts to improve the safety and quality of care are resource intensive and take continued commitment not only by those who deliver care, but also by agencies and foundations that fund this work. Advocates for children's health care must be at the table when key policy and regulatory issues are discussed. Only then will the voice of our most vulnerable groups of health care consumers be heard.

Health literacy

Health literacy is a common and serious safety concern. A study of 2,600 patients at two hospitals determined that between 26-60% of patients could not understand medication directions, a standard informed consent, or basic health care materials. This mismatch between a clinician's level of communication and a patient's ability to understand can lead to medication errors and adverse outcomes.

The Institute of Medicine (2004) report found low health literacy levels negatively affects healthcare outcomes. In particular, these patients have a higher risk of hospitalization and longer hospital stays, are less likely to comply with treatment, are more likely to make errors with medication, and are more ill when they seek medical care.

Pay for Performance (P4P)

Pay for performance systems link compensation to measures of work quality or goals. As of 2005, 75 percent of all U.S. companies connect at least part of an employee's pay to measures of performance, and in healthcare, over 100 private and federal pilot programmes are underway. Current methods of healthcare payment may actually reward less-safe care, since some insurance companies will not pay for new practices to reduce errors, while physicians and hospitals can bill for additional services that are needed when patients are injured by mistakes. However, early studies showed little gain in quality for the money spent, as well as evidence suggesting unintended consequences, like the avoidance of high-risk patients, when payment was linked to outcome improvements.

The 2006 Institute of Medicine report *Preventing Medication Errors* recommended "incentives...so that profitability of hospitals, clinics, pharmacies, insurance companies, and manufacturers (are) aligned with patient safety goals;...(to) strengthen the business case for quality and safety."

There is widespread international interest in health care pay-for-performance programmes in a range of countries, including the United Kingdom, United States, Australia, Canada, Germany, the Netherlands, and New Zealand.

United Kingdom

In the United Kingdom, the National Health Service (NHS) began an ambitious pay for performance initiative in 2004, known as the Quality and Outcomes Framework (QOF). General practitioners agreed to increases in existing income according to performance with respect to 146 quality indicators covering clinical care for 10 chronic diseases, organization of care, and patient experience. Unlike proposed quality incentive programmes in the United States, funding for primary care was increased 20% over previous levels.

This allowed practices to invest in extra staff and technology; 90% of general practitioners use the NHS Electronic Prescription Service, and up to 50% use electronic health records for the majority of clinical care. Early analysis showed that substantially increasing physicians' pay based on their success in meeting quality performance measures is successful. The 8,000 family practitioners included in the study earned an average of $40,000 more by collecting nearly 97% of the points available.

A component of this programme, known as *exception reporting*, allows physicians to use criteria to exclude individual patients from the quality calculations that determine physician reimbursement. There was initial concern that exception reporting would allow inappropriate exclusion of patients in whom targets were missed ("gaming"). However, a 2008 study has shown little evidence of widespread gaming.

United States

In the United States, Medicare has various pay-for-performance ("P4P") initiatives in offices, clinics and hospitals, seeking to improving quality and avoid unnecessary health care costs. The Centres for Medicare and Medicaid Services (CMS) has several demonstration projects underway offering compensation for improvements:

- Payments for better care coordination between home, hospital and offices for patients with chronic illnesses. In April 2005, CMS launched its first value-based purchasing pilot or "demonstration" project- the three-year Medicare Physician Group Practice (PGP) Demonstration. The project involves ten large, multi-speciality physician practices caring for more than 200,000 Medicare fee-for-service beneficiaries. Participating practices will phase in quality standards for preventive care and the management of common chronic illnesses such as diabetes. Practices meeting these standards will be eligible for rewards from savings due to resulting improvements in patient management. The *First Evaluation Report to Congress* in 2006 showed that the model rewarded high quality, efficient provision of health care, but the lack of up-front payment for the investment in new systems of case management "have made for an uncertain future with respect for any payments under the demonstration."
- A set of 10 hospital quality measures which, if reported to CMS, will increase the payments that hospitals receive for each discharge. By the third year of the demonstration, those hospitals that do not meet a threshold on quality will be subject to reductions in payment. Preliminary data from the second year of the study indicates that pay for performance was associated with a roughly 2.5% to 4.0% improvement in compliance with quality measures, compared with the control hospitals. Dr. Arnold Epstein of the Harvard School of Public Health commented in an accompanying editorial that pay-for-performance "is fundamentally a social experiment likely to have only modest incremental value." Unintended consequences of some publicly reported hospital quality measures have adversely affected patient care. The requirement to give the first antibiotic dose in the emergency department within 4 hours, if the patient has pneumonia, has caused an increase in pneumonia misdiagnosis.
- Rewards to physicians for improving health outcomes by the use of health information technology in the care of chronically ill Medicare patients.

- Disincentives: The Tax Relief & Health Care Act of 2006 required the HHS Inspector General to study ways that Medicare payments to hospitals could be recouped for "never events", as defined by the National Quality Forum, including hospital infections. In August 2007, CMS announced that it will stop payments to hospitals for several negative consequences of care that result in injury, illness or death. This rule, effective October 2008, would reduce hospital payments for eight serious types of preventable incidents: objects left in a patient during surgery, blood transfusion reaction, air embolism, falls, mediastinitis, urinary tract infections from catheters, pressure ulcer, and sepsis from catheters. Reporting of "never events" and creation of performance benchmarks for hospitals are also mandated. Other private health payers are considering similar actions; in 2005, HealthPartners, a Minnesota health insurer, chose not to cover 27 types of "never events". The Leapfrog Group has announced that will work with hospitals, health plans and consumer groups to advocate reducing payment for "never events", and will recognize hospitals that agree to certain steps when a serious avoidable adverse event occurs in the facility, including notifying the patient and patient safety organizations, and waiving costs. Physician groups involved in the management of complications, such as the Infectious Diseases Society of America, have voiced objections to these proposals, observing that "some patients develop infections despite application of all evidence-based practices known to avoid infection", and that a punitive response may discourage further study and slow the dramatic improvements that have already been made.

Complex Illness

Pay for performance programmes often target patients with serious and complex illnesses; such patients commonly interact with multiple healthcare providers and facilities. However, pilot programmes now underway focus on simple indicators such as improvement in lab values or use of emergency services, avoiding areas of complexity such as multiple complications or several treating specialists. A 2007 study analysing Medicare beneficiaries' healthcare visits showed that a median of two primary care physicians and five specialists provide care for a single patient. The authors doubt that pay-for-performance systems can accurately attribute responsibility for the outcome of care for such patients. The American College of Physicians Ethics has stated concerns about using a limited set of clinical practice parameters to assess quality, "especially if payment for good performance is grafted onto the current payment system, which does not reward robust comprehensive care...The elderly patient with multiple chronic conditions is especially vulnerable to this unwanted effect of powerful incentives." Present pay-for-performance systems measure good performance based on specified clinical measurements, such as glycohemoglobin for diabetic patients. Healthcare providers who are monitored by such limited criteria have a powerful incentive to *deselect* (dismiss or refuse to accept) patients whose outcome measures fall below the quality standard and therefore worsen the provider's assessment. Patients with low health literacy, inadequate financial resources to afford expensive medications or treatments, and ethnic groups traditionally subject to healthcare inequities may also be deselected by providers seeking improved performance measures.

Public Reporting

Mandatory Reporting

Denmark: The Danish Act on Patient Safety passed Parliament in June 2003, and on January 1, 2004, Denmark became the first country to introduce nation-wide mandatory reporting. The Act obligates frontline personnel to report adverse events to a national reporting system. Hospital owners are obligated to act on the reports and the National Board of Health is obligated to communicate the learning nationally. The reporting system is intended purely for learning and frontline personnel cannot experience sanctions for reporting. This is stated in Section 6 of the Danish Act on Patient Safety (as of January 1, 2007: Section 201 of the Danish Health Act): "A frontline person who reports an adverse event cannot as a result of that report be subjected to investigation or disciplinary action from the employer, the Board of Health or the Court of Justice." The reporting system and the Danish Patient Safety Database is described in further detail in a National Board of Health publication.

United Kingdom: The National Patient Safety Agency encourages voluntary reporting of health care errors, but has several specific instances, known as "Confidential Enquiries", for which investigation is routinely initiated: maternal or infant deaths, childhood deaths to age 16, deaths in persons with mental illness, and perioperative and unexpected medical deaths. Medical records and questionnaires are requested from the involved clinician, and participation has been high, since individual details are confidential.

United States: The 1999 Institute of Medicine (IOM) report recommended "a nationwide mandatory reporting system ... that provides for ... collection of standardized information by state governments about adverse events that result in death or serious harm." Professional organizations, such as the Anesthesia Patient Safety Foundation, responded negatively: "Mandatory reporting systems in general create incentives for individuals and institutions to play a numbers game. If such reporting becomes linked to punitive action or inappropriate public disclosure, there is a high risk of driving reporting "underground", and of reinforcing the cultures of silence and blame that many believe are at the heart of the problems of medical error..."

Although 23 states established mandatory reporting systems for serious patient injuries or death by 2005, the national database envisioned in the IOM report was delayed by the controversy over mandatory versus voluntary reporting. Finally in 2005, the US Congress passed the long-debated Patient Safety and Quality Improvement Act, establishing a federal reporting database. Hospitals reports of serious patient harm are voluntary, collected by patient safety organizations under contract to analyze errors and recommend improvements. The federal government serves to coordinate data collection and maintain the national database. Reports remain confidential, and cannot be used in liability cases. Consumer groups have objected to the lack of transparency, claiming it denies the public information on the safety of specific hospitals.

Individual Patient Disclosures

For a health care institution, disclosing an unanticipated event should be made as soon as possible. Some health care organizations may have a policy regarding the disclosure of unanticipated events. The amount of information presented to those affected is dependent on the family's readiness and the organization's culture. The employee disclosing the event to family requires support from risk management, patient safety officers and senior leadership. Disclosures are objectively documented in the medical record.

Voluntary Disclosure

In public surveys, a significant majority of those surveyed believe that health care providers should be required to report all serious medical errors publicly. However, reviews of the medical literature show little effect of publicly reported performance data on patient safety or the quality of care. Public reporting on the quality of individual providers or hospitals does not seem to affect selection of hospitals and individual providers. Some studies have shown that reporting performance data stimulates quality improvement activity in hospitals.

United States

Medical Error

Ethical standards of the Joint Commission on Accreditation of Healthcare Organizations (JCAHO), the American Medical Association (AMA) Council on Ethical and Judicial Affairs, and the American College of Physicians Ethics Manual require disclosure of the most serious adverse events. However, many doctors and hospitals do not report errors under the current system because of concerns about malpractice lawsuits; this prevents collection of information needed to find and correct the conditions that lead to mistakes. As of 2008, 35 US states have statutes allowing doctors and health care providers to apologize and offer expressions of regret without their words being used against them in court, and 7 states have also passed laws mandating written disclosure of adverse events and bad outcomes to patients and families.

In September 2005, US Senators Clinton and Obama introduced the National Medical Error Disclosure and Compensation (MEDiC) Bill, providing physicians protection from liability and a safe environment for disclosure, as part of a programme to notify and compensate patients harmed by medical errors. It is now the policy of several academic medical centres, including Johns Hopkins, University of Illinois and Stanford, to promptly disclose medical errors, offering apologies and compensation. This national initiative, hoping to restore integrity to dealings with patients, make it easier to learn from mistakes and avoid angry lawsuits, was modelled after a University of Michigan Hospital System programme that has reduced the number of lawsuits against the hospital by 75% and has decreased the average litigation cost. The Veterans Health Administration requires the disclosure of all adverse events to patients, even those that are not obvious. However, as of 2008 these initiatives have only included hospitals that are self-insured and that employ their staffs, thus limiting the number of parties involved.

Performance

In April 2008, consumer, employer and labour organizations announced an agreement with major physician organizations and health insurers on principles to measure and report doctors' performance on quality and cost.

United Kingdom

In the United Kingdom, whistleblowing is well recognised and is government sanctioned, as a way to protect patients by encouraging employees to call attention to deficient services. Health authorities are encouraged to put local policies in place to protect whistleblowers.

Studies of Patient Safety

Numerous organizations, government branches, and private companies conduct research studies to investigate the overall health of patient safety in America and across the globe. Despite the shocking and widely publicized statistics on preventable deaths due to medical errors in America's hospitals, the 2006 National Healthcare Quality Report assembled by the Agency for Healthcare Research and Quality (AHRQ) had the following sobering assessment:

- Most measures of Quality are improving, but the pace of change remains modest.
- Quality improvement varies by setting and phase of care.
- The rate of improvement accelerated for some measures while a few continued to show deterioration.
- Variation in health care quality remains high.

A 2011 study of more than 1,000 patients with advanced colon cancer found that one in eight was treated with at least one drug regimen with specific recommendations against their use in the National Comprehensive Cancer Network guidelines. The study focused on three chemotherapy regimens that were not supported by evidence from prior clinical studies or clinical practice guidelines. One treatment was rated "insufficient data to support," one had been "shown to be ineffective," and one was supported by "no data, nor is there a compelling rationale." Many of the patients received multiple cycles of non-beneficial chemotherapy and some received two or more unproven treatments. Potential side effects for the treatments include hypertension, heightened risk of bleeding and bowel perforation.

Organizations Advocating Patient Safety

Several authors of the 1999 Institute of Medicine report revisited the status of their recommendations and the state of patient safety, five years after "To Err is Human".[114] Discovering that patient safety had become a frequent topic for journalists, health care experts, and the public, it was harder to see overall improvements on a national level. What was noteworthy was the impact on attitudes and organizations. Few health care professionals now doubted that preventable medical injuries were a serious problem. The central concept of the report—that bad systems and not bad people lead to most errors—became established in patient safety efforts. A broad array of organizations now advance the cause of patient safety. For instance, in 2010 the principal European anaesthesiology organisations launched The Helsinki Declaration for Patient Safety in Anaesthesiology, which incorporates many of the principles described above.

Sanitation

Sanitation is the hygienic means of promoting health through prevention of human contact with the hazards of wastes as well as the treatment and proper disposal of sewage or wastewater. Hazards can be either physical, microbiological, biological or chemical agents of disease. Wastes that can cause health problems include human and animal excreta, solid wastes, domestic wastewater (sewage, sullage, greywater), industrial wastes and agricultural wastes. Hygienic means of prevention can be by using engineering solutions (e.g., sewerage, wastewater treatment, stormwater drainage, solid waste management, excreta management), simple technologies (e.g., pit latrines, dry toilets, UDDTs, septic tanks), or even simply by personal hygiene practices (e.g., hand washing with soap, behavior change).

The World Health Organization States That: "Sanitation generally refers to the provision of facilities and services for the safe disposal of human urine and feces. Inadequate sanitation is a major cause of disease world-wide and improving sanitation is known to have a significant beneficial impact on health both in households and across communities. The word 'sanitation' also refers to the maintenance of hygienic conditions, through services such as garbage collection and wastewater disposal.

Sanitation includes all four of these engineering infrastructure items (even though often only the first one is strongly associated with the term "sanitation"):

- Excreta management systems
- Wastewater management systems
- Solid waste management systems
- Drainage systems for rainwater, also called stormwater drainage

Despite the fact that sanitation *includes* wastewater treatment, the two terms are often use side by side: people tend to speak of sanitation *and* wastewater management which is why the differeantiation is also made in the sub-headings in this article. The term sanitation has been connected to several descriptors so that the terms sustainable sanitation, improved sanitation, unimproved sanitation, environmental sanitation, on-site sanitation, ecological sanitation, dry sanitation are all in use today. Sanitation should be regarded with a systems approach in mind which includes collection/containment, conveyance/transport, treatment and disposal or reuse.

Wastewater Management

Collection

The standard sanitation technology in urban areas is the collection of wastewater in sewers, its treatment in wastewater treatment plants for reuse or disposal in rivers, lakes or the sea. Sewers are either combined with storm drains or separated from them as sanitary sewers. Combined sewers are usually found in the central, older parts or urban areas. Heavy rainfall and inadequate maintenance can lead to combined sewer overflows or sanitary sewer overflows, i.e., more or less diluted raw sewage being discharged into the environment. Industries often discharge wastewater into municipal sewers, which can complicate wastewater treatment unless industries pre-treat their discharges.

The high investment cost of conventional wastewater collection systems are difficult to afford for many developing countries. Some countries have therefore promoted alternative wastewater collection systems such as condominial sewerage, which uses pipes with smaller diameters at lower depth with different network layouts from conventional sewerage.

Treatment

Centralised Treatment

In developed countries treatment of municipal wastewater is now widespread, but not yet universal (for an overview of technologies see wastewater treatment). In developing countries most wastewater is still discharged untreated into the environment. For example, in Latin America only about 15% of collected sewerage is being treated.

On-site Treatment, Decentralised Treatment

In many suburban and rural areas households are not connected to sewers. They discharge their wastewater into septic tanks or other types of on-site sanitation. On-site systems include drain fields, which require significant area of land. This makes septic systems unsuitable for most cities.

Constructed wetlands are another example for a possible decentralised treatment option.

Disposal or Reuse of Treated Wastewater

The reuse of untreated or partially treated wastewater in irrigated agriculture is common in developing countries. The reuse of treated wastewater in landscaping, especially on golf courses, irrigated agriculture and for industrial use is becoming increasingly widespread.

Types of Sanitation

The term sanitation is connected with various descriptors to signify certain types of sanitation systems. Here they are shown in alphabetical order:

Dry Sanitation

The term "dry sanitation" is somewhat misleading as sanitation as includes handwashing and can never be "dry". A more precise term would be "dry excreta management". When people speak of "dry sanitation" they usually mean sanitation systems with dry toilets with urine diversion, in particular the urine-diverting dry toilet (UDDT).

Ecological Sanitation

Ecological sanitation, which is commonly abbreviated to ecosan, is an approach, rather than a technology or a device which is characterized by a desire to "close the loop" (mainly for the nutrients and organic matter) between sanitation and agriculture in a safe manner. Put in other words: "Ecosan systems safely recycle excreta resources (plant nutrients and organic matter) to crop production in such a way that the use of non-renewable resources is minimised". When properly designed and operated, ecosan systems provide a hygienically safe, economical, and closed-loop system to convert human excreta into nutrients to be returned to the soil, and water to be returned to the land. Ecosan is also called resource-oriented sanitation.

Environmental Sanitation

Environmental sanitation is the control of environmental factors that form links in disease transmission. Subsets of this category are solid waste management, water and wastewater treatment, industrial waste treatment and noise and pollution control.

Improved and Unimproved Sanitation

Improved sanitation and unimproved sanitation refers to the management of human feces at the household level. This terminology is the indicator used to describe the target of the Millennium Development

Goal on sanitation, by the WHO/UNICEF Joint Monitoring Programme for Water Supply and Sanitation.

Lack of Sanitation

Lack of sanitation refers to the absence of sanitation. In practical terms it usually means lack of toilets or lack of hygienic toilets that anybody would want to use voluntarily. The result of lack of sanitation is usually open defecation (and open urination but this is of less concern) with the associated serious public health issues.

On-site Sanitation

Onsite sanitation is the collection and treatment of waste is done where it is deposited. Examples are the use of pit latrines, septic tanks, and Imhoff tanks

Sustainable Sanitation

Sustainable sanitation is a term that has been defined with five sustainability criteria by the Sustainable Sanitation Alliance. In order to be sustainable, a sanitation system has to be not only (i) economically viable, (ii) socially acceptable, and (iii) technically and (iv) institutionally appropriate, it should also (v) protect the environment and the natural resources. The main objective of a sanitation system is to protect and promote human health by providing a clean environment and breaking the cycle of disease.

Solid Waste Disposal

Disposal of solid waste is most commonly conducted in landfills, but incineration, recycling, composting and conversion to biofuels are also avenues. In the case of landfills, advanced countries typically have rigid protocols for daily cover with topsoil, where underdeveloped countries customarily rely upon less stringent protocols. The importance of daily cover lies in the reduction of vector contact and spreading of pathogens. Daily cover also minimises odour emissions and reduces windblown litter. Likewise, developed countries typically have requirements for perimeter sealing of the landfill with clay-type soils to minimize migration of leachate that could contaminate groundwater (and hence jeopardize some drinking water supplies).

For incineration options, the release of air pollutants, including certain toxic components is an attendant adverse outcome. Recycling and biofuel conversion are the sustainable options that generally have superior lifecycle costs, particularly when total ecological consequences are considered. Composting value will ultimately be limited by the market demand for compost product.

Food Preparation

Sanitation within the food industry means the adequate treatment of food-contact surfaces by a process that is effective in destroying vegetative cells of microorganisms of public health significance, and in substantially reducing numbers of other undesirable microorganisms, but without adversely affecting the food or its safety for the consumer (U.S. Food and Drug Administration, Code of Federal Regulations, 21CFR110, USA). Sanitation Standard Operating Procedures are mandatory for food industries in United States, which are regulated by 9 CFR part 416 in conjunction with 21 CFR part 178.1010. Similarly, in Japan, food hygiene has to be achieved through compliance with food sanitation law.

In the food and biopharmaceutical industries, the term "sanitary equipment" means equipment that is fully cleanable using clean-in-place (CIP) and sterilization-in-place (SIP) procedures: that is fully drainable from cleaning solutions and other liquids. The design should have a minimum amount of deadleg, or areas where the turbulence during cleaning is insufficient to remove product deposits. In general, to improve cleanability, this equipment is made from Stainless Steel 316L, (an alloy containing small amounts of molybdenum). The surface is usually electropolished to an effective surface roughness of less than 0.5 micrometre to reduce the possibility of bacterial adhesion.

Health Impacts

For any social and economic development, adequate sanitation in conjunction with good hygiene and safe water are essential to good health. Lack of proper sanitation causes diseases. Most of the diseases resulting from sanitation have a direct relation to poverty. The lack of clean water and poor sanitation has caused many diseases and the spread of diseases. Sanitation is very important in order to keep good health. One of the most significant diseases that arise from poor sanitation is diarrhea. Deaths resulting from diarrhea are estimated to be between 1.6 and 2.5 million deaths every year. Most of the affected are young children below the ages of five. Other diseases that are caused by poor sanitation include schistosomiasis, trachoma and intestinal worm infections (helminthiases).

Poor sanitation accounts for almost 50 percent of underweight child since it has a direct link to diarrhea. Children suffering from diarrhea are more vulnerable to become underweight which makes them more vulnerable to other diseases such as acute respiratory infections and malaria. Lack of sanitation is a serious issue that is affecting most developing countries and countries in transition. The importance of the isolation of excreta and waste lies in an effort to prevent diseases which can be transmitted through human waste, which afflict both developed countries as well as developing countries to differing degrees. It is estimated that up to 5 million people die each year from preventable waterborne diseases, as a result of inadequate sanitation and hygiene practices. The effects of sanitation has impacted the society of people throughout history. Sanitation is a necessity for a heathy life.

Relevant diseases and conditions caused by lack of sanitation and hygiene include:

- Waterborne diseases, which can contaminate drinking water
- Diseases transmitted by the fecal-oral route
  - o Infections with intestinal helminths (worms) - approximately two billion people are infected with soil-transmitted helminths worldwide; they are transmitted by eggs present in human faeces which in turn contaminate soil in areas where sanitation is poor.
- Stunted growth in children
- Malnutrition, particularly in children

The list of diseases that could be reduced with proper access to sanitation and hygiene practices is very long. For example in India, 15 diseases have been listed which could be stamped out by improving sanitation:

1. Anaemia, malnutrition
2. Ascariasis (a type of intestinal worm infection)
3. Campylobacteriosis
4. Cholera
5. Cyanobacteria toxins
6. Dengue
7. Hepatitis
8. Japanese encephalitis (JE)
9. Leptospirosis
10. Malaria
11. Ringworm or Tinea (a type of intestinal worm infection)
12. Scabies
13. Schistosomiasis
14. Trachoma
15. Typhoid and paratyphoid enteric fevers

Polio is in fact another diseases which is related to improper sanitation and hygiene.

Improving Global Access

The United Nations Millennium Development Goals (MDGs) include a target to reduce by half the proportion of people without access to basic sanitation by 2015. In December 2006, the United Nations General Assembly declared 2008 "The International Year of Sanitation", in recognition of the slow progress being made towards the MDGs sanitation target. The year aimed to develop awareness and action to meet the target. Particular concerns are:

- Removing the stigma around sanitation, so that the importance of sanitation can be more easily and publicly discussed.
- Highlighting the poverty reduction, health and other benefits that flow from better hygiene, household sanitation arrangements and wastewater treatment.

The Joint Monitoring Programme for Water Supply and Sanitation of WHO and UNICEF has defined improved sanitation as follows:

- Flush toilet or flush / pour-flush to a pit latrine whith are connected to either a sewer system or a septic system
- Ventilated improved pit latrine (VIP)
- Pit latrine with slab
- Composting toilet

The JMP publishes a report of updated estimates every two years on the use of various types of drinking-water sources and sanitation facilities at the national, regional and global levels. In March 2012, the JMP released its latest updates. According to the definition above, 1.8 billion more people used improved sanitation in 2010 than in 1990, bringing the percentage of people using improved sanitation to 63% globally. However, the world remains off track for the sanitation target of the Millennium Development Goals. 2.5 billion lack improved sanitation. According to the JMP, if current trends continue, in 2015 2.4 billion people will lack access to improved sanitation facilities. 15 per cent of the population still practise open defecation, defined as defecation in fields, forests, bushes, bodies of water or other open spaces. This represents 1.1 billion people. Though the proportion of people practising open defecation is decreasing, the absolute number has remained at over one billion for several years, due to population growth. In 2011 the Bill & Melinda Gates Foundation launched the Reinvent the Toilet Challenge to promote safer, more effective ways to treat human waste. The programme is aimed at developing technologies that might help bridge the global sanitation gap.

This outcome presents substantial public health risks as the waste could contaminate drinking water and cause life-threatening forms of diarrhea to infants. Most cities can neither afford a sewage drainage system, nor a sewage treatment system, as Sunita Narain spelled out in the magazine *D+C Development and Cooperation*. Improved sanitation, including hand washing and water purification, could save the lives of 1.5 million children who die from diarrheal diseases each year.

Research from the Overseas Development Institute suggests that sanitation and hygiene promotion needs to be better "mainstreamed" in development, if the MDG on sanitation is to be met. At present, promotion of sanitation and hygiene is mainly carried out through water institutions. The research argues that there are, in fact, many institutions that should carry out activities to develop better sanitation and hygiene in developing countries. For example, educational institutions can teach on hygiene, and health institutions can dedicate resources to preventative works (to avoid, for example, outbreaks of cholera). There are also civil society organisations providing the necessary infrastructure where national governments cannot do that on their own. In Ghana, there is an umbrella organisation for those programmes, called CONIWAS (Coalition of NGOs in Water and Sanitation) as reported in the magazine *D+C Development and Cooperation*.

The Institute of Development Studies (IDS) coordinated research programme on community-led total sanitation (CLTS) is a radically different approach to rural sanitation in developing countries and has shown promising successes where traditional rural sanitation programmes have failed. CLTS is an unsubsidized approach to rural sanitation that facilitates communities to recognize the problem of open defecation and take collective action to clean up and become "open defecation free". It uses community-led methods such as participatory mapping and analysing pathways between feces and mouth as a means of galvanizing communities into action. An IDS policy brief suggests that in many countries the MDG for sanitation is off track and asks how CLTS can be adopted and spread on a large scale in the many countries and regions where open defecation still prevails.

History

The earliest evidence of urban sanitation was seen in Harappa, Mohenjo-daro, and the recently discovered Rakhigarhi of Indus Valley civilization. This urban plan included the world's first urban sanitation systems. Within the city, individual homes or groups of homes obtained water from wells. From a room that appears to have been set aside for bathing, waste water was directed to covered drains, which lined the major streets.

Roman cities and Roman villas had elements of sanitation systems, delivering water in the streets of towns such as Pompeii, and building stone and wooden drains to collect and remove wastewater from populated areas. But there is little record of other sanitation in most of Europe until the High Middle Ages. Unsanitary conditions and overcrowding were widespread throughout Europe and Asia during the Middle Ages, resulting periodically in cataclysmic pandemics such as the Plague of Justinian (541-42) and the Black Death (1347–1351), which killed tens of millions of people and radically altered societies.

Very high infant and child mortality prevailed in Europe throughout medieval times, due not only to deficiencies in sanitation but to an insufficient food supply for a population which had expanded faster than agriculture. This was further complicated by frequent warfare and exploitation of civilians by autocratic rulers.

Community-led Total Sanitation

Community-led total sanitation (CLTS) is an innovative methodology for mobilising communities to completely eliminate open defecation (OD). Communities are facilitated to conduct their own appraisal and analysis of open defecation (OD) and take their own action to become open defecation free (ODF).

At the heart of CLTS lies the recognition that merely providing toilets does not guarantee their use, nor result in improved sanitation and hygiene. Earlier approaches to sanitation prescribed high initial standards and offered subsidies as an incentive. But this often led to uneven adoption, problems with long-term sustainability and only partial use. It also created a culture of dependence on subsidies. Open defecation and the cycle of fecal–oral contamination continued to spread disease.

In contrast, CLTS focuses on the behavioural change needed to ensure real and sustainable improvements – investing in community mobilisation instead of hardware, and shifting the focus from toilet construction for individual households to the creation of "open defecation-free" villages. By raising awareness that as long as even a minority continues to defecate in the open everyone is at risk of disease, CLTS triggers the community's desire for change, propels them into action and encourages innovation, mutual support and appropriate local solutions, thus leading to greater ownership and sustainability.

CLTS was pioneered by Kamal Kar (a development consultant from India) together with VERC (Village Education Resource Centre), partner of WaterAid Bangladesh, in 2000 in Mosmoil, a village in the Rajshahi district of Bangladesh, whilst evaluating a traditionally subsidised sanitation programme. Kar, who had years of experience in participatory approaches in a range of development projects, succeeded in persuading the local non-governmental organization (NGO) to stop top-down toilet construction through subsidy. He advocated change in institutional attitude and the need to draw on intense local mobilisation and facilitation to enable villagers to analyse their sanitation and waste situation and bring about collective decision-making to stop open defecation.

CLTS spread fast within Bangladesh, where informal institutions and NGOs are key. Both Bangladeshi and international NGOs adopted the approach. The Water and Sanitation Programme (WSP) of the World Bank played an important role in enabling spread to neighbouring India and then subsequently to Indonesia and parts of Africa. Plan International, WaterAid and UNICEF have become important disseminators and champions of CLTS. Today there is CLTS, in more than 40 countries of the world, especially in Asia, Africa, Latin America and the Middle East.

Benefits

CLTS has a great potential for contributing towards meeting the United Nations Development Programme goals, both directly on water and sanitation (goal 7) and indirectly through the knock-on impacts of improved sanitation on combating major diseases, particularly diarrhoea (goal 6), improving maternal health (goal 5) and reducing child mortality (goal 4). In addition to creating a culture of good sanitation, CLTS can also be an effective point for other livelihoods activities. It mobilizes community members towards collective action and empowers them to take further action in the future. CLTS outcomes illustrate what communities can achieve by undertaking further initiatives for their own development.

Recent Developments

More recently, it has also been adapted to the urban context. At the moment, the most exciting developments are taking place in Mathare 10, Nairobi where Plan together with CCS are doing an Urban Community-led Total Sanitation pilot.

Increasingly, there is also discussion about how CLTS could be adapted to post-emergency settings and there has been some experience with this in Haiti, Afghanistan and Indonesia.

Criticisms

CLTS's behavioural changes process is based on the use of shame, this is meant to promote collective consciousness-raising of the severe impacts of open defecation and trigger shock when participants realize the implications of their actions. There is quite a deal of evidence now that the triggering process has seen practices utilized, which infringe the human rights of recipients. There have been cases of fines (monetary and non-monetary), withholding of entitlements, public taunting, posting of humiliating pictures and even violence. It should be noted that the victims of these infringements are in most cases already the poorest and most vulnerable in their communities.

CLTS does not specify technical standards for toilets. This is a benefit in terms of keeping the costs of constructing toilets very low. However, it can produce two problems: first in flood plains or areas near water tables poorly constructed latrines are likely to contaminate the water table and thus represent little improvement. Second, long-term use of sanitation facilities is related to the pleasantness of the facilities, dirty overflowing pits are unlikely to be utilised in the longer term. A related issue here is that CLTS does note address the issue of latrine emptying services or where they exist, how they dispose of waste.

Occupational Hygiene

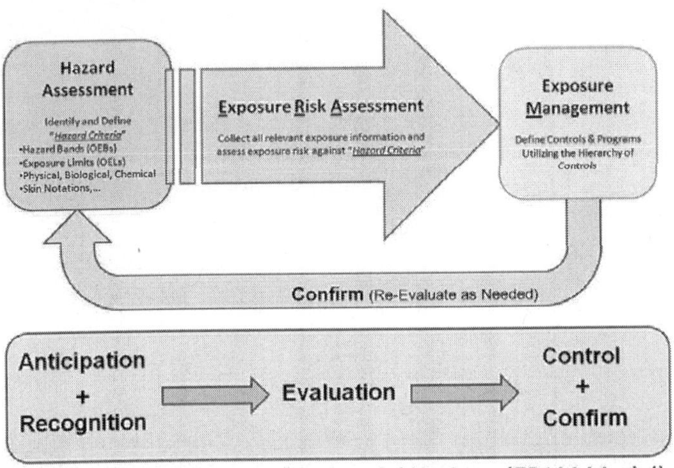

Fundamental Elements of Industrial Hygiene (ERAM Model)

Figure: *Illustration of Exposure Risk Assessment and Management related to anticipation, recognition, evaluation, control and confirm.*

Occupational (or "industrial" in the U.S.) hygiene (IH) is the anticipation, recognition, evaluation, control and prevention of hazards from work that may result in injury, illness, or affect the well being of workers. These hazards or stressors are typically divided into the categories biological, chemical, physical, ergonomic and psychosocial. The risk of a health effect from a given stressor is a function of the hazard multiplied by the exposure to the individual or group. For chemicals, the hazard can be understood by the dose response profile most often based on toxicological studies or models. Occupational hygienists work closely with toxicologists for understanding chemical hazards, physicists for physical hazards, and physicians and microbiologists for biological hazards. Environmental and occupational hygienists are considered experts in exposure science and exposure risk management. Depending on an individual's type of job, a hygienist will apply their exposure science expertise for the protection of workers, consumers and/or communities.

The British Occupational Hygiene Society (BOHS) defines that "occupational hygiene is about the prevention of ill-health from work, through recognizing, evaluating and controlling the risks". The International Occupational Hygiene Association (IOHA) refers to occupational hygiene as *the discipline of anticipating, recognizing, evaluating and controlling health hazards in the working environment with the objective of protecting worker health and well-being and safeguarding the community at large.* The term "occupational hygiene" (used in the UK and Commonwealth countries as well as much of Europe) is synonymous with *industrial hygiene* (used in the US, Latin America, and other countries that received initial technical support or training from US sources). The term "industrial hygiene" traditionally stems from industries with construction, mining or manufacturing and "occupational hygiene" refers to all types of industry such as those listed for "industrial hygiene" as well as financial and support services industries and refers to "work", "workplace" and "place of work" in general. *Environmental hygiene* addresses similar issues to *occupational hygiene,* but is likely to be about broad industry or broad issues affecting the local community, broader society, region or country.

The profession of occupational hygiene uses strict and rigorous scientific methodology and often requires professional judgement based on experience and education in determining the potential for hazardous exposure risks in workplace and environmental studies. These aspects of occupational hygiene can often be referred to as the "art" of occupational hygiene and is used in a similar sense to the "art" of medicine. In fact "occupational hygiene" is both an aspect of preventative medicine and in particular occupational medicine, in that its goal is to prevent industrial disease, using the science of risk management, exposure assessment and industrial safety. Ultimately professionals seek to implement "safe" systems, procedures or methods to be applied in the workplace or to the environment.

The Social Role of Occupational Hygiene

Occupational hygienists have been involved historically with changing the perception of society about the nature and extent of hazards and preventing exposures in the workplace and communities. Many occupational hygienists work day-to-day with industrial situations that require control or improvement to the workplace situation however larger social issues affecting whole industries have occurred in the past e.g. since 1900, asbestos exposures that have affected the lives of tens of thousands of people. Occupational hygienists have become more engaged in understanding and managing exposure risks to consumers from products with new regulations such as REACh (Registration, Evaluation, Authorisation and Restriction of Chemicals).

More recent issues affecting broader society are, for example in 1976, legionnaires' disease or legionellosis. More recently again in the 1990s radon and in the 2000s the effects of mold from indoor air quality situations in the home and at work. In the later part of the 2000s concern has been raised about the health effects of nanoparticles.

Many of these issues have required the coordination over a number of years of a number of medical and para professionals in detecting and then characterizing the nature of the issue, both in terms of the hazard and in terms of the risk to the workplace and ultimately to society. This has involved occupational hygienists in research, collection of data and to develop suitable and satisfactory control methodologies.

Workplace Assessment Methods

Although there are many aspects to occupational hygiene work the most known and sought after is in determining or estimating potential or actual exposures to hazards. For many chemicals and physical hazards, occupational exposure limits have been derived using toxicological, epidemiological and medical data allowing hygienists to reduce the risks of health effects by implementing the "Hierarchy of Hazard Controls". Several methods can be applied in assessing the workplace or environment for exposure to a known or suspected hazard. Occupational hygienists do not rely on the accuracy of the equipment or method used but in knowing with certainty and precision the limits of the equipment or method being used and the error or variance given by using that particular equipment or method. Well known methods for performing occupational exposure assessments can be found in "A Strategy for Assessing and Managing Occupational Exposures, Third Edition Edited by Joselito S. Ignacio and William H. Bullock".

The main steps outlined for assessing and managing occupational exposures:

- Basic Characterization (identify agents, hazards, people potentially exposed and existing exposure controls)
- Exposure Assessment (select occupational exposure limits, hazard bands, relevant toxicological data to determine if exposures are "acceptable", "unacceptable" or "uncertain")
- Exposure Controls (for "unacceptable" or "uncertain" exposures)
- Further Information Gathering (for "uncertain" exposures)
- Hazard Communication (for all exposures)
- Reassessment (as needed) / Management of Change

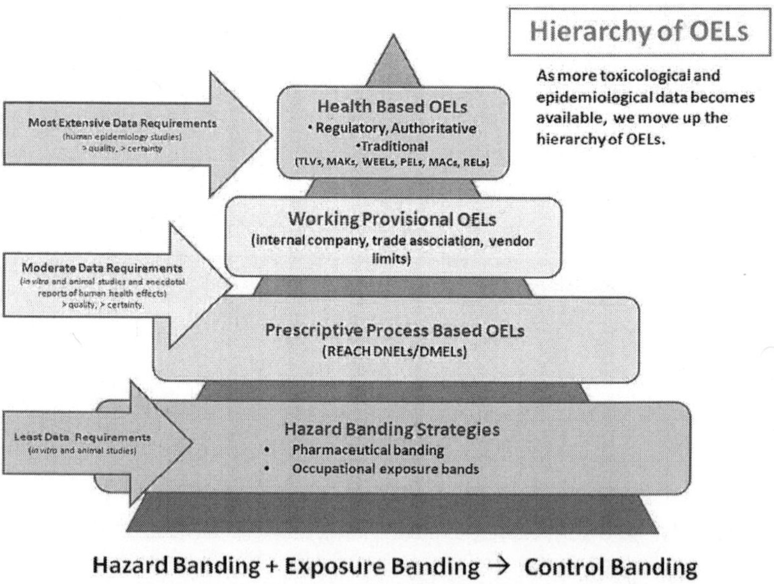

Figure: *Hierarchy of occupational exposure limits (OELs)*

Basic Characterization, Hazard Identification & Walk Through Surveys

The first step in understanding health risks related to exposures requires the collection of "basic characterization" information from available sources. A traditional method applied by occupational hygienists to initially survey a workplace or environment is used to determine both the types and possible exposures from hazards (e.g. noise, chemicals, radiation). The walk-through survey can be targeted or limited to particular hazards such as silica dust, or noise, to focus attention on control of all hazards to workers. A full walk-through survey is frequently used to provide information on establishing a framework for future investigations, prioritizing hazards, determining the requirements for measurement and establishing some immediate control of potential exposures. The Health Hazard Evaluation Programme from the National Institute for Occupational Safety and Health is an example of an industrial hygiene walk-through survey. Other sources of basic characterization information include worker interviews, observing exposure tasks, material safety data sheets, workforce scheduling, production data, equipment and maintenance schedules to identify potential exposure agents and people possibly exposed.

Sampling Survey Equipment

An occupational hygienist may use one or a number of commercially available electronic measuring devices to measure noise, vibration, ionizing and non-ionizing radiation, dust, solvents, gases, et cetera. Each device is often specifically designed to measure a specific or particular type of contaminant. Such devices are often subject to multiple interferences. Electronic devices need to be calibrated before and after use to ensure the accuracy of the measurements taken and often require a system of certifying the precision of the instrument.

Dust Sampling

Nuisance dust is considered to be the total dust in air including inhalable and respirable fractions.

Various dust sampling methods exist that are internationally recognised. Inhalable dust is determined using the modern equivalent of the Institute of Occupational Medicine (IOM) MRE 113A monitor. Inhalable dust is considered to be dust of less than 100 micrometers aerodynamic equivalent diameter (AED) that enters through the nose and or mouth.

Respirable dust is sampled using a cyclone dust sampler design to sample for a specific fraction of dust AED at a set flow rate. The respirable dust fraction is dust that enters the 'deep lung' and is considered to be less than 10 micrometers AED.

Nuisance, inhalable and respirable dust fractions are all sampled using a constant volumetric pump for a specific sampling period. By knowing the mass of the sample collected and the volume of air sampled a concentration for the fraction sampled can be given in milligrams (mg) per metre cubed (m3). From such samples the amount of inhalable or reespirable dust can be determined and compared to the relevant occupational exposure limits.

By use of inhalable, respirable or other suitable sampler (7 hole, 5 hole, et cetera) these dust sampling methods can also used to determine metal exposure in the air. This requires collection of the sample on a methyl-cellulose ester (MCE) filter and acid digestion of the collection media in the laboratory followed by measuring metal concentration though an atomic absorption (or emission) spectrophotometery. Both the UK Health and Safety Laboratory and NIOSH Manual of Analytical Methods have specific methodologies for a broad range of metals in air found in industrial processing (smelting, foundries, et cetera).

A further method exists for the determination of asbestos, fibreglass, synthetic mineral fibre and ceramic mineral fibre dust in air. This is the membrane filter method (MFM) and requires the collection of the dust on a grided filter for estimation of exposure by the counting of 'conforming' fibres in 100 fields through a microscope. Results are quantified on the basis of number of fibres per millilitre of air (f/ml). Many countries strictly regulate the methodology applied to the MFM.

Chemical Sampling

Two types of chemically absorbent tubes are used to sample for a wide range of chemical substances. Traditionally a chemical absorbent 'tube' (a glass or stainless steel tube of between 2 and 10 mm internal diameter) filled with very fine absorbent silica (hydrophilic) or carbon, such as coconut charcoal (lypophylic), is used in a sampling line where air is drawn through the absorbent material for between four hours (minimum workplace sample) to 24 hours (environmental sample) period. The hydrophilic material readily absorbs water-soluble chemical and the lypophylic material absorbs non water-soluble materials. The absorbent material is then chemically or physically extracted and measurements performed using various gas chromatograph or mass spectrometry methods. These absorbent tube methods have the advantage of being usable for a wide range of potential contaminates. However, they are relatively expensive methods, are time consuming and require significant expertise in sampling and chemical analysis. A frequent complaint of workers is in having to wear the sampling pump (up to 1 kg) for several days of work to provide adequate data for the required statistical certainty determination of the exposure.

In the last few decades, advances have been made in 'passive' badge technology. These samplers can now be purchased to measure one chemical (e.g. formaldehyde) or a chemical type (e.g. ketones) or a broad spectrum of chemicals (e.g. solvents). They are relatively easy to set up and use. However, considerable cost can still be incurred in analysis of the 'badge'. They weigh 20 to 30 grams and workers do not complain about their presence. Unfortunately 'badges' may not exist for all types of workplace sampling that may be required and the charcoal or silica method may sometimes have to be applied.

From the sampling method, results are expressed in milligrams per cubic meter (mg/m3) or parts per million (PPM) and compared to the relevant occupational exposure limits.

It is a critical part of the exposure determination that the method of sampling for the specific contaminate exposure is directly linked to the exposure standard used. Many countries regulate both the exposure standard, the method used to determine the exposure and the methods to be used for chemical or other analysis of the samples collected.

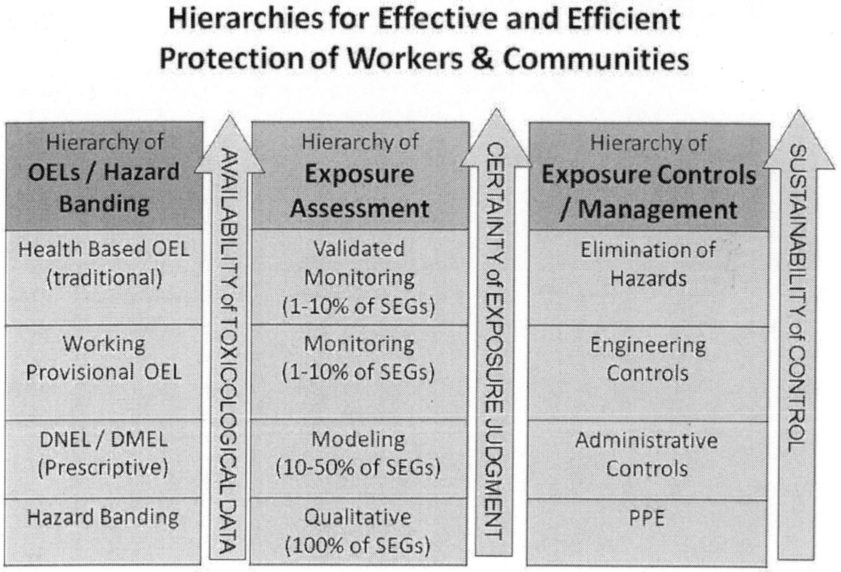

Figure: *Simple representation of exposure risk assessment and management hierarchy based on available information*

Exposure Management and Controls

The hierarchy of control defines the approach used to reduce exposure risks protecting workers and communities. These methods include elimination, substitution, engineering controls (isolation or ventilation), administrative controls and personal protective equipment.

Occupational hygienists, engineers, maintenance, management and employees should all be consulted for selecting and designing the most effective and efficient controls based on the hierarchy of control.

General Activities

The occupational hygienist may be involved with the assessment and control of physical, chemical, biological or environmental hazards in the workplace or community that could cause injury or disease. Physical hazards may include noise, temperature extremes, illumination extremes, ionizing or non-ionizing radiation, and ergonomics. Chemical hazards related to dangerous goods or hazardous substances are frequently investigated by occupational hygienists. Other related areas including indoor air quality (IAQ) and safety may also receive the attention of the occupational hygienist. Biological hazards may stem from the potential for legionella exposure at work or the investigation of biological injury or effects at work, such as dermatitis may be investigated.

As part of the investigation process, the occupational hygienist may be called upon to communicate effectively regarding the nature of the hazard, the potential for risk, and the appropriate methods of control. Appropriate controls are selected from the hierarchy of control: by elimination, substitution, engineering, administration and personal protective equipment (PPE) to control the hazard or eliminate the risk. Such controls may involve recommendations as simple as appropriate PPE such as a 'basic' particulate dust mask to occasionally designing dust extraction ventilation systems, work places or management systems to manage people and programmes for the preservation of health and well-being of those who enter a workplace.

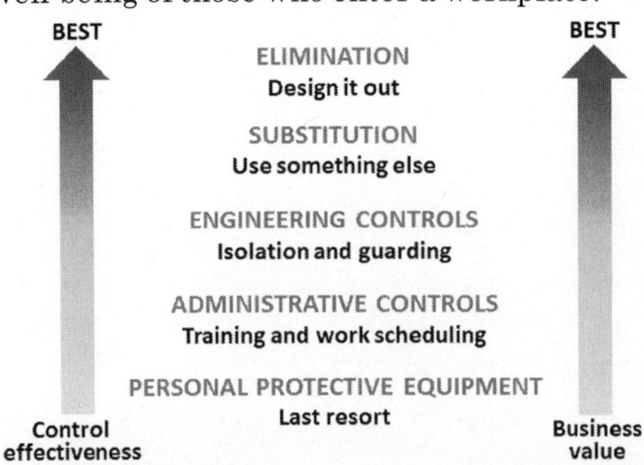

Figure: *The hierarchy of controls is an important tool to determine how to control hazards most efficiently and effectively in a workplace.*

Education

The basis of the technical knowledge of occupational hygiene is from competent training in the following areas of science and management.

- Basic Sciences (Biology, Chemistry, Mathematics (Statistics), Physics);
- Occupational Diseases (Illness, injury and health surveillance (biostatistics, epidemiology, toxicology));
- Health Hazards (Biological, Chemical and Physical hazards, Ergonomics and Human Factors);
- Working Environments (Mining, Industrial, Manufacturing, transport and storage, service industries and offices);
- Programme Management Principles (professional and business ethics, work site and incident investigation methods, exposure guidelines, Occupational exposure limits, jurisdictional based regulations, hazard identification, risk assessment and risk communication, data management, fire evacuation and other emergency responses);
- Sampling, measurement and evaluation practices (instrumentation, sampling protocols, methods or techniques, analytical chemistry);
- Hazard Controls (elimination, substitution, engineering, administrative, PPE and Air Conditioning and Extraction Ventilation);
- Environment (air pollution, hazardous waste).

However, it is not rote knowledge that identifies a competent occupational hygienist. There is an "art" to applying the technical principles in a manner that provides a reasonable solution for workplace and environmental issues. In effect an experienced "mentor", who has experience in occupational hygiene is required to show a new occupational hygienist how to apply the learned scientific and management knowledge in the workplace and to the environment issue to satisfactorily resolve the problem.

To be a professional occupational hygienist, experience in as wide a practice as possible is required to demonstrate knowledge in areas of occupational hygiene. This is difficult for "specialists" or those who practice in narrow subject areas. Limiting experience to individual subject like asbestos remediation, confined spaces, indoor air quality, or lead abatement, or learning only through a textbook or "review course" can be a disadvantage when required to demonstrate competence in other areas of occupational hygiene. Information presented in Wikipedia can be considered to be only an outline of the requirements for professional occupational hygiene training. This is because the actual requirements in any country, state or region may vary due to educational resources available, industry demand or regulatory mandated requirements.

During 2010, the Occupational Hygiene Training Association (OHTA) through sponsorship provided by the IOHA initiated a training scheme for those with an interest in or those requiring training in occupational hygiene. These training modules can be downloaded and used freely. The available subject modules (Basic Principles in Occupational Hygiene, Health Effects of Hazardous Substances, Measurement of Hazardous Substances, Thermal Environment, Noise, Asbestos, Control, Ergonomics) are aimed at the 'foundation' and 'intermediate' levels in Occupational Hygiene. Although the modules can be used freely without supervision attendance at an accredited training course is encouraged. These training modules are available from OH Learning.com

Academic programmes offering industrial hygiene Bachelors or Masters degrees in United States may apply to the Accreditation Board for Engineering and Technology (ABET) to have their programme accredited. As of October 1, 2006, 27 institutions have accredited their industrial hygiene programmes. Accreditation is not available for Doctoral programmes.

In the U.S. the training of IH professionals is supported by [National Institute for Occupational Safety and Health]] through their NIOSH Education and Research Centres.

Professional Societies

The development of industrial hygiene societies originated in the United States, beginning with the first convening of members for the American Conference of Governmental Industrial Hygienists in 1938, and the formation of the American Industrial Hygiene Association in 1939. In the United Kingdom, the British Occupational Hygiene Society started in 1953. Through the years, professional occupational societies have formed in many different countries, leading to the formation of the International Occupational Hygiene Association in 1987, in order to promote and develop occupational hygiene worldwide through the member organizations. The IOHA has grown to 29 member organizations, representing over 20,000 occupational hygienists worldwide, with representation from countries present in every continent.

Occupational Hygiene Peer-reviewed Literature

There are several academic journals specifically focused on publishing studies and research in the occupational health field. The *Journal of Occupational and Environmental Hygiene* (JOEH) has been published jointly since 2004 by the American Industrial Hygiene Association and the American Conference of Governmental Industrial Hygienists, replacing the former *American Industrial Hygiene Association Journal* and *Applied Occupational & Environmental Hygiene* journals. Another seminal occupational hygiene journal would be *The Annals of Occuapational Hygiene,* published by the British Occupational Hygiene Society since 1958. Further, The National Institute for Occupational Safety and Health maintains a searchable bibliographic database (NIOSHTIC-2) of occupational safety and health publications, documents, grant reports, and other communication products.

Chapter 4

Sociology of Health and Illness

The Sociology of Health and Illness, alternatively the Sociology of Health and Wellness, examines the interaction between society and health. The objective of this topic is to see how social life has an impact on morbidity and mortality rate, and vice versa. This aspect of sociology differs from medical sociology in that this branch of sociology discusses health and illness in relation to social institutions such as family, employment, and school. The sociology of medicine limits its concern to the patient-practitioner relationship and the role of health professionals in society. The sociology of health and illness covers sociological pathology (causes of disease and illness), reasons for seeking particular types of medical aid, and patient compliance or noncompliance with medical regimes.

Health, or lack of health, was once merely attributed to biological or natural conditions. Sociologists have demonstrated that the spread of diseases is heavily influenced by the socioeconomic status of individuals, ethnic traditions or beliefs, and other cultural factors. Where medical research might gather statistics on a disease, a sociological perspective on an illness would provide insight on what external factors caused the demographics who contracted the disease to become ill.

This topic requires a global approach of analysis because the influence of societal factors varies throughout the world. This will be demonstrated through discussion of the major diseases of each continent. These diseases are sociologically examined and compared based on the traditional medicine, economics, religion, and culture that is specific to each region. HIV/AIDS serves as a common basis of comparison among regions. While it is extremely problematic in certain areas, in others it has affected a relatively small percentage of the population. Sociological factors can help to explain why these discrepancies exist.

There are obvious differences in patterns of health and illness across societies, over time, and within particular society types. There has historically been a long-term decline in mortality within industrialized societies, and on average, life-expectancies are considerably higher in developed, rather than developing or undeveloped, societies. Patterns of global change in health care systems make it more imperative than ever to research and comprehend the sociology of health and illness. Continuous changes in economy, therapy, technology and insurance can affect the way individual communities view and respond to the medical care available. These rapid fluctuations cause the issue of health and illness within social life to be very dynamic in definition. Advancing information is vital because as patterns evolve, the study of the sociology of health and illness constantly needs to be updated.

Historical Background

The study of health and illness within society is not revolutionary and neither is its research a new feat. Humans have long sought after advice from those with the knowledge or skill in healing. Paleopathology, and other historical records, allowing an examination of how ancient societies dealt with illness and outbreak. Rulers in Ancient Egypt sponsored physicians that were specialists in specific diseases. Imhotep was the first medical doctor known by name. An Egyptian who lived around 2650 B.C., he was an adviser to King Zoser at a time when Egyptians were making progress in medicine. Among his contributions to medicine was a textbook on the treatment of wounds, broken bones, and even tumors.

Stopping the spread of the infectious disease was of utmost importance for maintaining a healthy society. The outbreak of disease during the Peloponnesian War was recorded by Thucydides who survived the epidemic. From his account it is shown how factors outside the disease itself can have an impact on society. The Athenians were under siege and concentrated within the city. Major city centres were the hardest hit. This made the outbreak even more deadly and with probable food shortages the fate of Athens was inevitable. Approximately 25% of the population died of the disease. Thucydides stated that the epidemic "carried away all alike". The disease attacked people of different ages, sexes and nationalities.

Ancient medical systems stressed that the importance of reducing illness through divination and ritual. Other codes of behavior and dietary protocols were widespread in the ancient world. During the Zhou Dynasty in China, doctors suggested exercise, meditation and temperance to preserve one's health.

The Chinese closely link health with spiritual well-being. Health regimes in ancient India focused on oral health as the best method for a healthy life. The Talmudic code created rules for health which stressed ritual cleanliness, connected disease with certain animals and created diets. Other examples include the Mosaic Code and Roman baths and aqueducts.

Figure: *Physician in Ancient Greece treating a patient 480–470 BC*

Those that were most concerned with health, sanitation and illness in the ancient world were those in the elite class. Good health was thought to reduce the risk of spiritual defilement and therefore enhanced the social status of the ruling class who saw themselves as the beacon of civilization. During the late Roman Period, sanitation for the lower classes were a concern for the leisured class. Those that had the means would donate to charities that focused on the health of non-elites. After the decline of the Roman Empire, physicians and concern with public health disappeared except in the largest cities. Health and public doctors remained in the Byzantine Empire. Focusing on preventing the spread of diseases such as small pox lead to a smaller mortality rate in much of the western world. Other factors that allowed the modern rise in population includes: better nutrition and environmental reforms (such as getting clean water supplies).

The present day sense of health being a public concern for the state began in the Middle Ages. A few state interventions include maintaining clean towns, enforcing quarantines during epidemics and supervising sewer systems. Private corporations also played a role in public health. The funding for research and the institutions for them to work were funded by governments and private firms. Epidemics were the cause of most government interventions. The early goal of public health was reactionary whereas the modern goal is to prevent disease before it becomes a problem. Despite the overall improvement of world health, there still has not been any decrease in the health gap between the affluent and the impoverished.

Today, society is more likely to blame health issues on the individual rather than society as a whole. This was the prevailing view in the late 20th century. In the 1980s the Black Report, published in the United Kingdom, went against this view and argued that the true root of the problem was material deprivation. This report proposed a comprehensive anti-poverty strategy to address these issues. Since this did not parallel the views of England's conservative government, it did not go into action immediately. The Conservative government was criticized by the Labour Party for not implementing the suggestions that the Black Report listed. This criticism gave the Black Report the exposure it needed and its arguments were considered a valid explanation for health inequality. There is also a debate over whether poverty causes ill-health or if ill-health causes poverty. Arguments by the National Health Services gave considerable emphasis on poverty and lack of access to health care. It has also been found that heredity has more of a bearing on health than social environment, but research has also proved that there is indeed a positive correlation between socioeconomic inequalities and illness.

Methodology

The Sociology of Health and Illness looks at three areas: the conceptualization, the study of measurement and social distribution, and the justification of patterns in health and illness. By looking at these things researchers can look at different diseases through a sociological lens. The prevalence and response to different diseases varies by culture. By looking at bad health, researchers can see if health affects different social regulations or controls. When measuring the distribution of health and illness, it is useful to look at official statistics and community surveys. Official statistics make it possible to look at people who have been treated. It shows that they are both willing and able to use health services. It also sheds light on the infected person's view of their illness. On the other hand, community surveys look at people's rating of their health. Then looking at the relation of clinically defined illness and self reports and find that there is often a discrepancy.

A great deal of the time, mortality statistics take the place of the morbidity statistics because in many developed societies where people typically die from degenerative conditions, the age in which they die sheds more light on their life-time health. This produces many limitations when looking at the pattern of sickness, but sociologists try to look at various data to analyze the distribution better. Normally, developing societies have lower life expectancies in comparison to developed countries. They have also found correlations between mortality and sex and age. Very young and old people are more susceptible to sickness and death. On average women typically live longer than men, although women are more likely to have bad health.

Disparities in health were also found between people in different social classes and ethnicities within the same society, even though in the medical profession they put more importance in "health related behaviours" such as alcohol consumption, smoking, diet, and exercise. There is a great deal of data supporting the conclusion that these behaviours affect health more significantly than other factors. Sociologists think that it is more helpful to look at health and illness through a broad lens. Sociologists agree that alcohol consumption, smoking, diet, and exercise are important issues, but they also see the importance of analysing the cultural factors that affect these patterns. Sociologists also look at the effects that the productive process has on health and illness. While also looking at things such as industrial pollution, environmental pollution, accidents at work, and stress-related diseases.

Social factors play a significant role in developing health and illness. Studies of epidemiology show that autonomy and control in the workplace are vital factors in the etiology of heart disease. One cause is an effort-reward imbalance. Decreasing career advancement opportunities and major imbalances in control over work have been coupled with various negative health costs. Various studies have shown that pension rights may shed light on mortality differences between retired men and women of different socioeconomic statuses. These studies show that there are outside factors that influence health and illness.

International Perspective

Africa

HIV/AIDS is the leading epidemic that affects the social welfare of Africa. Human Immunodeficiency virus (HIV) can cause AIDS which is an acronym for Acquired Immunodeficiency Syndrome (AIDS), a condition in humans in which the immune system begins to fail, leading to life-threatening infections. Two-thirds of the worlds HIV population is located in Sub-Saharan Africa. Since the epidemic started more than 15 million Africans have died by complications with HIV/AIDS.

People apart of religious sub-groups of Sub-Saharan Africa and those who actively and frequently participate in religious activities are more likely to be at a lower risk of contracting HIV/AIDS. On the opposite end, there are many beliefs that an infected male can be cured of the infection by having sex with a virgin. These beliefs increase the number of people with the virus and also increase the number of rapes against women.

Herbal treatment is one of the primary medicines used to treat HIV in Africa. It is used more than standard treatment because it is more affordable. Herbal treatment is more affordable but is not researched and is poorly regulated . This lack of research on whether the herbal medicines work and what the medicines consist of is a major flaw in the healing cycle of HIV in Africa.

Economically, HIV has a significant negative impact. The labour force in Africa is slowly diminishing, due to HIV-related deaths and illness. In response, government income declines and so does tax revenue. The government has to spend more money than it is making, in order to care for those affected with HIV/AIDS.

A major social problem in Africa in regards to HIV is the orphan epidemic. The orphan epidemic in Africa is a regional problem. In most cases, both of the parents are affected with HIV. Due to this, the children are usually raised by their grandmothers and in extreme cases they are raised by themselves. In order to care for the sick parents, the children have to take on more responsibility by working to produce an income. Not only do the children lose their parents but they also lose their childhood as well. Having to provide care for their parents, the children also miss out on an education which increases the risk of teen pregnancy and people affected with HIV. The most efficient way to diminish the orphan epidemic is prevention: preventing children from acquiring HIV from their mothers at birth, as well as educating them on the disease as they grow older. Also, educating adults about HIV and caring for the infected people adequately will lower the orphan population.

The HIV/AIDS epidemic is reducing the average life expectancy of people in Africa by twenty years. The age range with the highest death rates, due to HIV, are those between the ages of 20 and 49 years. The fact that this age range is when adults acquire most of their income they cannot afford to send their children to school, due to the high medication costs. It also removes the people who could help aid in responding to the epidemic.

Asia

Asian countries have wide variations of population, wealth, technology and health care, causing attitudes towards health and illness to differ. Japan, for example, has the third highest life expectancy (82 years old), while Afghanistan has the 11th worst (44 years old). Key issues in Asian health include childbirth and maternal health, HIV and AIDS, mental health, and aging and the elderly. These problems are influenced by the sociological factors of religion or belief systems, attempts to reconcile traditional medicinal practices with modern professionalism, and the economic status of the inhabitants of Asia.

Like the rest of the world, Asia is threatened by a possible pandemic of HIV and AIDS. Vietnam is a good example of how society is shaping Asian HIV/AIDS awareness and attitudes towards this disease. Vietnam is a country with feudal, traditional roots, which, due to invasion, wars, technology and travel is becoming increasingly globalized. Globalization has altered traditional viewpoints and values. It is also responsible for the spread of HIV and AIDS in Vietnam. Even early globalization has added to this problem – Chinese influence made Vietnam a Confucian society, in which women are of less importance than men. Men in their superiority have no need to be sexually responsible, and women, generally not well educated, are often unaware of the risk, perpetuating the spread of HIV and AIDS as well as other STIs.

Confucianism has had a strong influence on the belief system in Asia for centuries, particularly in China, Japan, and Korea, and its influence can be seen in the way people chose to seek, or not seek, medical care. An important issue in Asia is societal impact on the ability of disabled individuals to adjust to a disability. Cultural beliefs shape attitudes towards physical and mental disabilities. China exemplifies this problem. According to Chinese Confucian tradition (which is also applicable in other countries where Confucianism has been spread), people should always pursue good health in their lives, with an emphasis on health promotion and disease prevention. To the Chinese, having a disability signifies that one has not led a proper lifestyle and therefore there is a lack of opportunities for disabled individuals to explore better ways to accept or adapt to their disability.

Indigenous healing practices are extremely diverse throughout Asia but often follow certain patterns and are still prevalent today.

Many traditional healing practices include shamanism and herbal medicines, and may have been passed down orally in small groups or even institutionalized and professionalized. In many developing countries the only health care available until a few decades ago were those based on traditional medicine and spiritual healing. Now governments must be careful to create health policies that strike a balance between modernity and tradition. Organizations, like the World Health Organization, try to create policies that respect tradition without trying to replace it with modern science, instead regulating it to ensure safety but keeping it accessible. India in particular tries to make traditional medicines safe but still available to as many people as possible, adapting tradition to match modernization while still considering the economic positions and culture of its citizens.

Mental health issues are gaining an increasing amount of attention in the Asian countries. Many of these countries have a preoccupation with modernizing and developing their economies, resulting in cultural changes. In order to reconcile modern techniques with traditional practices, social psychologists in India are in the process of "indigenizing psychology". Indigenous psychology is that which is derived from the laws, theories, principals, and ideas of a culture and unique to each society.

In many Asian countries, childbirth is still treated by traditional means and is thought of with regional attitudes. For example, in Pakistan, decisions concerning pregnancy and antenatal care (ANC) are usually made by older women, often the pregnant woman's mother-in-law, while the mother and father to be are distanced from the process. They may or may not receive professional ANC depending on their education, class, and financial situation. Generally in Asia, childbirth is still a woman's area and male obstetricians are rare. Female midwives and healers are still the norm in most places. Western methods are overtaking the traditional in an attempt to improve maternal health and increase the number of live births.

Asian countries, which are mostly developing nations, are aging rapidly even as they are attempting to build their economies. Even wealthy Asian nations, such as Japan, Singapore, and Taiwan, also have very elderly populations and thus have to try to sustain their economies and society with small younger generations while caring for their elderly citizens. The elderly have been traditionally well respected and well cared for in most Asian cultures; experts predict that younger generations in the future are less likely to be concerned and involved in the health care of their older relatives due to various factors such as women joining the workforce more, the separation of families because of urbanization or migration, and the proliferation of Western ideals such as individualism.

Australia

The health patterns found on the continent of Australia which includes the Pacific Islands, have been very much influenced by European colonization. While indigenous medicinal beliefs are not significantly prevalent in Australia, traditional ideas are still influential in the health care problems in many of the islands of the Pacific. The rapid urbanization of Australia led to epidemics of typhoid fever and the Bubonic plague. Because of this, public health was professionalized beginning in the late 1870s in an effort to control these and other diseases. Since then Australia's health system has evolved similarly to Western countries and the main cultural influence affecting health care are the political ideologies of the parties in control of the government.

Australia has had treatment facilities for 'problem drinkers' since the 1870s. In the 1960s and 1970s it was recognized that Australia had several hundred thousand alcoholics and prevention became a priority over cures, as there was a societal consensus that treatments are generally ineffective. The government began passing laws attempting to curb alcohol consumption but consistently met opposition from the wine-making regions of southern Australia. The government has also waged a war on illegal drugs, particularly heroin, which in the 1950s became widely used as a pain reliever.

Experts believe that many of the History of the Pacific Islands health problems in the Pacific Islands can be traced back to European colonization and the subsequent globalization and modernization of island communities. European colonization and late independence meant modernization but also slow economic growth, which had an enormous impact on health care, particularly on nutrition in the Pacific Islands. The end of colonization meant a loss of medical resources, and the fledgling independent governments could not afford to continue the health policies put in place by the colonial governments. Nutrition was changed radically, contributing to various other health problems. While more prosperous, urban areas could afford food, they chose poor diets, causing 'overnourishment', and leading to extremely high levels of obesity, type 2 diabetes, and cardiovascular diseases. Poorer rural communities, on the other hand, continue to suffer from malnutrition and malaria.

Traditional diets in the Pacific are very low in fat, but since World War II there has been a significant increase in fat and protein in Pacific diets. Native attitudes towards weight contribute to the obesity problem. Tongan natives see obesity as a positive thing, especially in men. They also believe that women should do as little physical work as possible while the men provide for them, meaning they get very little exercise.

Europe

The largest endeavors to improve health across Europe is the World Health Organization European Region. The goal is to improve the health of poor and disadvantaged populations by promoting healthy lifestyles including environmental, economic, social and providing health care. Overall health in Europe is very high compared to the rest of the world. The average life expectancy is around 78 in EU countries but there is a wide gap between Western and Eastern Europe. It is as low as 67 in Russia and 73 in the Balkan states. Europe is seeing an increase in the spread of HIV/AIDS in Eastern Europe because of a worsening socioeconomic situation. Cardiovascular disease, cancer and diabetes mellitus are more prevalent is Eastern Europe. The WHO claims that poverty is the most important factor bringing on ill health across Europe. Those at low Socioeconomic status levels and many young people are also at risk because of their increased tobacco, alcohol and drug abuse. Health and illness prevention in Europe is largely funded by the governmental services including: regulating health care, insurance and social programmes. The role of religion and traditional medicine however, is often left unexamined in such reports.

The study of hypertension within the United Kingdom has turned to examining the role that beliefs play in its diagnosis and treatment. Hypertension is an essential topic for study since it is linked to increased risk of stroke and coronary heart disease. The most common treatment for hypertension is medication but compliance for this treatment plan is low. A study conducted in the UK examined the differences between 'white' patients and first generation immigrants from the West Indies. There were differing reasons for non-compliance that involve the patients' perception and beliefs about the diagnosis. Patients commonly believe that high levels of anxiety when first diagnosed are the major cause and think that when stress levels decline so too will their hypertension. Other respondents in this UK based study had varying beliefs concerning the necessity of medication while others still argued that it was the side effects of medication that made them end their prescribed regimen. West Indian respondents whose lay culture teaches them to reject long-term drug therapy opted instead for folk remedies in higher numbers than the 'white' respondents. What can be seen here is that some people will choose to ignore a doctor's expert advice and will employ 'lay consultation' instead.

Before people seek medical help they try to interpret the symptoms themselves and often consult people in their lives or use 'self-help' measures. A study of 'everyday illness' in Finland including: influenza, infections and musculo-skeletal problems focused on reasons for consulting medical experts and explanations of illness. These common illness were examined not because of their seriousness but because of their frequency. The researchers explain five possible triggers that people seek medical aid: 1- the occurrence of an interpersonal crisis 2- perceived interference with social and personal relations 3- perceived interference with vocational & physical activity 4- sanctioning by other people 5- sufferers ideas about how long certain complaints should last. These kind of explanatory models are part of the process that people use to construct medical culture. They give meaning to illness and health, answer questions about personal responsibility about health and most importantly are part of the dialogue between patients' and professionals' illness explanations. It can help explore why some patients will follow a doctors instructions to the letter and others ignore them completely. A patient's explanation or understanding of their illness can be much broader than a physician's and this dynamic has become a major criticism of modern medical practice since it normally excludes the "social, psychological and experiential dimensions of illness."

The Finnish study examined 127 patients and the results have been different from findings in other countries where there is more 'lay consultation'. Half of the respondents did not have any lay consultation before coming to the doctors office. One-third did not try any self-treatment and three-quarters of the sample consulted the doctor within three days of symptoms developing. Possible explanations are that in Finland there is an aspect "over-protectiveness" within their health care system. Many might conclude that the Finnish people are dependent and helpless but the researchers of this study found that people chose to consult professionals because they trusted them over some lay explanation. These results echo similar studies in Ireland that explain this phenomenon as being based in a strong work ethic. Illness in these countries will affect their work and Finnish people will quickly get treatment so they can return to work. This research out of Finland also describes that this relationship between patient and doctor is based on:

1. national and municipal administrative bureaucracies that demand more output and more satisfied patients
2. the public demanding better care
3. nurses criticizing physicians for not taking a holistic view of patients
4. hospital specialists wanting better/earlier screening for serious illnesses (e.g. cancer).

The conflict between medical and lay worlds is prominent. On one hand many patients believe they are the expert of their own body and view the Doctor-patient relationship as authoritarian. These people will often use knowledge outside the medical field to deal with health and illness. Others see the doctor as the expert and are shy about describing their symptoms and therefore rely on the doctor for diagnosis and treatment.

North America

North America is a fairly recent settled continent, made up of the United States, Canada, Mexico, Central America, and the Caribbean. It was built by an amalgamation of wealth, ideas, culture, and practices. North America is highly advanced intellectually, technologically, and traditionally. This advantageous character of North American nations has caused a high average life expectancy of 75 years for males and 80 years for females. This leads to the conclusion that North America has cultivated a comparatively healthy society. As North America contains several core nations, the growing economies in those nations are able to maintain and develop medical institutions. This subsequently provides more access to health care for American citizens but health care is not universal. North America is known for being a leading nation in regards to industrialization and modernization, but the United States lacks federal laws regarding health care as a basic human right. This lag of health care security causes subsequent issues with pharmaceutical competition, lack of care for the elderly, and little attention to alternative medicine. Health care and education are plentiful at a price and illness still persists for many reasons. A main reason is that a lower- and middle-class population still exists in plentiful numbers, maintaining a group that is highly vulnerable to physical ailment.

North America's primary risk factors for illness are currently alcohol abuse, malnutrition, obesity, tobacco use, and water sanitation. Obesity is a recent epidemic in North America. The 1990s brought a rise in the average Body Mass Index, or BMI. From the beginning and to the end of the decade, the median percent of adults who were obese rose from 12% to 20%. Alcoholism is the addiction of over-consumption of alcohol and is highly prevalent in the US. There are high incidence rates in many other world regions.

Roughly 61% of American adults drank in 2007, and 21% of current drinkers consumed five or more drinks at one point in the last year. There have also been 22,073 alcohol induced deaths in the United States in the past year, about 13,000 of which were related to liver disease. Alcoholism has many risk factors ingrained in North American culture, such as heredity, stress from competition or availability.

The Swine Flu (also known as (H1N1) epidemic is a recent disease emerging in the early 21st century. In April 2009, during the early days of the outbreak, a molecular biologist named Dr. Henry Miller wrote in the *Wall Street Journal* about New York City high-school students. These students apparently brought the virus back from Mexico and infected their classmates. All six cases so far reported in Canada were connected directly or indirectly with travel to Mexico as well. Flu viruses can be directly transmitted (via droplets from sneezing or coughing) from pigs to people, and vice versa. These cross-species infections occur most commonly when people are close to large numbers of pigs, such as in barns, livestock exhibits at fairs, and slaughterhouses. The flu is transmissible from human to human, either directly or via contaminated surfaces."

South America

There are many diseases that affect South America, but two major conditions are malaria and Hepatitis D. Malaria affects every country in South America except Uruguay, Chile, and The Falkland Islands. Elevation is a major factor in the areas where malaria is found. The disease is spread from person to person via mosquito bites. People are typically bitten by mosquitoes at dusk and dawn. Symptoms of this disorder are: high fever, chills, sweating, headaches, body aches, weakness, vomiting and diarrhea. If left untreated, new symptoms can occur; people that are infected may experience seizures, delirium and coma. Severe cases may end in death. Malaria can be cured, but the symptoms may not become noticeable until months later. There are three forms of medication that can cure Malaria. An infected person's accessibility to these drugs is dependent upon their access to medical care and their financial situation. Literature about Malaria treatment typically is focused toward people who are tourists. Most sources are not written with the native in mind.

The first sign of Hepatitis D was detected in 1978 when a strange and unrecognizable internuclear antigen was discovered during a liver biopsy of several Italians who suffered HBV infection. Scientists initially thought that it was an antigenic specificity of HBV, but they soon found that it was a protein from another disease altogether. They called it "Hepatitis Delta Virus" (HDV). This new virus was found to be defective. HDV needed HBV to act as a helper function in order for it to be detected. Normally Hepatitis B is transmitted through blood or any type of blood product. In South America Hepatitis D was found to be fatal. Scientists are still unsure in what way this disease was being transmitted throughout certain South American countries. Sexual contact and drug use are the most common means of transmission. HDV is still considered an unusual form of hepatitis. Agents of this virus resemble that of plant viroids. It is still hard to tell how many stereotypes exist because HDV is under the umbrella of HBV. HDV causes very high titers in the blood of people who are infected. Incubation of Hepatitis D typically lasts for thirty five days. Most often Hepatitis D is a co-infection with Hepatitis B or a super-infection with chronic hepatitis. In terms of super infections there are high mortality rates, ranging seventy to eighty percent; in contrast with co-infections which have a one to three percent mortality rate. There is little information with the ecology of Hepatitis D. Epidemics have been found in Venezuela, Peru, Columbia, and Brazil. People who are treated for Hepatitis B have been able to control Hepatitis D. People who have chronic HDB will continue to get HDV.

Another disease that affects South America is HIV and AIDS. In 2008 roughly two million people had HIV and AIDS. By the end of 2008 one hundred and seventy thousand people were infected with AIDS and HIV. Seventy seven thousand people died from this disease by the end of that year. Brazil has the most people that are affected with AIDS and HIV in South America. Forty-three percent of people in Brazil have HIV. In Brazil sixty percent of the inhabitants use drugs, are HIV positive, and are HIV positive because of their drug use. Usually this disease is transmitted by either drug use involving needles or unprotected sex. Sharing needles and being infected with HIV and AIDS is most common in Paraguay and Uruguay. South America is trying to get treatment to the thousands of people infected by this disease. Brazil is offering generic AIDS prescriptions that are much less expensive than the name brand drugs. One hundred and eighty-one thousand inhabitants in Brazil who were infected are being treated. That accounts for eighty percent of those who needed immediate help. This aid from the government has had positive results. Statistics show that there was a fifty percent decrease in mortality rates, approximately sixty to eighty percent decrease in morbidity rates and a seventy percent decrease in hospitalization of infected people.

In very remote areas of South America, traditional healers are the only forms of health care people have. In north Aymara and south Mapuche, where the indigenous groups have the strongest voices, they still heavily use traditional medicine. The government in Chile has implemented an Indigenous Health System to help strengthen the health care system. Even with Chile's indigenous groups, Chile still has the best public health services in South America. They also have the lowest mortality rates in the area. Their health care policies are centred around family and community wellbeing by focusing on the strategies for prevention health strategies. Reports have shown an increase in mental health issues, diabetes, and cardiovascular diseases.

South America's economy is developing rapidly and has a great deal of industries. The major industry in South America are agriculture. Other industries are fishing, handicrafts, and natural resources. Its trade and import-export market is continually thriving. In the past South American countries moved slowly in regards to economic development. South America began to build its economy ever since World War II. South America's largest economies are Brazil, Chile, Argentina, and Columbia. Venezuela, Peru, and Argentina's economy are growing very rapidly.

Medical Sociology

Medical sociology is the sociological analysis of medical organizations and institutions; the production of knowledge and selection of methods, the actions and interactions of healthcare professionals, and the social or cultural (rather than clinical or bodily) effects of medical practice. The field commonly interacts with the sociology of knowledge, science and technology studies, and social epistemology. Medical sociologists are also interested in the qualitative experiences of patients, often working at the boundaries of public health, social work, demography and gerontology to explore phenomena at the intersection of the social and clinical sciences. Health disparities commonly relate to typical categories such as class and race. Objective sociological research findings quickly become a normative and political issue.

Early work in medical sociology was conducted by Lawrence J Henderson whose theoretical interests in the work of Vilfredo Pareto inspired Talcott Parsons interests in sociological systems theory.

Parsons is one of the founding fathers of medical sociology, and applied social role theory to interactional relations between sick people and others. Key contributors to medical sociology since the 1950s include Howard S. Becker, Mike Bury, Peter Conrad, Jack Douglas, David Silverman, Phil Strong, Bernice Pescosolido, Carl May, Anne Rogers, Anselm Strauss, Renee Fox, and Joseph W. Schneider.

The field of medical sociology is usually taught as part of a wider sociology, clinical psychology or health studies degree course, or on dedicated Master's degree courses where it is sometimes combined with the study of medical ethics/bioethics. In Britain, sociology was introduced into the medical curriculum following the Goodenough report in 1944: "In medicine, 'social explanations' of the aetiology of disease meant for some doctors a redirection of medical thought from the purely clinical and psychological criteria of illness. The introduction of 'social' factors into medical explanation was most strongly evidenced in branches of medicine closely related to the community — Social Medicine and, later, General Practice" (Reid 1976).

History

Medical sociology can trace its intellectual lineage to the late 1800s. In the nineteenth century, two nascent disciplines — sociology and allopathic medicine — began to cross paths. For allopathic medicine, this time period witnessed the beginnings of medicine's ongoing attempts to consolidate its professional powers and social legitimacy. Meanwhile, sociology (the term being first coined by Auguste Comte in 1838) was beginning to emerge as a distinct discipline. The first publication which formally linked medicine and sociology was The Importance of the Study of Medical Sociology", authored by Charles McIntire and first published in 1894. Two key books followed, Elizabeth Blackwell's (1902) "Essays in Medical Sociology" and the James P. Warbasse (1909) "Medical Sociology". The first journal to focus on medical sociology was the Journal of Sociologic Medicine, which was published by the American Academy of Medicine, and existing for four years between 1915 and 1919. The American Public Health Association hosted a similar "Section of Sociology" between 1909 and 1921. It took another quarter century before the next medical sociology journal (Journal of Health and Human Behavior) would appear.

The initial timing and brief duration of these links between medicine and sociology reflected a much broader transformation taking place within allopathic medicine and between medicine and society, as both rushed to affirm the validity of scientific medicine. As medicine grew in clinical effectiveness and organizational complexity, the social-psychological and behavioural sides of medicine began to lose attention, with instruction, research, and principles relegated to "second order" of medical fields such as psychiatry and public health. Scattered "sociology of medicine" articles would continue to appear infrequently in medical journals between 1920 and 1950.

In 1960, Austin Porterfield published what would become the first substantive disciplinary journal in medical sociology, the Journal of Health & Human Behavior (JHHB). In the spring of 1967, the American Sociological Association (ASA) took JHHB under its organizational wing where it was renamed the Journal of Health and Social Behavior (JHSB). Eliot Freidson was the first editor. This same year also marked the first issue of Social Science & Medicine (SS&M), with its distinctively international and multidisciplinary social science focus.

By the early 1970s, the medical sociology section of the British Sociological Association had established its own organizational footprint, and in 1979 published its own "medical sociology" journal (Sociology of Health & Illness). During the 1950s and 1960s, the field of medical sociology underwent an explosive period of growth—before peaking in the early 1970s. During these two decades, the field enjoyed considerable academic excitement and success, including what today might be considered a lavish amount of grant support, both from private foundations and the federal government. At its peak in the early 1970s, for example, the National Institute of Mental Health subcommittee for social science training was awarding 1,500 graduate student stipends per year — 80% of which went to sociology departments. The number of stipends was well in excess of what was needed to support medical sociology graduate students, and the entire field of sociology benefited from this philanthropic and federal largess.

Even the founding of the medical sociology section itself and the ASA's decision to adopt the JHSB were underwritten by outside funding. Membership in the new ASA section (established in 1959) was mercurial. In less than a year, the medical sociology section grew to 561 members. By 1964, membership had soared to nearly 900 (which, not incidentally, is close to the section's membership today). In less than a half dozen years, the field went from publishing introductions to the field to summative reviews (one notable example is Eliot Freidson's[1961] "The Sociology of Medicine: A Trend Report and Bibliography," published as a special issue in Current Sociology).

By the mid-1970s, however, there were signs of trouble. Established funding streams had dried up and were not replaced by alternative resources. Section membership had plateaued and coverage of medical/

health issues in flagship sociology journals, such as the AJS and the American Sociological Review, became more infrequent. Meanwhile, colleges and universities were undergoing their own upheavals. Faced with considerable financial pressures, schools looked to trim programmes, and sociology was high on a number of lists. As one small but indicative example, Yale University's Department of Sociology, which housed the first medical sociology programme in the United States, decided in the 1990s to eliminate that programme.

The 1980s and 1990s were a difficult time for allopathic medicine as well. The rise of managed care, the commodification of medical services, and the discovery of medicine by Wall Street and corporate America during 1985 and 1997 earth-shattering implications for the future of medicine as an autonomous profession. The 1970s through early 1990s also were a time of vigorous debates within academic sociology about the fate and future of allopathic medicine as a profession (Hafferty and Light 1995; Hafferty and Wolinsky 1991). Beginning with Eliot Freidson's (1970a, 1970b) transformative Profession of Medicine and Professional Dominance, a number of distinguished medical sociologists in the United States (Mark Field, David Frankford, Marie Haug, Eliot Krause, Donald Light, John McKinlay, Fredric Wolinsky) and elsewhere (David Coburn, Julio Frenk, Rudolf Klein, Magali Larson, Gerald Larkin, ElianneRiska, Evan Willis) began to debate the changing fortunes of organized medicine's status as a profession (Hafferty and McKinlay 1993). Once again medicine and sociology crossed paths. It is worth noting, however, that by the time organized medicine began to mount a campaign to reestablish its professional status and stature, sociologists had moved on to other debates (Castellani and Hafferty 2006).

Issues of Identity and Identification From its very conception as an academic entity, medical sociology has been plagued by issues of identity (self) and of identification (others). On the one hand, the study of medical and health issues offered sociology great challenges and opportunities. On the other hand, these same opportunities had the potential to strip sociology of its unique perspective. One hallmark of this tension is the now 50-year-old debate about whether the ASA's section should be named "medical sociology" or whether it should sport some other marquee such as "health sociology" or the "sociology of health and illness." Many of these tensions are reflected in Robert Straus's (1957) famous distinction between sociology of and sociology in medicine.

The problem is one of placement and perspective. The former (of) reflects situations where sociologists maintain their disciplinary base (an academic sociology department for example) and train their sociological lens on fields of enquiry (such as medicine) for the purpose of answering sociological questions. The latter (in) connotes a state of affairs where sociologists work, for example, in a medical setting and employ sociological concepts and perspectives to solve problems that are defined as such by medicine. Sociology of medicine thus became considered (by academically based sociologists) as more in keeping with the sociological tradition, with the presumption being that those operating from a sociology in medicine ran the risk of being co-opted or at least corrupted by the medical perspective.

More recently, there have been efforts to "retire" this distinction by insisting that sociology has passed through its of/in phase and has graduated into a sociology with medicine (Levine 1987). Organized medicine remains one of the most powerful social institutions in modern times—forces of deprofessionalization not withstanding. Furthermore, medicine has little incentive (then or now) to welcome sociology to its table unless it feels that sociology can help solve issues or problems—as defined by medicine (and not sociology).

Under such circumstances (and expectations), any working relationship between sociology and medicine involves considerable potential for sociology to undergo disciplinary co-option. Sociologists who work in medical settings must be particularly sensitive to these issues. Often they function betwixt and between, receiving little respect from physicians or from their academically based peers who consider their "wayward" colleges to be too "applied." Whatever the particulars, organized medicine retains considerable institutional power and social legitimacy within today's society. Medicine has been able to establish its knowledge, skills, and culture as the everyday, taken-for-granted order of things and this is what makes the medical perspective so potentially corrupting.

The move to introduce medical sociology into the medical school and nursing curriculum played an important role in the discipline's evolution as an institutional entity. The first beachhead came in 1959, when Robert Straus founded the first Department of Behavioural Science at the University of Kentucky. Straus also helped to found, in 1970, the discipline's first professional association (Association for the Behavioural Sciences and Medical Education). For Straus, "behavioural science" (note the singular form) reflected the intersection of medical sociology, medical anthropology, and medical psychology—and therefore represented a unique and transcending social science discipline. The field quickly established a presence within a number (but not all) of medical schools during the 1960s and 1970s, particularly in those 40+ community medical schools that were being founded during the 1970s and 1980s.

Key Themes

We see two emergent lines of sociological investigation as we move to examine the future of medical sociology — each related to the other. The first is globalization. It is clear that the world in which we live is going through major transformation. This is particularly true of health and health care. We now live in a world where the spread of disease is global and where the poor health of one country affects the well-being of others. Global financial markets and economic competition are challenging the ability of business and governments to provide affordable health care. As such, we can expect that as globalization increases, so will its importance as a major theme in medical sociology (Bury 2005). There are an increasing number of studies examining issues of health and illness in countries other than the United States or Britain—far more than can be listed here.

Resources such as Mechanic and Rochefort's (1996) "Comparative Medical Systems" and Cockerham's (2004) The Blackwell Companion to Medical Sociology (with its 17 chapters on the United States, Canada, Mexico, Brazil, the United Kingdom, France, Germany, Sweden, Russia, Poland, the Czech Republic, South Africa, the Arab world, Israel, Australia, Japan, and the People's Republic of China) provide an excellent beginning. The second and related theme is "complexity science." As argued by a growing list of scholars, and due to key factors such as the information revolution and globalization, and emerging theme within twentieth-first-century science is complexity (Capra 1996, 2002). One example is the study of complex health networks (Freeman 2004; Scott 2000).

While this perspective has been an important part of medical sociology since the 1970s, primarily in terms of explaining the role that social support and kinship networks play in promoting health and well-being, the latest advances in the study of complex networks (e.g., small worlds, scale-free networks) are providing new insights into the processes by which diseases spread and the ways that health care providers can improve the health and well-being of large populations (Watts 2004). As these two new themes suggest, the theoretical framework of medical sociology continues to change to meet the new and contextually grounded needs of health care providers and patients. Medical sociology is—and remains—a theoretically rich area of study.

Role of Medical Sociologist in Hospital

Medical Sociology is a specialization within the field of sociology.Its main interest is in the study of health,health behavior and medical institutions. Illness is viewed not only as a medical problems but also psychological and social problem. The problems presented by patients are not always purely medical but also psycho-social. Diseases such as tuberculosis, leprosy, sexually transmitted diseases have a big social component in their aetiology.

Medical sociologist study of social behavioural and cultural factors of illness. A social approach to disease treatment is also emphasized. A successful Medical Sociologist must possess a knowledge of the community and the factors which affects the health of the community. Medical Sociologist will look at the patient illness in a social dimensions. They try to find out root causes of the illness on social ground, rectify the reasons and they will help the physician to understand the actual reasons for the diseases and illness that occurred to the patients. Mostly, Medical sociologist will be functioning as a "Doctor Patient Relationship Officers" in hospital sectors.

DPRO role is to associate with the patients and physician to bridge the gap and to provide the holistic health to the patients. Medical sociologist are all like a counsellors who council the patient and to understand the social problem. They will try to guide them and make them to realize the actual root cause of the problem.

School Hygiene

School hygiene or school hygiene education is a healthcare science, a form of the wider school health education. School hygiene is a study of school environment influence; it explores affection of schooling to mental and physical health of students.

The primary aims of school hygiene education is to improve behavior through useful practices connected to personal, water, food, domestic and public hygiene. Also, it aims to protect water and food supplies and to safely manage environmental factors.

History of School Hygiene

School hygiene expert Fletcher B. Dresslar explained in his 1915 work *School Hygiene* that "School Hygiene is the branch of this science [hygiene] which has to do with the conservation and development of the health of school children." The school was looked upon as existing "not only for the welfare of each child in attendance, but also for the welfare of the state and the nation." Dresslar broke school hygiene up into two essential parts: "the physical environment of the child during his school life" and "the laws of mental hygiene as illustrated by the proper adjustment of the subjects of the curriculum to the mental powers and needs of the children."

School hygiene as a major discipline was at its zenith in the United States and England in the late 19th and early 20th century, with major works of the subject being offered by various authors, among them Sir Arthur Newsholme, Edward R. Shaw, Robert A. Lyster, and G.G. Groff. After this time period, the school hygiene discipline became part of a comprehensive look at school health education; the American School Hygiene Association became inactive, and the American School Health Association was founded. Exclusive focus on hygiene was no longer prominent.

School hygiene still appears to be an active, separate discipline in other parts of the world, like Eastern Europe and developing countries where school sanitation norms are not as well established.

School Environment

Schools can determine children's health and well-being by their exposure to a healthy or unhealthy school environment. There are lot of architectural and aesthetic aspects related to a school's hygienic needs, such as: school's building plan, safe water supply, disposition of waste, emergency lighting, heating and ventilation, as well as adequate school facilities (halls, classrooms, and common areas) and furniture.

School Location

Due to health reasons (influence of noise, exhaust gases from vehicles, and potential risk of accident), schools in an urban and suburban areas should be located more than 100 meters away from major traffic and causeways. Some studies suggest it is best to orient and design a school building so that natural light can be a part of the lighting scheme of the school, and that buildings should avoid being placed in a valley, due to air quality issues.

Importance of School Hygiene

Schools have a central place in the health of a community. Inappropriate hygiene in schools can cause many diseases. If there are no school sanitation and hygiene facilities, or if they aren't maintained and used adequately, schools become places where diseases are likely transmitted.

Industrial Hygiene

What is Industrial Hygiene?

Industrial hygiene is the science of anticipating, recognizing, evaluating, and controlling workplace conditions that may cause workers' injury or illness. Industrial hygienists use environmental monitoring and analytical methods to detect the extent of worker exposure and employ engineering, work practice controls, and other methods to control potential health hazards.

There has been an awareness of industrial hygiene since antiquity. The environment and its relation to worker health was recognized as early as the fourth century BC when Hippocrates noted lead toxicity in the mining industry. In the first century AD, Pliny the Elder, a Roman scholar, perceived health risks to those working with zinc and sulphur. He devised a face mask made from an animal bladder to protect workers from exposure to dust and lead fumes. In the second century AD, the Greek physician, Galen, accurately described the pathology of lead poisoning and also recognized the hazardous exposures of copper miners to acid mists.

In the Middle Ages, guilds worked at assisting sick workers and their families. In 1556 the German scholar, Agricola, advanced the science of industrial hygiene even further when, in his book *De Re Metallica,* he described the diseases of miners and prescribed preventive measures. The book included suggestions for mine ventilation and worker protection, discussed mining accidents, and described diseases associated with mining occupations such as silicosis.

Industrial hygiene gained further respectability in 1700 when Bernardo Ramazzini, known as the "father of industrial medicine," published in Italy the first comprehensive book on industrial medicine, *De Morbis Artificum Diatriba (The Diseases of Workmen).* The book contained accurate descriptions of the occupational diseases of most of the workers of his time. Ramazzini greatly affected the future of industrial hygiene because he asserted that occupational diseases should be studied in the work environment rather than in hospital wards.

Industrial hygiene received another major boost in 1743 when Ulrich Ellenborg published a pamphlet on occupational diseases and injuries among gold miners. Ellenborg also wrote about the toxicity of carbon monoxide, mercury, lead, and nitric acid.

In England in the 18th century, Percival Pott, as a result of his findings on the insidious effects of soot on chimney sweepers, was a major force in getting the British Parliament to pass the *Chimney-Sweepers Act of 1788.* The passage of the English Factory Acts beginning in 1833 marked the first effective legislative acts in the field of industrial safety. The Acts, however, were intended to provide compensation for accidents rather than to control their causes. Later, various other European nations developed workers' compensation acts, which stimulated the adoption of increased factory safety precautions and the establishment of medical services within industrial plants.

In the early 20th century in the U. S., Dr. Alice Hamilton, led efforts to improve industrial hygiene. She observed industrial conditions first hand and startled mine owners, factory managers, and state officials with evidence that there was a correlation between worker illness and their exposure to toxins. She also presented definitive proposals for eliminating unhealthful working conditions.

At about the same time, U.S. federal and state agencies began investigating health conditions in industry. In 1908, the public's awareness of occupationally related diseases stimulated the passage of compensation acts for certain civil employees. States passed the first workers' compensation laws in 1911. And in 1913, the New York Department of Labour and the Ohio Department of Health established the first state industrial hygiene programmes. All states enacted such legislation by 1948. In most states, there is some compensation coverage for workers contracting occupational diseases.

What is a Worksite Analysis?

A worksite analysis is an essential first step that helps an industrial hygienist determine what jobs and work stations are the sources of potential problems. During the worksite analysis, the industrial hygienist measures and identifies exposures, problem tasks, and risks. The most effective worksite analyses include all jobs, operations, and work activities. The industrial hygienist inspects, researches, or analyses how the particular chemicals or physical hazards at that worksite affect worker health. If a situation hazardous to health is discovered, the industrial hygienist recommends the appropriate corrective actions.

How do IH's Recognize and Control Hazards?

Industrial hygienists recognize that engineering, work practice, and administrative controls are the primary means of reducing employee exposure to occupational hazards. Engineering controls minimize employee exposure by either reducing or removing the hazard at the source or isolating the worker from the hazards.

Engineering controls include eliminating toxic chemicals and replacing harmful toxic materials with less hazardous ones, enclosing work processes or confining work operations, and installing general and local ventilation systems.

Work practice controls alter the manner in which a task is performed. Some fundamental and easily implemented work practice controls include (1) following proper procedures that minimize exposures while operating production and control equipment; (2) inspecting and maintaining process and control equipment on a regular basis; (3) implementing good house-keeping procedures; (4) providing good supervision and (5) mandating that eating, drinking, smoking, chewing tobacco or gum, and applying cosmetics in regulated areas be prohibited.

Administrative controls include controlling employees' exposure by scheduling production and workers' tasks, or both, in ways that minimize exposure levels. For example, the employer might schedule operations with the highest exposure potential during periods when the fewest employees are present.

When effective work practices and/or engineering controls are not feasible to achieve the permissible exposure limit, or while such controls are being instituted, and in emergencies, appropriate respiratory equipment must be used. In addition, personal protective equipment such as gloves, safety goggles, helmets, safety shoes, and protective clothing may also be required. To be effective, personal protective equipment must be individually selected, properly fitted and periodically refitted; conscientiously and properly worn; regularly maintained; and replaced as necessary.

What Are Some Examples of Job Hazards?

To be effective in recognizing and evaluating on-the-job hazards and recommending controls, industrial hygienists must be familiar with the hazards' characteristics. Major job risks can include air contaminants, and chemical, biological, physical, and ergonomic hazards.

Air Contaminants

These are commonly classified as either particulate or gas and vapour contaminants. The most common particulate contaminants include dusts, fumes, mists, aerosols, and fibers. Dusts are solid particles that are formed or generated from solid organic or inorganic materials by reducing their size through mechanical processes such as crushing, grinding, drilling, abrading or blasting.

Fumes are formed when material from a volatilized solid condenses in cool air. In most cases, the solid particles resulting from the condensation react with air to form an oxide.

The term mist is applied to a finely divided liquid suspended in the atmosphere. Mists are generated by liquids condensing from a vapour back to a liquid or by breaking up a liquid into a dispersed state such as by splashing, foaming or atomizing. Aerosols are also a form of a mist characterized by highly respirable, minute liquid particles.

Fibres are solid particles whose length is several times greater than their diameter.

Gases are formless fluids that expand to occupy the space or enclosure in which they are confined. Examples are welding gases such as acetylene, nitrogen, helium, and argon; and carbon monoxide generated from the operation of internal combustion engines or by its use as a reducing gas in a heat treating operation. Another example is hydrogen sulfide which is formed wherever there is decomposition of materials containing sulphur under reducing conditions.

Liquids change into vapours and mix with the surrounding atmosphere through evaporation. Vapours are the volatile form of substances that are normally in a solid or liquid state at room temperature and pressure. Vapours are the gaseous form of substances which are normally in the solid or liquid state at room temperature and pressure. They are formed by evaporation from a liquid or solid and can be found where parts cleaning and painting takes place and where solvents are used.

Chemical Hazards

Harmful chemical compounds in the form of solids, liquids, gases, mists, dusts, fumes, and vapours exert toxic effects by inhalation (breathing), absorption (through direct contact with the skin), or ingestion (eating or drinking). Airborne chemical hazards exist as concentrations of mists, vapours, gases, fumes, or solids. Some are toxic through inhalation and some of them irritate the skin on contact; some can be toxic by absorption through the skin or through ingestion, and some are corrosive to living tissue.

The degree of worker risk from exposure to any given substance depends on the nature and potency of the toxic effects and the magnitude and duration of exposure.

Information on the risk to workers from chemical hazards can be obtained from the Material Safety Data Sheet (MSDS) that OSHA'S *Hazard Communication Standard* requires be supplied by the manufacturer or importer to the purchaser of all hazardous materials. The MSDS is a summary of the important health, safety, and toxicological information on the chemical or the mixture's ingredients. Other provisions of the *Hazard Communication Standard* require that all containers of hazardous substances in the workplace have appropriate warning and identification labels.

Biological Hazards

These include bacteria, viruses, fungi, and other living organisms that can cause acute and chronic infections by entering the body either directly or through breaks in the skin. Occupations that deal with plants or animals or their products or with food and food processing may expose workers to biological hazards. Laboratory and medical personnel also can be exposed to biological hazards. Any occupations that result in contact with bodily fluids pose a risk to workers from biological hazards.

In occupations where animals are involved, biological hazards are dealt with by preventing and controlling diseases in the animal population as well as proper care and handling of infected animals. Also, effective personal hygiene, particularly proper attention to minor cuts and scratches, especially those on the hands and forearms, helps keep worker risks to a minimum. In occupations where there is potential exposure to biological hazards, workers should practice proper personal hygiene, particularly hand washing. Hospitals should provide proper ventilation, proper personal protective equipment such as gloves and respirators, adequate infectious waste disposal systems, and appropriate controls including isolation in instances of particularly contagious diseases such as tuberculosis.

Physical Hazards

These include excessive levels of ionizing and nonionizing electromagnetic radiation, noise, vibration, illumination, and temperature. In occupations where there is exposure to ionizing radiation, time, distance, and shielding are important tools in ensuring worker safety. Danger from radiation increases with the amount of time one is exposed to it; hence, the shorter the time of exposure the smaller the radiation danger.

Distance also is a valuable tool in controlling exposure to both ionizing and non-ionizing radiation. Radiation levels from some sources can be estimated by comparing the squares of the distances between the worker and the source. For example, at a reference point of 10 feet from a source, the radiation is 1/100 of the intensity at 1 foot from the source. Shielding also is a way to protect against radiation. The greater the protective mass between a radioactive source and the worker, the lower the radiation exposure.

Nonionizing radiation also is dealt with by shielding workers from the source. Sometimes limiting exposure times to nonionizing radiation or increasing the distance is not effective. Laser radiation, for example, cannot be controlled effectively by imposing time limits. An exposure can be hazardous that is faster than the blinking of an eye. Increasing the distance from a laser source may require miles before the energy level reaches a point where the exposure would not be harmful.

Noise, another significant physical hazard, can be controlled by various measures. Noise can be reduced by installing equipment and systems that have been engineered, designed, and built to operate quietly; by enclosing or shielding noisy equipment; by making certain that equipment is in good repair and properly maintained with all worn or unbalanced parts replaced; by mounting noisy equipment on special mounts to reduce vibration; and by installing silencers, mufflers, or baffles.

Substituting quiet work methods for noisy ones is another significant way to reduce noise, for example, welding parts rather than riveting them. Also, treating floors, ceilings, and walls with acoustical material can reduce reflected or reverberant noise. In addition, erecting sound barriers at adjacent work stations around noisy operations will reduce worker exposure to noise generated at adjacent work stations.

It is also possible to reduce noise exposure by increasing the distance between the source and the receiver, by isolating workers in acoustical booths, limiting workers' exposure time to noise, and by providing hearing protection. OSHA requires that workers in noisy surroundings be periodically tested as a precaution against hearing loss.

Another physical hazard, radiant heat exposure in factories such as steel mills, can be controlled by installing reflective shields and by providing protective clothing.

Ergonomic Hazards

The science of ergonomics studies and evaluates a full range of tasks including, but not limited to, lifting, holding, pushing, walking, and reaching. Many ergonomic problems result from technological changes such as increased assembly line speeds, adding specialized tasks, and increased repetition; some problems arise from poorly designed job tasks. Any of those conditions can cause ergonomic hazards such as excessive vibration and noise, eye strain, repetitive motion, and heavy lifting problems. Improperly designed tools or work areas also can be ergonomic hazards. Repetitive motions or repeated shocks over prolonged periods of time as in jobs involving sorting, assembling, and data entry can often cause irritation and inflammation of the tendon sheath of the hands and arms, a condition known as carpal tunnel syndrome.

Ergonomic hazards are avoided primarily by the effective design of a job or jobsite and better designed tools or equipment that meet workers' needs in terms of physical environment and job tasks. Through thorough worksite analyses, employers can set up procedures to correct or control ergonomic hazards by using the appropriate engineering controls (e.g., designing or re-designing work stations, lighting, tools, and equipment); teaching correct work practices (e.g., proper lifting methods); employing proper administrative controls (e.g., shifting workers among several different tasks, reducing production demand, and increasing rest breaks); and, if necessary, providing and mandating personal protective equipment. Evaluating working conditions from an ergonomics standpoint involves looking at the total physiological and psychological demands of the job on the worker.

Overall, industrial hygienists point out that the benefits of a well-designed, ergonomic work environment can include increased efficiency, fewer accidents, lower operating costs and more effective use of personnel.

In sum, industrial hygiene encompasses a broad spectrum of the working environment. Early in its history OSHA recognized industrial hygiene as an integral part of a healthful work setting. OSHA places a high priority on using industrial hygiene concepts in its health standards and as a tool for effective enforcement of job safety and health regulations. By recognizing and applying the principles of industrial hygiene to the work environment, America's workplaces will become more healthful and safer.

Food Safety

Food safety is a scientific discipline describing handling, preparation, and storage of food in ways that prevent foodborne illness. This includes a number of routines that should be followed to avoid potentially severe health hazards. The tracks within this line of thought are safety between industry and the market and then between the market and the consumer. In considering industry to market practices, food safety considerations include the origins of food including the practices relating to food labeling, food hygiene, food additives and pesticide residues, as well as policies on biotechnology and food and guidelines for the management of governmental import and export inspection and certification systems for foods. In considering market to consumer practices, the usual thought is that food ought to be safe in the market and the concern is safe delivery and preparation of the food for the consumer.

Food can transmit disease from person to person as well as serve as a growth medium for bacteria that can cause food poisoning. In developed countries there are intricate standards for food preparation, whereas in lesser developed countries the main issue is simply the availability of adequate safe water, which is usually a critical item. In theory, food poisoning is 100% preventable. The five key principles of food hygiene, according to WHO, are:

1. Prevent contaminating food with pathogens spreading from people, pets, and pests.
2. Separate raw and cooked foods to prevent contaminating the cooked foods.
3. Cook foods for the appropriate length of time and at the appropriate temperature to kill pathogens.
4. Store food at the proper temperature.
5. Do use safe water and cooked materials.

ISO 22000

ISO 22000 is a standard developed by the International Organization for Standardization dealing with food safety. This is a general derivative of ISO 9000. ISO 22000 standard: The ISO 22000 international standard specifies the requirements for a food safety management system that involves interactive communication, system management, prerequisite programmes, HACCP principles.

Incidence

A 2003 World Health Organization (WHO) report concluded that about 30% of reported food poisoning outbreaks in the WHO European Region occur in private homes. According to the WHO and CDC, in the USA alone, annually, there are 76 million cases of foodborne illness leading to 325,000 hospitalizations and 5,000 deaths.

Chapter 5

Regulatory Agencies

WHO and FAO

In 2003, the WHO and FAO published the Codex Alimentarius which serves as a guideline to food safety.

However, according to Unit 04 - Communication of Health & Consumers Directorate-General of the European Commission (SANCO): "The Codex, while being recommendations for voluntary application by members, Codex standards serve in many cases as a basis for national legislation. The reference made to Codex food safety standards in the World Trade Organizations' Agreement on Sanitary and Phytosanitary measures (SPS Agreement) means that Codex has far reaching implications for resolving trade disputes. WTO members that wish to apply stricter food safety measures than those set by Codex may be required to justify these measures scientifically." So, an agreement made in 2003, signed by all member states, inclusive all EU, in the codex Stan Codex 240 – 2003 for coconut milk, sulphite containing additives like E223 and E 224 are allowed till 30 mg/kg, does NOT mean, they are allowed into the EU, "sulphite unauthorised in coconut milk from Thailand ". Same for polysorbate E 435, unauthorised polysorbates in coconut milk and, 2007. AIC from France. Only for the latter the EU amended its regulations with (EU) No 583/2012 per 2 July 2012 to allow this additive, already used for decades and absolutely necessary.

Australia

Food Standards Australia New Zealand requires all food businesses to implement food safety systems. These systems are designed to ensure food is safe to consume and halt the increasing incidence of food poisoning, and they include basic food safety training for at least one person in each business. Food safety training is delivered in various forms by Registered Training Organizations (RTOs), after which staff are issued a nationally recognised unit of competency code on their certificate. Basic food safety training includes:

- Understanding the hazards associated with the main types of food and the conditions to prevent the growth of bacteria which can cause food poisoning and to prevent illness.
- Potential problems associated with product packaging such as leaks in vacuum packs, damage to packaging or pest infestation, as well as problems and diseases spread by pests.
- Safe food handling. This includes safe procedures for each process such as receiving, re-packing, food storage, preparation and cooking, cooling and re-heating, displaying products, handling products when serving customers, packaging, cleaning and sanitizing, pest control, transport and delivery. Also covers potential causes of cross contamination.
- Catering for customers who are particularly at risk of food-borne illness, as well as those with allergies or intolerance.
- Correct cleaning and sanitizing procedures, cleaning products and their correct use, and the storage of cleaning items such as brushes, mops and cloths.
- Personal hygiene, hand washing, illness, and protective clothing.

New legislation means that people responsible for serving unsafe food may be liable for heavy fines.

China

Food safety is a growing concern in Chinese agriculture. The Chinese government oversees agricultural production as well as the manufacture of food packaging, containers, chemical additives, drug production, and business regulation. In recent years, the Chinese government attempted to consolidate food regulation with the creation of the State Food and Drug Administration in 2003, and officials have also been under increasing public and international pressure to solve food safety problems. However, it appears that regulations are not well known by the trade. Labels used for "green" food, "organic" food and "pollution-free" food are not well recognized by traders and many are unclear about their meaning. A survey by the World Bank found that supermarket managers had difficulty in obtaining produce that met safety requirements and found that a high percentage of produce did not comply with established standards.

Traditional marketing systems, whether in China or the rest of Asia, presently provide little motivation or incentive for individual farmers to make improvements to either quality or safety as their produce tends to get grouped together with standard products as it progresses through the marketing channel. Direct linkages between farmer groups and traders or ultimate buyers, such as supermarkets, can help avoid this problem. Governments need to improve the condition of many markets through upgrading management and reinvesting market fees in physical infrastructure. Wholesale markets need to investigate the feasibility of developing separate sections to handle fruits and vegetables that meet defined safety and quality standards.

European Union

The parliament of the European Union (EU) makes legislation in the form of directives and regulations, many of which are mandatory for member states and which therefore must be incorporated into individual countries' national legislation. As a very large organisation that exists to remove barriers to trade between member states, and into which individual member states have only a proportional influence, the outcome is often seen as an excessively bureaucratic 'one size fits all' approach. However, in relation to food safety the tendency to err on the side of maximum protection for the consumer may be seen as a positive benefit. The EU parliament is informed on food safety matters by the European Food Safety Authority.

Individual member states may also have other legislation and controls in respect of food safety, provided that they do not prevent trade with other states, and can differ considerably in their internal structures and approaches to the regulatory control of food safety.

France

Agence nationale de sécurité sanitaire de l'alimentation, de l'environnement et du travail (anses) is a French governmental agency dealing with food safety.

Germany

The Federal Ministry of Food, Agriculture and Consumer Protection (BMELV) is a Federal Ministry of the Federal Republic of Germany. History: Founded as Federal Ministry of Food, Agriculture and Foresting in 1949, this name did not change until 2001. Then the name changed to Federal Ministry of Consumer Protection, Food and Agriculture. At the 22nd of November 2005, the name got changed again to its current state: Federal Ministry of Food, Agriculture and

Consumer Protection. The reason for this last change was that all the resorts should get equal ranking which was achieved by sorting the resorts alphabetically. Vision: A balanced and healthy diet with safe food, distinct consumer rights and consumer information for various areas of life, and a strong and sustainable agriculture as well as perspectives for our rural areas are important goals of the Federal Ministry of Food, Agriculture and Consumer Protection (BMELV). The Federal Office of Consumer Protection and Food Safety is under the control of the Federal Ministry of Food, Agriculture and Consumer Protection. It exercises several duties, with which it contributes to safer food and thereby intensifies health-based consumer protection in Germany. Food can be manufactured and sold within Germany without a special permission, as long as it does not cause any damage on consumers' health and meets the general standards set by the legislation. However, manufacturers, carriers, importers and retailers are responsible for the food they pass into circulation. They are obliged to ensure and document the safety and quality of their food with the use of in-house control mechanisms.

Hong Kong

In Hong Kong SAR, the Centre for Food Safety is in charge of ensuring food sold is safe and fit for consumption.

India

Food Safety and Standards Authority of India, established under the Food Safety and Standards Act, 2006, is the regulating body related to food safety and laying down of standards of food in India.

New Zealand

The New Zealand Food Safety Authority (NZFSA), or Te Pou Oranga Kai O Aotearoa is the New Zealand government body responsible for food safety. NZFSA is also the controlling authority for imports and exports of food and food-related products. The NZFSA as of 2012 is now a division of the Ministry for Primary Industries (MPI) and is no longer its own organization.

Pakistan

Pakistan does not have an integrated legal framework but has a set of laws, which deals with various aspects of food safety. These laws, despite the fact that they were enacted long time ago, have tremendous capacity to achieve at least minimum level of food safety. However, like many other laws, these laws remain very poorly enforced. There are four laws that specifically deal with food safety. Three of these laws directly focus issues related to food safety, while the fourth, the Pakistan Standards and Quality Control Authority Act, is indirectly relevant to food safety.

The Pure Food Ordinance 1960 consolidates and amends the law in relation to the preparation and the sale of foods. All provinces and some northern areas have adopted this law with certain amendments. Its aim is to ensure purity of food being supplied to people in the market and, therefore, provides for preventing adulteration. The Pure Food Ordinance 1960 does not apply to cantonment areas. There is a separate law for cantonments called "The Cantonment Pure Food Act, 1966". There is no substantial difference between the Pure Food Ordinance 1960 and The Cantonment Pure Food Act. Even the rules of operation are very much similar.

Pakistan Hotels and Restaurant Act, 1976 applies to all hotels and restaurants in Pakistan and seeks to control and regulate the rates and standard of service(s) by hotels and restaurants. In addition to other provisions, under section 22(2), the sale of food or beverages that are contaminated, not prepared hygienically or served in utensils that are not hygienic or clean is an offence. There are no express provisions for consumer complaints in the Pakistan Restaurants Act, 1976, Pakistan Penal Code, 1860 and Pakistan Standards and Quality Control Authority Act, 1996. The laws do not prevent citizens from lodging complaints with the concerned government officials; however, the consideration and handling of complaints is a matter of discretion of the officials.

South Korea

Korea Food & Drug Administration

Korea Food & Drug Administration (KFDA) is working for food safety since 1945. It is part of the Government of South Korea.

IOAS-Organic Certification Bodies Registered in KFDA: "Organic" or related claims can be labelled on food products when organic certificates are considered as valid by KFDA. KFDA admits organic certificates which can be issued by 1) IFOAM (International Federation of Organic Agriculture Movement) accredited certification bodies 2) Government accredited certification bodies – 328 bodies in 29 countries have been registered in KFDA.

Food Import Report: According to Food Import Report, it is supposed to report or register what you import. Competent authority is as follows:

Product	*Authority*
Imported Agricultural Products, Processed Foods, Food Additives, Utensils, Containers & Packages or Health Functional Foods	KFDA (Korea Food and Drug Administration)
Imported Livestock, Livestock products (including Dairy products)	NVRQS (National Veterinary Research and Quarantine Service)
Packaged meat, milk & dairy products (butter, cheese), hamburger patties, meat ball and other processed products which are stipulated by Livestock Sanitation Management Act	NVRQS (National Veterinary Research and Quarantine Service)
Imported Marine products; fresh, chilled, frozen, salted, dehydrated, eviscerated marine produce which can be recognized its characteristics	NFIS (National Fisheries Products Quality Inspection Service)

National Institute of Food and Drug Safety Evaluation

National Institute of Food and Drug Safety Evaluation (NIFDS) is functioning as well. The National Institute of Food and Drug Safety Evaluation is a national organization for toxicological tests and research. Under the Korea Food & Drug Administration, the Institute performs research on toxicology, pharmacology, and risk analysis of foods, drugs, and their additives.

The Institute strives primarily to understand important biological triggering mechanisms and improve assessment methods of human exposure, sensitivities, and risk by (1) conducting basic, applied, and policy research that closely examines biologically triggering harmful effects on the regulated products such as foods, food additives, and drugs, and operating the national toxicology programme for the toxicological test development and inspection of hazardous chemical substances assessments.

The Institute ensures safety by investigation and research on safety by its own researchers, contract research by external academicians and research centres.

United Kingdom

In the UK the Food Standards Agency is an independent government department responsible for food safety and hygiene across the UK. They work with businesses to help them produce safe food, and with local authorities to enforce food safety regulations. In 2006 food hygiene legislation changed and new requirements came into force. The main requirement resulting from this change is that if you own or run a food business in the UK, you must have a documented Food Safety Management System, which is based on the principles of Hazard Analysis Critical Control Point HACCP.

United States

The US food system is regulated by numerous federal, state and local officials. It has been criticized as lacking in "organization, regulatory tools, and not addressing food borne illness."

Federal Level Regulation

The Food and Drug Administration publishes the Food Code, a model set of guidelines and procedures that assists food control jurisdictions by providing a scientifically sound technical and legal basis for regulating the retail and food service industries, including restaurants, grocery stores and institutional foodservice providers such as nursing homes. Regulatory agencies at all levels of government in the United States use the FDA Food Code to develop or update food safety rules in their jurisdictions that are consistent with national food regulatory policy. According to the FDA, 48 of 56 states and territories, representing 79% of the U.S. population, have adopted food codes patterned after one of the five versions of the Food Code, beginning with the 1993 edition.

In the United States, federal regulations governing food safety are fragmented and complicated, according to a February 2007 report from the Government Accountability Office. There are 15 agencies sharing oversight responsibilities in the food safety system, although the two primary agencies are the U.S. Department of Agriculture (USDA) Food Safety and Inspection Service (FSIS), which is responsible for the safety of meat, poultry, and processed egg products, and the Food and Drug Administration (FDA), which is responsible for virtually all other foods.

The Food Safety and Inspection Service has approximately 7,800 inspection programme personnel working in nearly 6,200 federally inspected meat, poultry and processed egg establishments. FSIS is charged with administering and enforcing the Federal Meat Inspection Act, the Poultry Products Inspection Act, the Egg Products Inspection Act, portions of the Agricultural Marketing Act, the Humane Slaughter Act, and the regulations that implement these laws. FSIS inspection programme personnel inspect every animal before slaughter, and each carcass after slaughter to ensure public health requirements are met. In fiscal year (FY) 2008, this included about 50 billion pounds of livestock carcasses, about 59 billion pounds of poultry carcasses, and about 4.3 billion pounds of processed egg products. At U.S. borders, they also inspected 3.3 billion pounds of imported meat and poultry products.

Industry Pressure

There have been concerns over the efficacy of safety practices and food industry pressure on U.S. regulators. A study reported by Reuters found that "the food industry is jeopardizing U.S. public health by withholding information from food safety investigators or pressuring regulators to withdraw or alter policy designed to protect consumers". A survey found that 25% of U.S. government inspectors and scientists surveyed have experienced during the past year corporate interests forcing their food safety agency to withdraw or to modify agency policy or action that protects consumers. Scientists have observed that management undercuts field inspectors who stand up for food safety against industry pressure. According to Dr. Dean Wyatt, a USDA veterinarian who oversees federal slaughter house inspectors, "Upper level management does not adequately support field inspectors and the actions they take to protect the food supply. Not only is there lack of support, but there's outright obstruction, retaliation and abuse of power."

State and Local Regulation

A number of U.S. states have their own meat inspection programmes that substitute for USDA inspection for meats that are sold only in-state. Certain state programmes have been criticized for undue leniency to bad practices.

However, other state food safety programmes supplement, rather than replace, Federal inspections, generally with the goal of increasing consumer confidence in the state's produce. For example, state health departments have a role in investigating outbreaks of food-borne disease bacteria, as in the case of the 2006 outbreak of *Escherichia coli* O157:H7 (a pathogenic strain of the ordinarily harmless bacteria, *E. coli*) from processed spinach. Health departments also promote better food processing practices to eliminate these threats.

In addition to the US Food and Drug Administration, several states that are major producers of fresh fruits and vegetables (including California, Arizona and Florida) have their own state programmes to test produce for pesticide residues.

Restaurants and other retail food establishments fall under state law and are regulated by state or local health departments. Typically these regulations require official inspections of specific design features, best food-handling practices, and certification of food handlers. In some places a letter grade or numerical score must be prominently posted following each inspection. In some localities, inspection deficiencies and remedial action are posted on the Internet.

Consumer Labeling

United Kingdom

Foodstuffs in the UK have one of two labels to indicate the nature of the deterioration of the product and any subsequent health issues. EHO Food Hygiene certification is required to prepare and distribute food. While there is no specified expiry date of such a qualification the changes in legislation it is suggested to update every five years.

Best before indicates a future date beyond which the food product *may* lose quality in terms of taste or texture amongst others, but does not imply any serious health problems if food is consumed beyond this date (within reasonable limits).

Use by indicates a legal date beyond which it is not permissible to sell a food product (usually one that deteriorates fairly rapidly after production) due to the potential serious nature of consumption of pathogens. Leeway is sometimes provided by producers in stating display until dates so that products are not at their limit of safe consumption on the actual date stated (this latter is voluntary and not subject to regulatory control). This allows for the variability in production, storage and display methods.

United States

With the exception of infant formula and baby foods which must be withdrawn by their expiration date, Federal law does not require expiration dates. For all other foods, except dairy products in some states, freshness dating is strictly voluntary on the part of manufacturers. In response to consumer demand, perishable foods are typically labelled with a Sell by date. It is up to the consumer to decide how long after the Sell by date a package is usable. Other common dating statements are Best if used by, Use-by date, Expiration date, Guaranteed fresh <date>, and Pack date.

Australia and New Zealand

Guide to Food Labelling and Other Information Requirements: This guide provides background information on the general labelling requirements in the Code. The information in this guide applies both to food for retail sale and to food for catering purposes. Foods for catering purposes means those foods for use in restaurants, canteens, schools, caterers or self-catering institutions, where food is offered for immediate consumption. Labelling and information requirements in the new Code apply both to food sold or prepared for sale in Australia and New Zealand and food imported into Australia and New Zealand. Warning and Advisory Declarations, Ingredient Labelling, Date Marking, Nutrition Information Requirements, Legibility Requirements for Food Labels, Percentage Labelling, Information Requirements for Foods Exempt from Bearing a Label.

Waste Management

Waste management is the "generation, prevention, characterization, monitoring, treatment, handling, reuse and residual disposition of solid wastes". There are various types of solid waste including municipal (residential, institutional, commercial), agricultural, and special (health care, household hazardous wastes, sewage sludge). The term usually relates to materials produced by human activity, and the process is generally undertaken to reduce their effect on health, the environment or aesthetics.

There is a wide array of issues relating to waste management and those areas include:

- Generation of waste
- Waste minimization
- Waste removal
- Waste transportation
- Waste treatment
- Recycling and reuse
- Storage, collection, transport, and transfer
- Treatment
- Landfill disposal
- Environmental considerations
- Financial and marketing aspects
- Policy and regulations
- Education and training
- Planning and implementation.

Waste management practices are not uniform among: countries (developed and developing nations); regions (urban and rural area), and sectors (residential and industrial).

History

Throughout most of history, the amount of waste generated by humans was insignificant due to low population density and low societal levels of the exploitation of natural resources. Common waste produced during pre-modern times was mainly ashes and human biodegradable waste, and these were released back into the ground locally, with minimum environmental impact. Tools made out of wood or metal were generally reused or passed down through the generations.

However, some civilizations do seem to have been more profligate in their waste output than others. In particular, the Maya of Central America had a fixed monthly ritual, in which the people of the village would gather together and burn their rubbish in large dumps.

Modern Era

Following the onset of industrialisation and the sustained urban growth of large population centres in England, the buildup of waste in the cities caused a rapid deterioration in levels of sanitation and the general quality of urban life. The streets became choked with filth due to the lack of waste clearance regulations. Calls for the establishment of a municipal authority with waste removal powers were mooted as early as 1751 by Corbyn Morris in London, who proposed that "...as the preservation of the health of the people is of great importance, it is proposed that the cleaning of this city, should be put under one uniform public management, and all the filth be...conveyed by the Thames to proper distance in the country".

However, it was not until the mid-19th century, spurred by increasingly devastating cholera outbreaks and the emergence of a public health debate that the first legislation on the issue emerged. Highly influential in this new focus was the report *The Sanitary Condition of the Labouring Population* in 1842 of the social reformer, Edwin Chadwick, in which he argued for the importance of adequate waste removal and management facilities to improve the health and wellbeing of the city's population.

In the UK, the Nuisance Removal and Disease Prevention Act of 1846 began what was to be a steadily evolving process of the provision of regulated waste management in London. The Metropolitan Board of Works was the first city-wide authority that centralized sanitation regulation for the rapidly expanding city and the Public Health Act 1875 made it compulsory for every household to deposit their weekly waste in "moveable receptacles: for disposal—the first concept for a dust-bin.

The dramatic increase in waste for disposal led to the creation of the first incineration plants, or, as they were then called, "destructors". In 1874, the first incinerator was built in Nottingham by Manlove, Alliott & Co. Ltd. to the design of Albert Fryer. However, these were met with opposition on account of the large amounts of ash they produced and which wafted over the neighbouring areas. Similar municipal systems of waste disposal sprung up at the turn of the 20th century in other large cities of Europe and North America. In 1895, New York City became the first U.S. city with public-sector garbage management.

Early garbage removal trucks were simply open bodied dump trucks pulled by a team of horses. They became motorized in the early part of the 20th century and the first close body trucks to eliminate odours with a dumping lever mechanism were introduced in the 1920s in Britain. These were soon equipped with 'hopper mechanisms' where the scooper was loaded at floor level and then hoisted mechanically to deposit the waste in the truck. The Garwood Load Packer was the first truck in 1938, to incorporate a hydraulic compactor.

Methods of Disposal

Landfill

Disposal of waste in a landfill involves burying the waste and this remains a common practice in most countries. Landfills were often established in abandoned or unused quarries, mining voids or borrow pits. A properly designed and well-managed landfill can be a hygienic and relatively inexpensive method of disposing of waste materials. Older, poorly designed or poorly managed landfills can create a number of adverse environmental impacts such as wind-blown litter, attraction of vermin, and generation of liquid leachate. Another common product of landfills is gas (mostly composed of methane and carbon dioxide), which is produced from anaerobic breakdown of organic waste. This gas can create odour problems, kill surface vegetation and is a greenhouse gas.

Design characteristics of a modern landfill include methods to contain leachate such as clay or plastic lining material. Deposited waste is normally compacted to increase its density and stability and covered to prevent attracting vermin (such as mice or rats). Many landfills also have landfill gas extraction systems installed to extract the landfill gas. Gas is pumped out of the landfill using perforated pipes and flared off or burnt in a gas engine to generate electricity.

Incineration

Incineration is a disposal method in which solid organic wastes are subjected to combustion so as to convert them into residue and gaseous products. This method is useful for disposal of residue of both solid waste management and solid residue from waste water management. This process reduces the volumes of solid waste to 20 to 30 percent of the original volume. Incineration and other high temperature waste treatment systems are sometimes described as "thermal treatment". Incinerators convert waste materials into heat, gas, steam and, ash.

Incineration is carried out both on a small scale by individuals and on a large scale by industry. It is used to dispose of solid, liquid and gaseous waste. It is recognized as a practical method of disposing of certain hazardous waste materials (such as biological medical waste). Incineration is a controversial method of waste disposal, due to issues such as emission of gaseous pollutants.

Incineration is common in countries such as Japan where land is more scarce, as these facilities generally do not require as much area as landfills. Waste-to-energy (WtE) or energy-from-waste (EfW) are broad terms for facilities that burn waste in a furnace or boiler to generate heat, steam or electricity. Combustion in an incinerator is not always perfect and there have been concerns about pollutants in gaseous emissions from incinerator stacks. Particular concern has focused on some very persistent organic compounds such as dioxins, furans, and PAHs, which may be created and which may have serious environmental consequences.

Recycling

Recycling is a resource recovery practice that refers to the collection and reuse of waste materials such as empty beverage containers. The materials from which the items are made can be reprocessed into new products. Material for recycling may be collected separately from general waste using dedicated bins and collection vehicles, a procedure called kerbside collection. In some communities, the owner of the waste is required to separate the materials into various different bins (e.g. for paper, plastics, metals) prior to its collection. In other communities, all recyclable materials are placed in a single bin for collection, and the sorting is handled later at a central facility. The latter method is known as "single-stream recycling."

The most common consumer products recycled include aluminium such as beverage cans, copper such as wire, steel from food and aerosol cans, old steel furnishings or equipment, polyethylene and PET bottles, glass bottles and jars, paperboard cartons, newspapers, magazines and light paper, and corrugated fibreboard boxes.

PVC, LDPE, PP, and PS are also recyclable. These items are usually composed of a single type of material, making them relatively easy to recycle into new products. The recycling of complex products (such as computers and electronic equipment) is more difficult, due to the additional dismantling and separation required. The type of material accepted for recycling varies by city and country. Each city and country has different recycling programmes in place that can handle the various types of recyclable materials. However, certain variation in acceptance is reflected in the resale value of the material once it is reprocessed.

Sustainability

The management of waste is a key component in a business' ability to maintaining ISO14001 accreditation. Companies are encouraged to improve their environmental efficiencies each year by eliminating waste through resource recovery practices, which are sustainability-related activities. One way to do this is by shifting away from waste management to resource recovery practices like recycling materials such as glass, food scraps, paper and cardboard, plastic bottles and metal.

Biological Reprocessing

Recoverable materials that are organic in nature, such as plant material, food scraps, and paper products, can be recovered through composting and digestion processes to decompose the organic matter. The resulting organic material is then recycled as mulch or compost for agricultural or landscaping purposes. In addition, waste gas from the process (such as methane) can be captured and used for generating electricity and heat (CHP/cogeneration) maximising efficiencies. The intention of biological processing in waste management is to control and accelerate the natural process of decomposition of organic matter.

Energy Recovery

Energy recovery from waste is the conversion of non-recyclable waste materials into usable heat, electricity, or fuel through a variety of processes, including combustion, gasification, pyrolyzation, anaerobic digestion, and landfill gas recovery. This process is often called waste-to-energy. Energy recovery from waste is part of the non-hazardous waste management hierarchy. Using energy recovery to convert non-recyclable waste materials into electricity and heat, generates a renewable energy source and can reduce carbon emissions by offsetting the need for energy from fossil sources as well as reduce methane generation from landfills. Globally, waste-to-energy accounts for 16% of waste management.

The energy content of waste products can be harnessed directly by using them as a direct combustion fuel, or indirectly by processing them into another type of fuel. Thermal treatment ranges from using waste as a fuel source for cooking or heating and the use of the gas fuel, to fuel for boilers to generate steam and electricity in a turbine. Pyrolysis and gasification are two related forms of thermal treatment where waste materials are heated to high temperatures with limited oxygen availability. The process usually occurs in a sealed vessel under high pressure. Pyrolysis of solid waste converts the material into solid, liquid and gas products. The liquid and gas can be burnt to produce energy or refined into other chemical products (chemical refinery). The solid residue (char) can be further refined into products such as activated carbon. Gasification and advanced Plasma arc gasification are used to convert organic materials directly into a synthetic gas (syngas) composed of carbon monoxide and hydrogen. The gas is then burnt to produce electricity and steam. An alternative to pyrolysis is high temperature and pressure supercritical water decomposition (hydrothermal monophasic oxidation).

Resource Recovery

Resource recovery is the systematic diversion of waste, which was intended for disposal, for a specific next use. It is the processing of recyclables to extract or recover materials and resources, or convert to energy. These activities are performed at a resource recovery facility. Resource recovery is not only environmentally important, but it is also cost effective. It decreases the amount of waste for disposal, saves space in landfills, and conserves natural resources. Resource recovery (as opposed to waste management) uses LCA (life cycle analysis) attempts to offer alternatives to waste management. For mixed MSW (Municipal Solid Waste) a number of broad studies have indicated that administration, source separation and collection followed by reuse and recycling of the non-organic fraction and energy and compost/fertilizer production of the organic material via anaerobic digestion to be the favoured path.

Avoidance and Reduction Methods

An important method of waste management is the prevention of waste material being created, also known as waste reduction. Methods of avoidance include reuse of second-hand products, repairing broken items instead of buying new, designing products to be refillable or reusable (such as cotton instead of plastic shopping bags), encouraging consumers to avoid using disposable products (such as disposable cutlery), removing any food/liquid remains from cans and packaging, and designing products that use less material to achieve the same purpose (for example, lightweighting of beverage cans).

Waste Handling and Transport

Waste collection methods vary widely among different countries and regions. Domestic waste collection services are often provided by local government authorities, or by private companies for industrial and commercial waste. Some areas, especially those in less developed countries, do not have a formal waste-collection system.

Waste Handling Systems

- Vacuum collection in which waste is transported from the home or commercial premises by vacuum along small bore tubes. Systems are in use in Europe and North America
- Curbside collection is the most common method of disposal in most European countries, Canada, New Zealand and many other parts of the developed world in which waste is collected at regular intervals by specialised trucks. This is often associated with curb-side waste segregation. In rural areas waste may need to be taken to a transfer station. Waste collected is then transported to a regional landfill.
- In many areas, pyrolysis is used to dispose of some wastes including tires, a process that can produce recovered fuels, steel and heat. In some cases tires can provide the feedstock for cement manufacture. Such systems are used in USA, California, Australia, Greece, Mexico, the United Kingdom and in Israel. The RESEM pyrolysis plant that has been operational at Texas USA since December 2011, and processes up to 60 tons per day.
- In some areas such as Taipei, the city government charges its households and industries for the volume of rubbish they produce. Waste will only be collected by the city council if waste is disposed in government issued rubbish bags. This policy has successfully reduced the amount of waste the city produces and increased the recycling rate. A similar system operates in New Zealand where waste must be packed in specially identified bags.
- In some jurisdictions unsegregated waste is collected at the curb-side or from waste transfer stations and then sorted into recyclables and unusable waste. Such systems are capable of sorting large volumes of solid waste, salvaging recyclables, and turning the rest into bio-gas and soil conditioner.
- In San Francisco, the local government established its Mandatory Recycling and Composting Ordinance in support of its goal of zero waste by 2020, requiring everyone in the city to keep recyclables and compostables out of the landfill. The three

streams are collected with the curbside "Fantastic 3" bin system - blue for recyclables, green for compostables, and black for landfill-bound materials - provided to residents and businesses and serviced by San Francisco's sole refuse hauler, Recology.

The City's "Pay-As-You-Throw" system charges customers by the volume of landfill-bound materials, which provides a financial incentive to separate recyclables and compostables from other discards. The City's Department of the Environment's Zero Waste Programme has led the City to achieve 80 % diversion, the highest diversion rate in North America.

International Waste Movement

While waste transport within a given country falls under national regulations, trans-boundary movement of waste is often subject to international treaties. A major concern to many countries in the world has been hazardous waste. The Basel Convention, ratified by 172 countries, deprecates movement of hazardous waste from developed to less developed countries. The provisions of the Basel convention have been integrated into the EU waste shipment regulation. Nuclear waste, although considered hazardous, does not fall under the jurisdiction of the Basel Convention.

Benefits

Waste is not something that should be discarded or disposed of with no regard for future use. It can be a valuable resource if addressed correctly, through policy and practice. With rational and consistent waste management practices there is an opportunity to reap a range of benefits. Those benefits include:

1. Economic - Improving economic efficiency through the means of resource use, treatment and disposal and creating markets for recycles can lead to efficient practices in the production and consumption of products and materials resulting in valuable materials being recovered for reuse and the potential for new jobs and new business opportunities.
2. Social - By reducing adverse impacts on health by proper waste management practices, the resulting consequences are more appealing settlements. Better social advantages can lead to new sources of employment and potentially lifting communities out of poverty especially in some of the developing poorer countries and cities.

3. *Environmental* - Reducing or eliminating adverse impacts on the environmental through reducing, reusing and recycling, and minimizing resource extraction can provide improved air and water quality and help in the reduction of greenhouse emissions.
4. *Inter-generational Equity* - Following effective waste management practices can provide subsequent generations a more robust economy, a fairer and more inclusive society and a cleaner environment.

Challenges in Developing Countries

Waste management in cities with developing economies and economies in transition experience exhausted waste collection services, inadequately managed and uncontrolled dumpsites and the problems are worsening. Problems with governance also complicate the situation.

Waste management, in these countries and cities, is an ongoing challenge and many struggle due to weak institutions, chronic under-resourcing and rapid urbanization.

All of these challenges along with the lack of understanding of different factors that contribute to the hierarchy of waste management, affect the treatment of waste.

Technologies

Traditionally the waste management industry has been slow to adopt new technologies such as RFID (Radio Frequency Identification) tags, GPS and integrated software packages which enable better quality data to be collected without the use of estimation or manual data entry.

- Technologies like RFID tags are now being used to collect data on presentation rates for curb-side pick-ups.
- Benefits of GPS tracking is particularly evident when considering the efficiency of ad hoc pick-ups (like skip bins or dumpsters) where the collection is done on a consumer request basis.
- Integrated software packages are useful in aggregating this data for use in optimisation of operations for waste collection operations.
- Rear vision cameras are commonly used for OH&S (Occupational Health & Safety) reasons and video recording devices are becoming more widely used, particularly concerning residential services.

Central Principles of Waste Management

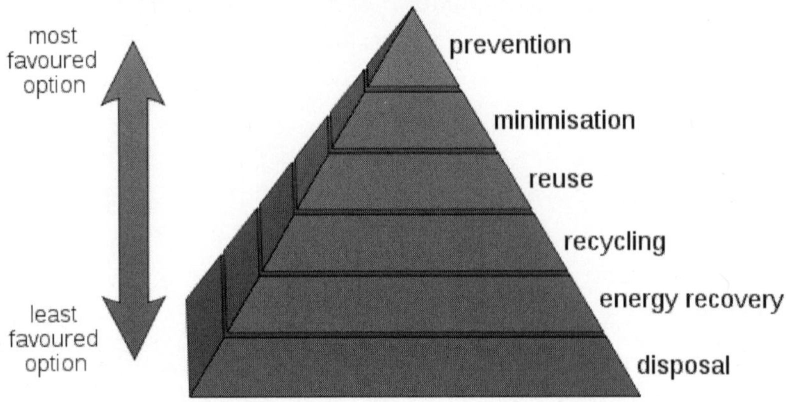

Figure: *Diagram of the waste hierarchy*

There are a number of concepts about waste management which vary in their usage between countries or regions. Some of the most general, widely used concepts include:

1. Waste hierarchy - The waste hierarchy refers to the "3 Rs" reduce, reuse and recycle, which classify waste management strategies according to their desirability in terms of waste minimization. The waste hierarchy remains the cornerstone of most waste minimization strategies. The aim of the waste hierarchy is to extract the maximum practical benefits from products and to generate the minimum amount of waste. The waste hierarchy is represented as a pyramid because the basic premise is for policy to take action first and prevent the generation of waste. The next step or preferred action is to reduce the generation of waste i.e. by reuse. The next is recycling which would include composting. Following this step is material recovery and waste-to-energy. Energy can be recovered from processes i.e. landfill and combustion, at this level of the hierarchy. The final action is disposal, in landfills or through incineration without energy recovery. This last step is the final resort for waste which has not been prevented, diverted or recovered. The waste hierarchy represents the progression of a product or material through the sequential stages of the pyramid of waste management. The hierarchy represents the latter parts of the life-cycle for each product.
2. Life-cycle of a Product - The life-cycle begins with design, then proceeds through manufacture, distribution, use and then

follows through the waste hierarchy's stages of reuse, recovery, recycling and disposal. Each of the above stages of the life-cycle offers opportunities for policy intervention, to rethink the need for the product, to redesign to minimize waste potential, to extend its use. The key behind the life-cycle of a product is to optimize the use of the world's limited resources by avoiding the unnecessary generation of waste.

3. Resource efficiency - the current, global, economic growth and development can not be sustained with the current production and consumption patterns. Globally, we are extracting more resources to produce goods than the planet can replenish. Resource efficiency is the reduction of the environmental impact from the production and consumption of these goods, from final raw material extraction to last use and disposal. This process of resource efficiency can address sustainability.

4 Polluter pays principle - the Polluter Pays Principle is a principle where the polluting party pays for the impact caused to the environment. With respect to waste management, this generally refers to the requirement for a waste generator to pay for appropriate disposal of the unrecoverable material.

Chapter 6

Infection

Infection is the invasion of a host organism's body tissues by disease-causing agents, their multiplication, and the reaction of host tissues to these organisms and the toxins they produce. Infectious diseases, also known as transmissible diseases or communicable diseases, comprise clinically evident illness (i.e., characteristic medical signs and/or symptoms of disease) resulting from the infection, presence and growth of pathogenic biological agents in an individual host organism. Infections are caused by infectious agents such as viruses, viroids, and prions, microorganisms such as bacteria, nematodes such as roundworms and pinworms, arthropods such as ticks, mites, fleas, and lice, fungi such as ringworm, and other macroparasites such as tapeworms.

Hosts can fight infections using their immune system. Mammalian hosts react to infections with an innate response, often involving inflammation, followed by an adaptive response.

The branch of medicine that focuses on infections and pathogens is *infectious disease medicine.* Physicians and veterinarians may use specific pharmaceutical drugs to treat infections (antibiotics, antivirals, antifungals, antiprotozoals, antihelminthics).

Classification

Bacterial infections are classified by the causative agent, as well as the symptoms and medical signs produced.

Symptomatic infections are *apparent,* whereas an infection that is active but does not produce noticeable symptoms may be called *inapparent, silent,* or *subclinical.* An infection that is inactive or dormant is called a *latent infection.*

A short-term infection is an *acute* infection. A long-term infection is a chronic infection.

Primary Versus Opportunistic

Among the vast varieties of microorganisms, relatively few cause disease in otherwise healthy individuals. Infectious disease results from the interplay between those few pathogens and the defences of the hosts they infect.

The appearance and severity of disease resulting from any pathogen, depends upon the ability of that pathogen to damage the host as well as the ability of the host to resist the pathogen. Clinicians therefore classify infectious microorganisms or microbes according to the status of host defences - either as *primary pathogens* or as *opportunistic pathogens*:

- Primary pathogens cause disease as a result of their presence or activity within the normal, healthy host, and their intrinsic virulence (the severity of the disease they cause) is, in part, a necessary consequence of their need to reproduce and spread. Many of the most common primary pathogens of humans only infect humans, however many serious diseases are caused by organisms acquired from the environment or which infect non-human hosts.
- Opportunistic pathogens can cause an infectious disease in a host with depressed resistance. Opportunistic infection may be caused by microbes ordinarily in contact with the host, such as pathogenic bacteria or fungi in the gastrointestinal or the upper respiratory tract, and they may also result from (otherwise innocuous) microbes acquired from other hosts (as in *Clostridium difficile* colitis) or from the environment as a result of traumatic introduction (as in surgical wound infections or compound fractures).

  An opportunistic disease requires impairment of host defences, which may occur as a result of genetic defects (such as Chronic granulomatous disease), exposure to antimicrobial drugs or immunosuppressive chemicals (as might occur following poisoning or cancer chemotherapy), exposure to ionizing radiation, or as a result of an infectious disease with immunosuppressive activity (such as with measles, malaria or HIV disease). Primary pathogens may also cause more severe disease in a host with depressed resistance than would normally occur in an immunosufficient host.

Occult Infection

Occult infection is a hidden infection first recognized by secondary manifestations. Fran Giampietro discovered this type, and coined the term "occult infection" in the late 1930s.

Infectious or Not

One way of proving that a given disease is "infectious", is to satisfy Koch's postulates (first proposed by Robert Koch), which demands that the infectious agent be identified only in patients and not in healthy controls, and that patients who contract the agent also develop the disease. These postulates were first used in the discovery that Mycobacteria species cause tuberculosis. Koch's postulates can not be applied ethically for many human diseases because they require experimental infection of a healthy individual with a pathogen produced as a pure culture. Often, even clearly infectious diseases do not meet the infectious criteria. For example, *Treponema pallidum*, the causative spirochete of syphilis, cannot be cultured *in vitro* - however the organism can be cultured in rabbit testes. It is less clear that a pure culture comes from an animal source serving as host than it is when derived from microbes derived from plate culture. Epidemiology is another important tool used to study disease in a population. For infectious diseases it helps to determine if a disease outbreak is sporadic (occasional occurrence), endemic (regular cases often occurring in a region), epidemic (an unusually high number of cases in a region), or pandemic (a global epidemic).

Contagiousness

Infectious diseases are sometimes called "contagious disease" when they are easily transmitted by contact with an ill person or their secretions (e.g., influenza). Thus, a contagious disease is a subset of infectious disease that is especially infective or easily transmitted. Other types of infectious/transmissible/communicable diseases with more specialized routes of infection, such as vector transmission or sexual transmission, are usually not regarded as "contagious," and often do not require medical isolation (sometimes loosely called quarantine) of victims. However, this specialized connotation of the word "contagious" and "contagious disease" (easy transmissibility) is not always respected in popular use.

By Anatomic Location

Infections can be classified by the anatomic location or organ system infected, including:

- Urinary tract infection
- Skin infection
- Respiratory tract infection
- Odontogenic infection (an infection that originates within a tooth or in the closely surrounding tissues)
- Vaginal infections
- Intra-amniotic infection

In addition, locations of inflammation where infection is the most common cause include pneumonia, meningitis and salpingitis.

Signs and Symptoms

The symptoms of an infection depend on the type of disease. Some signs of infection affect the whole body generally, such as fatigue, loss of appetite, weight loss, fevers, night sweats, chills, aches and pains. Others are specific to individual body parts, such as skin rashes, coughing, or a runny nose.

In certain cases, infectious diseases may be asymptomatic for much or even all of their course in a given host. In the latter case, the disease may only be defined as a "disease" (which by definition means an illness) in hosts who secondarily become ill after contact with an asymptomatic carrier. An infection is not synonymous with an infectious disease, as some infections do not cause illness in a host.

Bacterial or Viral

Bacterial and viral infections can both cause the same kinds of symptoms. It can be difficult to distinguish which is the cause of a specific infection. It's important to distinguish, because viral infections cannot be cured by antibiotic

Comparison of viral and bacterial infection		
Characteristic	***Viral infection***	***Bacterial infection***
Typical symptoms	In general, viral infections are systemic. This means they involve many different parts of the body or more than one body system at the same time; i.e. a runny nose, sinus congestion, cough, body aches etc. They can be local at times as in viral conjunctivitis or "pink eye" and herpes. Only a few viral infections are painful, like herpes. The pain of viral infections is often described as itchy or burning.[6]	The classic symptoms of a bacterial infection are localized redness, heat, swelling and pain. One of the hallmarks of a bacterial infection is local pain, pain that is in a specific part of the body. For example, if a cut occurs and is infected with bacteria, pain occurs at the site of the infection. Bacterial throat pain is often characterized by more pain on one side of the throat. An ear infection is more likely to be diagnosed as bacterial if the pain occurs in only one ear.[6] A cut that produces pus and milky-colored liquid is most likely infected.[8]
Cause	Pathogenic viruses	Pathogenic bacteria

Pathophysiology

There is a general chain of events that applies to infections. For infections to occur, a given chain of events must occur. The chain of events involves several steps—which include the infectious agent, reservoir, entering a susceptible host, exit and transmission to new hosts. Each of the links must be present in a chronological order for an infection to develop. Understanding these steps helps health care workers target the infection and prevent it from occurring in the first place.

Colonization

Infection begins when an organism successfully colonizes by entering the body, growing and multiplying. Most humans are not easily infected. Those who are weak, sick, malnourished, have cancer or are diabetic have increased susceptibility to chronic or persistent infections. Individuals who have a suppressed immune system are particularly susceptible to opportunistic infections. Entrance to the host at host-pathogen interface, generally occurs through the mucosa in orifices like the oral cavity, nose, eyes, genitalia, anus, or the microbe can enter through open wounds. While a few organisms can grow at the initial site of entry, many migrate and cause systemic infection in different organs. Some pathogens grow within the host cells (intracellular) whereas others grow freely in bodily fluids.

Wound colonization refers to nonreplicating microorganisms within the wound, while in infected wounds, replicating organisms exist and tissue is injured. All multicellular organisms are colonized to some degree by extrinsic organisms, and the vast majority of these exist in either a mutualistic or commensal relationship with the host. An example of the former is the anaerobic bacteria species, which colonizes the mammalian colon, and an example of the latter is various species of staphylococcus that exist on human skin. Neither of these colonizations are considered infections. The difference between an infection and a colonization is often only a matter of circumstance. Non-pathogenic organisms can become pathogenic given specific conditions, and even the most virulent organism requires certain circumstances to cause a compromising infection. Some colonizing bacteria, such as *Corynebacteria sp.* and *viridans streptococci*, prevent the adhesion and colonization of pathogenic bacteria and thus have a symbiotic relationship with the host, preventing infection and speeding wound healing.

The variables involved in the outcome of a host becoming inoculated by a pathogen and the ultimate outcome include:

- the route of entry of the pathogen and the access to host regions that it gains
- the intrinsic virulence of the particular organism
- the quantity or load of the initial inoculant
- the immune status of the host being colonized

As an example, the staphylococcus species remains harmless on the skin, but, when present in a normally sterile space, such as in the capsule of a joint or the peritoneum, multiplies without resistance and creates a burden on the host.

It can be difficult to know which chronic wounds are infected. Despite the huge number of wounds seen in clinical practice, there are limited quality data for evaluated symptoms and signs. A review of chronic wounds in the Journal of the American Medical Association's "Rational Clinical Examination Series" quantified the importance of increased pain as an indicator of infection. The review showed that the most useful finding is an increase in the level of pain [likelihood ratio (LR) range, 11-20] makes infection much more likely, but the absence of pain (negative likelihood ratio range, 0.64-0.88) does not rule out infection (summary LR 0.64-0.88).

Disease

Disease can arise if the host's protective immune mechanisms are compromised and the organism inflicts damage on the host. Microorganisms can cause tissue damage by releasing a variety of toxins or destructive enzymes. For example, Clostridium tetani releases a toxin that paralyzes muscles, and staphylococcus releases toxins that produce shock and sepsis. Not all infectious agents cause disease in all hosts. For example less than 5% of individuals infected with polio develop disease. On the other hand, some infectious agents are highly virulent. The prion causing mad cow disease and Creutzfeldt–Jakob disease kills almost all animals and people that are infected.

Persistent infections occur because the body is unable to clear the organism after the initial infection. Persistent infections are characterized by the continual presence of the infectious organism, often as latent infection with occasional recurrent relapses of active infection. There are some viruses that can maintain a persistent infection by infecting different cells of the body. Some viruses once acquired never leave the body. A typical example is the herpes virus, which tends to hide in nerves and become reactivated when specific circumstances arise.

Persistent infections cause millions of deaths globally each year. Chronic infections by parasites account for a high morbidity and mortality in many underdeveloped countries.

Transmission

For infecting organisms to survive and repeat the infection cycle in other hosts, they (or their progeny) must leave an existing reservoir and cause infection elsewhere. Infection transmission can take place via many potential routes:

- Droplet contact, also known as the *respiratory route*, and the resultant infection can be termed airborne disease. If an infected person coughs or sneezes on another person the microorganisms, suspended in warm, moist droplets, may enter the body through the nose, mouth or eye surfaces.
- Fecal-oral transmission, wherein foodstuffs or water become contaminated (by people not washing their hands before preparing food, or untreated sewage being released into a drinking water supply) and the people who eat and drink them become infected. Common fecal-oral transmitted pathogens include *Vibrio cholerae, Giardia* species, rotaviruses, *Entameba histolytica, Escherichia coli,* and tape worms. Most of these pathogens cause gastroenteritis.
- Sexual transmission, with the resulting disease being called sexually transmitted disease
- Oral transmission; Diseases that are transmitted primarily by oral means may be caught through direct oral contact such as kissing, or by indirect contact such as by sharing a drinking glass or a cigarette.
- Transmission by direct contact; Some diseases that are transmissible by direct contact include athlete's foot, impetigo and warts
- Vertical transmission'; directly from the mother to an embryo, fetus or baby during pregnancy or childbirth. It can occur when the mother gets an infection as an intercurrent disease in pregnancy.
- Iatrogenic transmission, due to medical procedures such as injection or transplantation of infected material.
- Vector-borne transmission, transmitted by a vector, which is an organism that does not cause disease itself but that transmits infection by conveying pathogens from one host to another.

The relationship between *virulence versus transmissibility* is complex; if a disease is rapidly fatal, the host may die before the microbe can get passed along to another host.

Prevention

Techniques like hand washing, wearing gowns, and wearing face masks can help prevent infections from being passed from the surgeon to the patient or vice versa. Frequent hand washing remains the most important defense against the spread of unwanted organisms. Nutrition must be improved and one has to make changes in life style- such as avoiding the use of illicit drugs, using a condom, and entering an exercise programme. Cooking foods well and avoiding foods that have been left outside for a long time is also important.

Antimicrobial substances used to prevent transmission of infections include:

- antiseptics, which are applied to living tissue/skin
- disinfectants, which destroy microorganisms found on non-living objects.
- antibiotics, called prophylactic when given as prevention rather as treatment of infection. However, long term use of antibiotics leads to resistance and chances of developing opportunistic infections like clostridium difficile colitis. Thus, avoiding using antibiotics longer than necessary helps preventing such infectious diseases.

One of the ways to prevent or slow down the transmission of infectious diseases is to recognize the different characteristics of various diseases. Some critical disease characteristics that should be evaluated include virulence, distance traveled by victims, and level of contagiousness. The human strains of Ebola virus, for example, incapacitate their victims extremely quickly and kill them soon after. As a result, the victims of this disease do not have the opportunity to travel very far from the initial infection zone. Also, this virus must spread through skin lesions or permeable membranes such as the eye. Thus, the initial stage of Ebola is not very contagious since its victims experience only internal hemorrhaging. As a result of the above features, the spread of Ebola is very rapid and usually stays within a relatively confined geographical area. In contrast, the Human Immunodeficiency Virus (HIV) kills its victims very slowly by attacking their immune system. As a result, many of its victims transmit the virus to other individuals before even realizing that they are carrying the disease. Also, the relatively low virulence allows its victims to travel long distances, increasing the likelihood of an epidemic.

Another effective way to decrease the transmission rate of infectious diseases is to recognize the effects of small-world networks. In epidemics, there are often extensive interactions within hubs or groups of infected individuals and other interactions within discrete hubs of susceptible individuals. Despite the low interaction between discrete hubs, the disease can jump to and spread in a susceptible hub via a single or few interactions with an infected hub. Thus, infection rates in small-world networks can be reduced somewhat if interactions between individuals within infected hubs are eliminated. However, infection rates can be drastically reduced if the main focus is on the prevention of transmission jumps between hubs. The use of needle exchange programmes in areas with a high density of drug users with HIV is an example of the successful implementation of this treatment method. Another example is the use of ring culling or vaccination of potentially susceptible livestock in adjacent farms to prevent the spread of the foot-and-mouth virus in 2001.

A general method to prevent transmission of vector-borne pathogens is pest control.

Immunity

Infection with most pathogens does not result in death of the host and the offending organism is ultimately cleared after the symptoms of the disease have waned. This process requires immune mechanisms to kill or inactivate the inoculum of the pathogen. Specific acquired immunity against infectious diseases may be mediated by antibodies and/or T lymphocytes. Immunity mediated by these two factors may be manifested by:

- a direct effect upon a pathogen, such as antibody-initiated complement-dependent bacteriolysis, opsonoization, phagocytosis and killing, as occurs for some bacteria,
- neutralization of viruses so that these organisms cannot enter cells,
- or by T lymphocytes which will kill a cell parasitized by a microorganism.

The immune system response to a microorganism often causes symptoms such as a high fever and inflammation, and has the potential to be more devastating than direct damage caused by a microbe.

Resistance to infection (immunity) may be acquired following a disease, by asymptomatic carriage of the pathogen, by harbouring an organism with a similar structure (crossreacting), or by vaccination. Knowledge of the protective antigens and specific acquired host immune factors is more complete for primary pathogens than for opportunistic pathogens. Immune resistance to an infectious disease requires a critical level of either antigen-specific antibodies and/or T cells when the host encounters the pathogen. Some individuals develop natural serum antibodies to the surface polysaccharides of some agents although they have had little or no contact with the agent, these natural antibodies confer specific protection to adults and are passively transmitted to newborns.

Host Genetic Factors

The clearance of the pathogens, either treatment-induced or spontaneous, it can be influenced by the genetic variants carried by the individual patients. For instance, for genotype 1 hepatitis C treated with Pegylated interferon-alpha-2a or Pegylated interferon-alpha-2b (brand names Pegasys or PEG-Intron) combined with ribavirin, it has been shown that genetic polymorphisms near the human IL28B gene, encoding interferon lambda 3, are associated with significant differences in the treatment-induced clearance of the virus. This finding, originally reported in Nature, showed that genotype 1 hepatitis C patients carrying certain genetic variant alleles near the IL28B gene are more possibly to achieve sustained virological response after the treatment than others. Later report from Nature demonstrated that the same genetic variants are also associated with the natural clearance of the genotype 1 hepatitis C virus.

Diagnosis

Diagnosis of infectious disease sometimes involves identifying an infectious agent either directly or indirectly. In practice most minor infectious diseases such as warts, cutaneous abscesses, respiratory system infections and diarrheal diseases are diagnosed by their clinical presentation. Conclusions about the cause of the disease are based upon the likelihood that a patient came in contact with a particular agent, the presence of a microbe in a community, and other epidemiological considerations. Given sufficient effort, all known infectious agents can be specifically identified. The benefits of identification, however, are often greatly outweighed by the cost, as often there is no specific treatment, the cause is obvious, or the outcome of an infection is benign.

Diagnosis of infectious disease is nearly always initiated by medical history and physical examination. More detailed identification techniques involve the culture of infectious agents isolated from a patient. Culture allows identification of infectious organisms by examining their microscopic features, by detecting the presence of substances produced by pathogens, and by directly identifying an organism by its genotype. Other techniques (such as X-rays, CAT scans, PET scans or NMR) are used to produce images of internal abnormalities resulting from the growth of an infectious agent. The images are useful in detection of, for example, a bone abscess or a spongiform encephalopathy produced by a prion.

Symptomatic Diagnostics

The diagnosis is aided by the presenting symptoms in any individual with an infectious disease, yet it usually needs additional diagnostic techniques to confirm the suspicion. Some signs are specifically characteristic and indicative of a disease and are called pathognomonic signs; but these are rare.

In children the presence of cyanosis, rapid breathing, poor peripheral perfusion, or a petechial rash increases the risk of a serious infection by greater than 5 fold. Other important indicators include parental concern, clinical instinct, and temperature greater than 40 °C.

Microbial Culture

Microbiological culture is a principal tool used to diagnose infectious disease. In a microbial culture, a growth medium is provided for a specific agent. A sample taken from potentially diseased tissue or fluid is then tested for the presence of an infectious agent able to grow within that medium. Most pathogenic bacteria are easily grown on nutrient agar, a form of solid medium that supplies carbohydrates and proteins necessary for growth of a bacterium, along with copious amounts of water. A single bacterium will grow into a visible mound on the surface of the plate called a colony, which may be separated from other colonies or melded together into a "lawn". The size, colour, shape and form of a colony is characteristic of the bacterial species, its specific genetic makeup (its strain), and the environment which supports its growth. Other ingredients are often added to the plate to aid in identification. Plates may contain substances that permit the growth of some bacteria and not others, or that change colour in response to certain bacteria and not others. Bacteriological plates such as these are commonly used in the clinical identification of infectious bacterium. Microbial culture may also be used in the identification of viruses: the medium in this case being cells grown in culture that the virus can infect, and then alter or kill. In the case of viral identification, a region of dead cells results from viral growth, and is called a "plaque". Eukaryotic parasites may also be grown in culture as a means of identifying a particular agent.

In the absence of suitable plate culture techniques, some microbes require culture within live animals. Bacteria such as *Mycobacterium leprae* and *Treponema pallidum* can be grown in animals, although serological and microscopic techniques make the use of live animals unnecessary. Viruses are also usually identified using alternatives to growth in culture or animals. Some viruses may be grown in embryonated eggs. Another useful identification method is Xenodiagnosis, or the use of a vector to support the growth of an infectious agent. Chagas disease is the most significant example, because it is difficult to directly demonstrate the presence of the causative agent, *Trypanosoma cruzi* in a patient, which therefore makes it difficult to definitively make a diagnosis. In this case, xenodiagnosis involves the use of the vector of the Chagas agent *T. cruzi*, an uninfected triatomine bug, which takes a blood meal from a person suspected of having been infected. The bug is later inspected for growth of *T. cruzi* within its gut.

Microscopy

Another principal tool in the diagnosis of infectious disease is microscopy. Virtually all of the culture techniques discussed above rely, at some point, on microscopic examination for definitive identification of the infectious agent. Microscopy may be carried out with simple instruments, such as the compound light microscope, or with instruments as complex as an electron microscope. Samples obtained from patients may be viewed directly under the light microscope, and can often rapidly lead to identification. Microscopy is often also used in conjunction with biochemical staining techniques, and can be made exquisitely specific when used in combination with antibody based techniques. For example, the use of antibodies made artificially fluorescent (fluorescently labelled antibodies) can be directed to bind to and identify a specific antigens present on a pathogen. A fluorescence microscope is then used to detect fluorescently labelled antibodies bound to internalized antigens within clinical samples or cultured cells. This technique is especially useful in the diagnosis of viral diseases, where the light microscope is incapable of identifying a virus directly.

Other microscopic procedures may also aid in identifying infectious agents. Almost all cells readily stain with a number of basic dyes due to the electrostatic attraction between negatively charged cellular molecules and the positive charge on the dye. A cell is normally transparent under a microscope, and using a stain increases the contrast of a cell with its background. Staining a cell with a dye such as Giemsa stain or crystal violet allows a microscopist to describe its size, shape, internal and external components and its associations with other cells. The response of bacteria to different staining procedures is used in the taxonomic classification of microbes as well. Two methods, the Gram stain and the acid-fast stain, are the standard approaches used to classify bacteria and to diagnosis of disease. The Gram stain identifies the bacterial groups Firmicutes and Actinobacteria, both of which contain many significant human pathogens. The acid-fast staining procedure identifies the Actinobacterial genera *Mycobacterium* and *Nocardia*.

Biochemical Tests

Biochemical tests used in the identification of infectious agents include the detection of metabolic or enzymatic products characteristic of a particular infectious agent. Since bacteria ferment carbohydrates in patterns characteristic of their genus and species, the detection of fermentation products is commonly used in bacterial identification. Acids, alcohols and gases are usually detected in these tests when bacteria are grown in selective liquid or solid media.

The isolation of enzymes from infected tissue can also provide the basis of a biochemical diagnosis of an infectious disease. For example, humans can make neither RNA replicases nor reverse transcriptase, and the presence of these enzymes are characteristic of specific types of viral infections. The ability of the viral protein hemagglutinin to bind red blood cells together into a detectable matrix may also be characterized as a biochemical test for viral infection, although strictly speaking hemagglutinin is not an *enzyme* and has no metabolic function.

Serological methods are highly sensitive, specific and often extremely rapid tests used to identify microorganisms. These tests are based upon the ability of an antibody to bind specifically to an antigen. The antigen, usually a protein or carbohydrate made by an infectious agent, is bound by the antibody. This binding then sets off a chain of events that can be visibly obvious in various ways, dependent upon the test. For example, "Strep throat" is often diagnosed within minutes, and is based on the appearance of antigens made by the causative agent, *S. pyogenes*, that is retrieved from a patients throat with a cotton swab. Serological tests, if available, are usually the preferred route of identification, however the tests are costly to develop and the reagents used in the test often require refrigeration. Some serological methods are extremely costly, although when commonly used, such as with the "strep test", they can be inexpensive.

Complex serological techniques have been developed into what are known as Immunoassays. Immunoassays can use the basic antibody

– antigen binding as the basis to produce an electro - magnetic or particle radiation signal, which can be detected by some form of instrumentation. Signal of unknowns can be compared to that of standards allowing quantitation of the target antigen. To aid in the diagnosis of infectious diseases, immunoassays can detect or measure antigens from either infectious agents or proteins generated by an infected organism in response to a foreign agent. For example, immunoassay A may detect the presence of a surface protein from a virus particle. Immunoassay B on the other hand may detect or measure antibodies produced by an organism's immune system which are made to neutralize and allow the destruction of the virus.

Instrumentation can be used to read extremely small signals created by secondary reactions linked to the antibody – antigen binding. Instrumentation can control sampling, reagent use, reaction times, signal detection, calculation of results, and data management to yield a cost effective automated process for diagnosis of infectious disease.

Molecular Diagnostics

Technologies based upon the polymerase chain reaction (PCR) method will become nearly ubiquitous gold standards of diagnostics of the near future, for several reasons. First, the catalogue of infectious agents has grown to the point that virtually all of the significant infectious agents of the human population have been identified. Second, an infectious agent must grow within the human body to cause disease; essentially it must amplify its own nucleic acids in order to cause a disease. This amplification of nucleic acid in infected tissue offers an opportunity to detect the infectious agent by using PCR. Third, the essential tools for directing PCR, primers, are derived from the genomes of infectious agents, and with time those genomes will be known, if they are not already.

Thus, the technological ability to detect any infectious agent rapidly and specifically are currently available. The only remaining blockades to the use of PCR as a standard tool of diagnosis are in its cost and application, neither of which is insurmountable. The diagnosis of a few diseases will not benefit from the development of PCR methods, such as some of the clostridial diseases (tetanus and botulism). These diseases are fundamentally biological poisonings by relatively small numbers of infectious bacteria that produce extremely potent neurotoxins. A significant proliferation of the infectious agent does not occur, this limits the ability of PCR to detect the presence of any bacteria.

Indication of Tests

There is usually an indication for a specific identification of an infectious agent only when such identification can aid in the treatment or prevention of the disease, or to advance knowledge of the course of an illness prior to the development of effective therapeutic or preventative measures. For example, in the early 1980s, prior to the appearance of AZT for the treatment of AIDS, the course of the disease was closely followed by monitoring the composition of patient blood samples, even though the outcome would not offer the patient any further treatment options.

In part, these studies on the appearance of HIV in specific communities permitted the advancement of hypotheses as to the route of transmission of the virus. By understanding how the disease was transmitted, resources could be targeted to the communities at greatest risk in campaigns aimed at reducing the number of new infections. The specific serological diagnostic identification, and later genotypic or molecular identification, of HIV also enabled the development of hypotheses as to the temporal and geographical origins of the virus, as well as a myriad of other hypothesis. The development of molecular diagnostic tools have enabled physicians and researchers to monitor the efficacy of treatment with anti-retroviral drugs. Molecular diagnostics are now commonly used to identify HIV in healthy people long before the onset of illness and have been used to demonstrate the existence of people who are genetically resistant to HIV infection. Thus, while there still is no cure for AIDS, there is great therapeutic and predictive benefit to identifying the virus and monitoring the virus levels within the blood of infected individuals, both for the patient and for the community at large.

Anti-infective Treatments

When infection attacks the body, *anti-infective* drugs can suppress the infection. Four types of *anti-infective* or drugs exist: antibacterial (antibiotic), antiviral, antitubercular, and antifungal. Depending on the severity and the type of infection, the antibiotic may be given by mouth, injection or may be applied topically. Severe infections of the brain are usually treated with intravenous antibiotics. Sometimes, multiple antibiotics are used to decrease the risk of resistance and increase efficacy. Antibiotics only work for bacteria and do not affect viruses. Antibiotics work by slowing down the multiplication of bacteria or killing the bacteria. The most common classes of antibiotics used in medicine include penicillin, cephalosporins, aminoglycosides, macrolides, quinolones and tetracyclines.

Epidemiology

"About 10 million people around the world died of communicable diseases in 2010," CBC News reports, citing data from the Institute for Health Metrics and Evaluation.

The World Health Organization collects information on global deaths by International Classification of Disease (ICD) code categories. The following table lists the top infectious disease killers which caused more than 100,000 deaths in 2002 (estimated). 1993 data is included for comparison.

Worldwide mortality due to infectious diseases

Rank	***Cause of death***	***Deaths 2002 (in millions)***	***Percentage of all deaths***	***Deaths 1993 (in millions)***	***1993 Rank***
N/A	All infectious diseases	14.7	25.9%	16.4	32.2%
1	Lower respiratory infections	3.9	6.9%	4.1	1
2	HIV/AIDS	2.8	4.9%	0.7	7
3	Diarrheal diseases	1.8	3.2%	3.0	2
4	Tuberculosis (TB)	1.6	2.7%	2.7	3
5	Malaria	1.3	2.2%	2.0	4
6	Measles	0.6	1.1%	1.1	5
7	Pertussis	0.29	0.5%	0.36	7
8	Tetanus	0.21	0.4%	0.15	12
9	Meningitis	0.17	0.3%	0.25	8
10	Syphilis	0.16	0.3%	0.19	11
11	Hepatitis B	0.10	0.2%	0.93	6
12-17	Tropical diseases (6)	0.13	0.2%	0.53	9, 10, 16-18
Note: Other causes of death include maternal and perinatal conditions (5.2%), nutritional deficiencies (0.9%), noncommunicable conditions (58.8%), and injuries (9.1%).					

Note: Other causes of death include maternal and perinatal conditions (5.2%), nutritional deficiencies (0.9%), noncommunicable conditions (58.8%), and injuries (9.1%).

The top three single agent/disease killers are HIV/AIDS, TB and malaria. While the number of deaths due to nearly every disease have decreased, deaths due to HIV/AIDS have increased fourfold. Childhood diseases include pertussis, poliomyelitis, diphtheria, measles and tetanus. Children also make up a large percentage of lower respiratory and diarrheal deaths.

Historic Pandemics

A pandemic (or global epidemic) is a disease that affects people over an extensive geographical area.

- Plague of Justinian, from 541 to 750, killed between 50% and 60% of Europe's population.

- The Black Death of 1347 to 1352 killed 25 million in Europe over 5 years. The plague reduced the world population from an estimated 450 million to between 350 and 375 million in the 14th century.
- The introduction of smallpox, measles, and typhus to the areas of Central and South America by European explorers during the 15th and 16th centuries caused pandemics among the native inhabitants. Between 1518 and 1568 disease pandemics are said to have caused the population of Mexico to fall from 20 million to 3 million.
- The first European influenza epidemic occurred between 1556 and 1560, with an estimated mortality rate of 20%.
- Smallpox killed an estimated 60 million Europeans during the 18th century (approximately 400,000 per year). Up to 30% of those infected, including 80% of the children under 5 years of age, died from the disease, and one-third of the survivors went blind.
- In the 19th century, tuberculosis killed an estimated one-quarter of the adult population of Europe; by 1918 one in six deaths in France were still caused by TB.
- The Influenza Pandemic of 1918 (or the Spanish Flu) killed 25-50 million people (about 2% of world population of 1.7 billion). Today Influenza kills about 250,000 to 500,000 worldwide each year.

Emerging Diseases

In most cases, microorganisms live in harmony with their hosts via mutual or commensal interactions. Diseases can emerge when existing parasites become pathogenic or when new pathogenic parasites enter a new host.

1. Coevolution between parasite and host can lead to hosts becoming resistant to the parasites or the parasites may evolve greater virulence, leading to immunopathological disease.
2. Human activity is involved with many emerging infectious diseases, such as environmental change enabling a parasite to occupy new niches. When that happens, a pathogen that had been confined to a remote habitat has a wider distribution and possibly a new host organism. Parasites jumping from nonhuman to human hosts are known as zoonoses. Under disease invasion, when a parasite invades a new host species, it may become pathogenic in the new host.

Several human activities have led to the emergence of zoonotic human pathogens, including viruses, bacteria, protozoa, and rickettsia, and spread of vector-borne diseases:

- Encroachment on wildlife habitats. The construction of new villages and housing developments in rural areas force animals to live in dense populations, creating opportunities for microbes to mutate and emerge.
- Changes in agriculture. The introduction of new crops attracts new crop pests and the microbes they carry to farming communities, exposing people to unfamiliar diseases.
- The destruction of rain forests. As countries make use of their rain forests, by building roads through forests and clearing areas for settlement or commercial ventures, people encounter insects and other animals harbouring previously unknown microorganisms.
- Uncontrolled urbanization. The rapid growth of cities in many developing countries tends to concentrate large numbers of people into crowded areas with poor sanitation. These conditions foster transmission of contagious diseases.
- Modern transport. Ships and other cargo carriers often harbour unintended "passengers", that can spread diseases to faraway destinations. While with international jet-airplane travel, people infected with a disease can carry it to distant lands, or home to their families, before their first symptoms appear.

History

Ideas of contagion became more popular in Europe during the Renaissance, particularly through the writing of the Italian physician Girolamo Fracastoro.

Anton van Leeuwenhoek (1632–1723) advanced the science of microscopy by being the first to observe microorganisms, allowing for easy visualization of bacteria.

In the mid-19th century John Snow and William Budd did important work demonstrating the contagiousness of typhoid and cholera through contaminated water. Both are credited with decreasing epidemics of cholera in their towns by implementing measures to prevent contamination of water.

Louis Pasteur proved beyond doubt that certain diseases are caused by infectious agents, and developed a vaccine for rabies.

Robert Koch, provided the study of infectious diseases with a scientific basis known as Koch's postulates.

Edward Jenner, Jonas Salk and Albert Sabin developed effective vaccines for smallpox and polio, which would later result in the eradication and near-eradication of these diseases, respectively.

Alexander Fleming discovered the world's first antibiotic Penicillin which Florey and Chain then developed.

Gerhard Domagk developed sulphonamides, the first broad spectrum synthetic antibacterial drugs.

Medical Specialists

The medical treatment of infectious diseases falls into the medical field of Infectiology and in some cases the study of propagation pertains to the field of Epidemiology. Generally, infections are initially diagnosed by primary care physicians or internal medicine specialists. For example, an "uncomplicated" pneumonia will generally be treated by the internist or the pulmonologist (lung physician). The work of the infectiologist therefore entails working with both patients and general practitioners, as well as laboratory scientists, immunologists, bacteriologists and other specialists.

An infectious disease team may be alerted when:

- The disease has not been definitively diagnosed after an initial workup
- The patient is immunocompromised (for example, in AIDS or after chemotherapy);
- The infectious agent is of an uncommon nature (e.g. tropical diseases);
- The disease has not responded to first line antibiotics;
- The disease might be dangerous to other patients, and the patient might have to be isolated

Society and Culture

A number of studies have reported associations between pathogen load in an area and human behavior. Higher pathogen load is associated with decreased size of ethnic and religious groups in an area. This may be due high pathogen load favoring avoidance other groups which may reduce pathogen transmission or a high pathogen load preventing the creation of large settlements and armies which enforce a common culture. Higher pathogen load is also associated with more restricted sexual behavior which may reduce pathogen transmission. It also associated with higher preferences for health and attractiveness in mates. Higher fertility rates and shorter or less parental care per child is another association which may be a compensation for the higher mortality rate. There is also an association with polygyny which may be due to higher pathogen load making selecting males with a high genetic resistance increasingly important. Higher pathogen load is also associated with more collectivism and less individualism which may limit contacts with outside groups and infections. There are alternative explanations for at least some of the associations although some of these explanations may in turn ultimately be due to pathogen load. Thus, polygny may also be due to a lower male:female ratio in these areas but this may ultimately be due to male infants having increased mortality from infectious diseases. Another example is that poor socioeconomic factors may ultimately in part be due to high pathogen load preventing economic development.

Fossil Record

Evidence of infection in fossil remains is a subject of interest for paleopathologists, scientists who study occurrences of injuries and illness in extinct life forms. Signs of infection have been discovered in the bones of carnivorous dinosaurs. When present, however, these infections seem to tend to be confined to only small regions of the body. A skull attributed to the early carnivorous dinosaur *Herrerasaurus ischigualastensis* exhibits pit-like wounds surrounded by swollen and porous bone. The unusual texture of the bone around the wounds suggests they were afflicted by a short-lived, non-lethal infection. Scientists who studied the skull speculated that the bite marks were received in a fight with another *Herrerasaurus*. Other carnivorous dinosaurs with documented evidence of infection include *Acrocanthosaurus*, *Allosaurus*, *Tyrannosaurus* and a tyrannosaur from the Kirtland Formation. The infections from both tyrannosaurs were received by being bitten during a fight, like the *Herrerasaurus* specimen.

Malaria

Malaria is a mosquito-borne infectious disease of humans and other animals caused by parasitic protozoans (a type of single cell microorganism) of the *Plasmodium* type. Malaria causes symptoms that typically include fever, fatigue, vomiting and headaches. In severe cases it can cause yellow skin, seizures, coma or death. These symptoms usually begin ten to fifteen days after being bitten. In those who have not been appropriately treated disease may recur months later. In those who have recently survived an infection, re-infection typically causes milder symptoms. This partial resistance disappears over months to years if there is no ongoing exposure to malaria.

Commonly, the disease is transmitted by the bite of an infected female *Anopheles* mosquito. This bite introduces the parasites from the mosquito's saliva into a person's blood. The parasites then travel to the liver where they mature and reproduce. Five species of *Plasmodium* can infect and be spread by humans. Most deaths are caused by *P. falciparum* because *P. vivax, P. ovale,* and *P. malariae* generally cause a milder form of malaria. The species *P. knowlesi* rarely causes disease in humans. Malaria is typically diagnosed by the microscopic examination of blood using blood films, or with antigen-based rapid diagnostic tests. Methods that use the polymerase chain reaction to detect the parasite's DNA have been developed, but are not widely used in areas where malaria is common due to their cost and complexity.

The risk of disease can be reduced by preventing mosquito bites by using mosquito nets and insect repellents, or with mosquito-control measures such as spraying insecticides and draining standing water. Several medications are available to prevent malaria in travellers to areas where the disease is common. Occasional doses of the medication sulfadoxine/pyrimethamine are recommended in infants and after the first trimester of pregnancy in areas with high rates of malaria. Despite a need, no effective vaccine exists, although efforts to develop one are ongoing. The recommended treatment for malaria is a combination of antimalarial medications that includes an artemisinin. The second medication may be either mefloquine, lumefantrine, or sulfadoxine/ pyrimethamine. Quinine along with doxycycline may be used if an artemisinin is not available. It is recommended that in areas where the disease is common, malaria is confirmed if possible before treatment is started due to concerns of increasing drug resistance. Resistance has developed to several antimalarial medications; for example, chloroquine-resistant *P. falciparum* has spread to most malarial areas, and resistance to artemisinin has become a problem in some parts of Southeast Asia.

The disease is widespread in tropical and subtropical regions that are present in a broad band around the equator. This includes much of Sub-Saharan Africa, Asia, and Latin America. The World Health Organization estimates that in 2012, there were 207 million cases of malaria. That year, the disease is estimated to have killed between 473,000 and 789,000 people, many of whom were children in Africa. Malaria is commonly associated with poverty and has a major negative effect on economic development. In Africa it is estimated to result in losses of $12 billion USD a year due to increased healthcare costs, lost ability to work and effects on tourism.

Signs and Symptoms

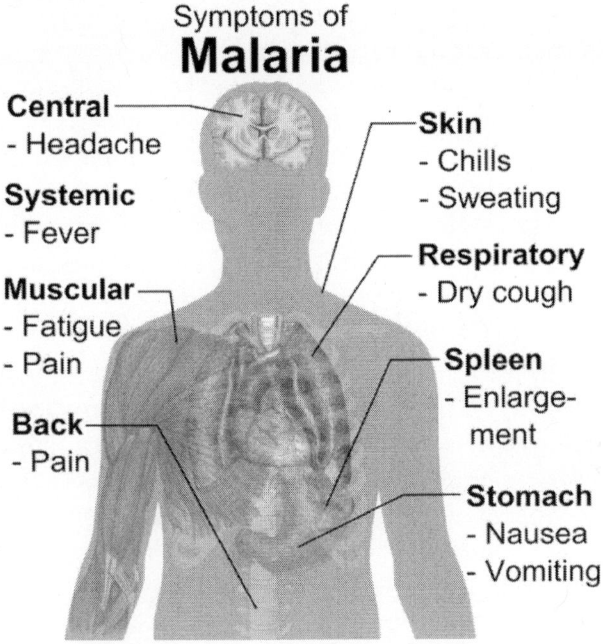

Figure: *Main symptoms of malaria*

The signs and symptoms of malaria typically begin 8–25 days following infection; however, symptoms may occur later in those who have taken antimalarial medications as prevention. Initial manifestations of the disease—common to all malaria species—are similar to flu-like symptoms, and can resemble other conditions such as septicemia, gastroenteritis, and viral diseases. The presentation may include headache, fever, shivering, joint pain, vomiting, hemolytic anemia, jaundice, hemoglobin in the urine, retinal damage, and convulsions.

The classic symptom of malaria is paroxysm—a cyclical occurrence of sudden coldness followed by shivering and then fever and sweating, occurring every two days (tertian fever) in *P. vivax* and *P. ovale* infections, and every three days (quartan fever) for *P. malariae. P. falciparum* infection can cause recurrent fever every 36–48 hours or a less pronounced and almost continuous fever.

Severe malaria is usually caused by *P. falciparum* (often referred to as falciparum malaria). Symptoms of falciparum malaria arise 9–30 days after infection. Individuals with cerebral malaria frequently exhibit neurological symptoms, including abnormal posturing, nystagmus, conjugate gaze palsy (failure of the eyes to turn together in the same direction), opisthotonus, seizures, or coma.

Complications

There are several serious complications of malaria. Among these is the development of respiratory distress, which occurs in up to 25% of adults and 40% of children with severe *P. falciparum* malaria. Possible causes include respiratory compensation of metabolic acidosis, noncardiogenic pulmonary oedema, concomitant pneumonia, and severe anaemia. Although rare in young children with severe malaria, acute respiratory distress syndrome occurs in 5–25% of adults and up to 29% of pregnant women. Coinfection of HIV with malaria increases mortality. Renal failure is a feature of blackwater fever, where hemoglobin from lysed red blood cells leaks into the urine.

Infection with *P. falciparum* may result in cerebral malaria, a form of severe malaria that involves encephalopathy. It is associated with retinal whitening, which may be a useful clinical sign in distinguishing malaria from other causes of fever. Splenomegaly, severe headache, hepatomegaly (enlarged liver), hypoglycemia, and hemoglobinuria with renal failure may occur.

Malaria in pregnant women is an important cause of stillbirths, infant mortality and low birth weight, particularly in *P. falciparum* infection, but also with *P. vivax*.

Cause

Malaria parasites belong to the genus *Plasmodium* (phylum Apicomplexa). In humans, malaria is caused by *P. falciparum*, *P. malariae*, *P. ovale*, *P. vivax* and *P. knowlesi*. Among those infected, *P. falciparum* is the most common species identified (~75%) followed by *P. vivax* (~20%). Although *P. falciparum* traditionally accounts for the majority of deaths, recent evidence suggests that *P. vivax* malaria is associated with potentially life-threatening conditions about as often as with a diagnosis of *P. falciparum* infection. *P. vivax* proportionally is more common outside of Africa. There have been documented human infections with several species of *Plasmodium* from higher apes; however, except for *P. knowlesi*—a zoonotic species that causes malaria in macaques—these are mostly of limited public health importance.

Climate change is likely to affect malaria transmission, but the severity and geographic distribution of such effects is currently uncertain.

Life Cycle

In the life cycle of *Plasmodium*, a female *Anopheles* mosquito (the definitive host) transmits a motile infective form (called the sporozoite) to a vertebrate host such as a human (the secondary host), thus acting as a transmission vector. A sporozoite travels through the blood vessels to liver cells (hepatocytes), where it reproduces asexually (tissue schizogony), producing thousands of merozoites. These infect new red blood cells and initiate a series of asexual multiplication cycles (blood schizogony) that produce 8 to 24 new infective merozoites, at which point the cells burst and the infective cycle begins anew.

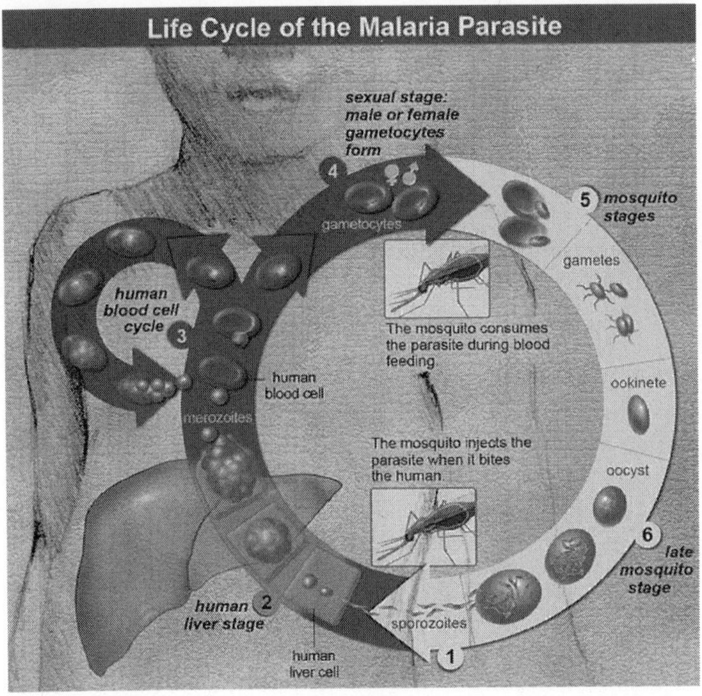

Figure: *The life cycle of malaria parasites. A mosquito causes an infection by a bite. First, sporozoites enter the bloodstream, and migrate to the liver. They infect liver cells, where they multiply into merozoites, rupture the liver cells, and return to the bloodstream. Then, the merozoites infect red blood cells, where they develop into ring forms, trophozoites and schizonts that in turn produce further merozoites. Sexual forms are also produced, which, if taken up by a mosquito, will infect the insect and continue the life cycle.*

Other merozoites develop into immature gametocytes, which are the precursors of male and female gametes. When a fertilised mosquito bites an infected person, gametocytes are taken up with the blood and mature in the mosquito gut. The male and female gametocytes fuse and form an ookinete—a fertilized, motile zygote. Ookinetes develop into new sporozoites that migrate to the insect's salivary glands, ready to infect a new vertebrate host. The sporozoites are injected into the skin, in the saliva, when the mosquito takes a subsequent blood meal.

Only female mosquitoes feed on blood; male mosquitoes feed on plant nectar, and thus do not transmit the disease. The females of the *Anopheles* genus of mosquito prefer to feed at night. They usually start searching for a meal at dusk, and will continue throughout the night until taking a meal. Malaria parasites can also be transmitted by blood transfusions, although this is rare.

Recurrent Malaria

Symptoms of malaria can recur after varying symptom-free periods. Depending upon the cause, recurrence can be classified as either recrudescence, relapse, or reinfection. Recrudescence is when symptoms return after a symptom-free period. It is caused by parasites surviving in the blood as a result of inadequate or ineffective treatment. Relapse is when symptoms reappear after the parasites have been eliminated from blood but persist as dormant hypnozoites in liver cells. Relapse commonly occurs between 8–24 weeks and is commonly seen with *P. vivax* and *P. ovale* infections. *P. vivax* malaria cases in temperate areas often involve overwintering by hypnozoites, with relapses beginning the year after the mosquito bite. Reinfection means the parasite that caused the past infection was eliminated from the body but a new parasite was introduced. Reinfection cannot readily be distinguished from recrudescence, although recurrence of infection within two weeks of treatment for the initial infection is typically attributed to treatment failure. People may develop some immunity when exposed to frequent infections.

Pathophysiology

Malaria infection develops via two phases: one that involves the liver (exoerythrocytic phase), and one that involves red blood cells, or erythrocytes (erythrocytic phase). When an infected mosquito pierces a person's skin to take a blood meal, sporozoites in the mosquito's saliva enter the bloodstream and migrate to the liver where they infect hepatocytes, multiplying asexually and asymptomatically for a period of 8–30 days.

After a potential dormant period in the liver, these organisms differentiate to yield thousands of merozoites, which, following rupture of their host cells, escape into the blood and infect red blood cells to begin the erythrocytic stage of the life cycle. The parasite escapes from the liver undetected by wrapping itself in the cell membrane of the infected host liver cell.

Within the red blood cells, the parasites multiply further, again asexually, periodically breaking out of their host cells to invade fresh red blood cells. Several such amplification cycles occur. Thus, classical descriptions of waves of fever arise from simultaneous waves of merozoites escaping and infecting red blood cells.

Some *P. vivax* sporozoites do not immediately develop into exoerythrocytic-phase merozoites, but instead produce hypnozoites that remain dormant for periods ranging from several months (7–10 months is typical) to several years. After a period of dormancy, they reactivate and produce merozoites. Hypnozoites are responsible for long incubation and late relapses in *P. vivax* infections, although their existence in *P. ovale* is uncertain.

The parasite is relatively protected from attack by the body's immune system because for most of its human life cycle it resides within the liver and blood cells and is relatively invisible to immune surveillance. However, circulating infected blood cells are destroyed in the spleen. To avoid this fate, the *P. falciparum* parasite displays adhesive proteins on the surface of the infected blood cells, causing the blood cells to stick to the walls of small blood vessels, thereby sequestering the parasite from passage through the general circulation and the spleen. The blockage of the microvasculature causes symptoms such as in placental malaria. Sequestered red blood cells can breach the blood–brain barrier and cause cerebral malaria.

Genetic Resistance

According to a 2005 review, due to the high levels of mortality and morbidity caused by malaria—especially the *P. falciparum* species—it has placed the greatest selective pressure on the human genome in recent history. Several genetic factors provide some resistance to it including sickle cell trait, thalassaemia traits, glucose-6-phosphate dehydrogenase deficiency, and the absence of Duffy antigens on red blood cells.

The impact of sickle cell trait on malaria immunity illustrates some evolutionary trade-offs that have occurred because of endemic malaria. Sickle cell trait causes a defect in the hemoglobin molecule in the blood. Instead of retaining the biconcave shape of a normal red blood cell, the modified hemoglobin S molecule causes the cell to sickle or distort into a curved shape. Due to the sickle shape, the molecule is not as effective in taking or releasing oxygen. Infection causes red cells to sickle more, and so they are removed from circulation sooner. This reduces the frequency with which malaria parasites complete their life cycle in the cell. Individuals who are homozygous (with two copies of the abnormal hemoglobin beta allele) have sickle-cell anaemia, while those who are heterozygous (with one abnormal allele and one normal allele) experience resistance to malaria. Although the shorter life expectancy for those with the homozygous condition would not sustain the trait's survival, the trait is preserved because of the benefits provided by the heterozygous form.

Liver Dysfunction

Liver dysfunction as a result of malaria is uncommon and usually only occurs in those with other liver condition such as viral hepatitis or chronic liver disease. The syndrome is sometimes called *malarial hepatitis*. While it has been considered a rare occurrence, malarial hepatopathy has seen an increase, particularly in Southeast Asia and India. Liver compromise in people with malaria correlates with a greater likelihood of complications and death.

Diagnosis

Owing to the non-specific nature of the presentation of symptoms, diagnosis of malaria in non-endemic areas requires a high degree of suspicion, which might be elicited by any of the following: recent travel history, enlarged spleen, fever, low number of platelets in the blood, and higher-than-normal levels of bilirubin in the blood combined with a normal level of white blood cells.

Malaria is usually confirmed by the microscopic examination of blood films or by antigen-based rapid diagnostic tests (RDT). Microscopy is the most commonly used method to detect the malarial parasite—about 165 million blood films were examined for malaria in 2010. Despite its widespread usage, diagnosis by microscopy suffers from two main drawbacks: many settings (especially rural) are not equipped to perform the test, and the accuracy of the results depends on both the skill of the person examining the blood film and the levels of the parasite in the blood. The sensitivity of blood films ranges from 75–90% in optimum conditions, to as low as 50%. Commercially available RDTs are often more accurate than blood films at predicting the presence of malaria parasites, but they are widely variable in diagnostic sensitivity and specificity depending on manufacturer, and are unable to tell how many parasites are present.

In regions where laboratory tests are readily available, malaria should be suspected, and tested for, in any unwell person who has been in an area where malaria is endemic. In areas that cannot afford laboratory diagnostic tests, it has become common to use only a history of fever as the indication to treat for malaria—thus the common teaching "fever equals malaria unless proven otherwise". A drawback of this practice is overdiagnosis of malaria and mismanagement of non-malarial fever, which wastes limited resources, erodes confidence in the health care system, and contributes to drug resistance. Although polymerase chain reaction-based tests have been developed, they are not widely used in areas where malaria is common as of 2012, due to their complexity.

Classification

Malaria is classified into either "severe" or "uncomplicated" by the World Health Organization (WHO). It is deemed severe when *any* of the following criteria are present, otherwise it is considered uncomplicated.

- Decreased consciousness
- Significant weakness such that the person is unable to walk
- Inability to feed
- Two or more convulsions
- Low blood pressure (less than 70 mmHg in adults and 50 mmHg in children)
- Breathing problems
- Circulatory shock
- Kidney failure or hemoglobin in the urine
- Bleeding problems, or hemoglobin less than 50 g/L (5 g/dL)
- Pulmonary oedema
- Blood glucose less than 2.2 mmol/L (40 mg/dL)
- Acidosis or lactate levels of greater than 5 mmol/L
- A parasite level in the blood of greater than 100,000 per microlitre (μL) in low-intensity transmission areas, or 250,000 per μL in high-intensity transmission areas

Cerebral malaria is defined as a severe *P. falciparum*-malaria presenting with neurological symptoms, including coma (with a Glasgow coma scale less than 11, or a Blantyre coma scale greater than 3), or with a coma that lasts longer than 30 minutes after a seizure.

Prevention

Methods used to prevent malaria include medications, mosquito elimination and the prevention of bites. There is no vaccine for malaria. The presence of malaria in an area requires a combination of high human population density, high anopheles mosquito population density and high rates of transmission from humans to mosquitoes and from mosquitoes to humans. If any of these is lowered sufficiently, the parasite will eventually disappear from that area, as happened in North America, Europe and parts of the Middle East. However, unless the parasite is eliminated from the whole world, it could become re-established if conditions revert to a combination that favours the parasite's reproduction. Furthermore, the cost per person of eliminating anopheles mosquitoes rises with decreasing population density, making it economically unfeasible in some areas.

Prevention of malaria may be more cost-effective than treatment of the disease in the long run, but the initial costs required are out of reach of many of the world's poorest people. There is a wide difference in the costs of control (i.e. maintenance of low endemicity) and elimination programmes between countries. For example, in China—whose government in 2010 announced a strategy to pursue malaria elimination in the Chinese provinces—the required investment is a small proportion of public expenditure on health. In contrast, a similar programme in Tanzania would cost an estimated one-fifth of the public health budget.

Mosquito Control

Vector control refers to methods used to decrease malaria by reducing the levels of transmission by mosquitoes. For individual protection, the most effective insect repellents are based on DEET or picaridin. Insecticide-treated mosquito nets (ITNs) and indoor residual spraying (IRS) have been shown to be highly effective in preventing malaria among children in areas where malaria is common. Prompt treatment of confirmed cases with artemisinin-based combination therapies (ACTs) may also reduce transmission.

Mosquito nets help keep mosquitoes away from people and reduce infection rates and transmission of malaria. Nets are not a perfect barrier and are often treated with an insecticide designed to kill the mosquito before it has time to find a way past the net. Insecticide-treated nets are estimated to be twice as effective as untreated nets and offer greater than 70% protection compared with no net. Between 2000 and 2008, the use of ITNs saved the lives of an estimated 250,000 infants in Sub-Saharan Africa. About 13% of households in Sub-Saharan countries own ITNs. In 2000, 1.7 million (1.8%) African children living in areas of the world where malaria is common were protected by an ITN. That number increased to 20.3 million (18.5%) African children using ITNs in 2007, leaving 89.6 million children unprotected. An increased percentage of African households (31%) are estimated to own at least one ITN in 2008. Most nets are impregnated with pyrethroids, a class of insecticides with low toxicity. They are most effective when used from dusk to dawn. It is recommended to hang a large "bed net" above the centre of a bed and either tuck the edges under the mattress or make sure it is large enough such that it touches the ground.

Indoor residual spraying is the spraying of insecticides on the walls inside a home. After feeding, many mosquitoes rest on a nearby surface while digesting the bloodmeal, so if the walls of houses have been coated with insecticides, the resting mosquitoes can be killed before they can bite another person and transfer the malaria parasite. As of 2006, the World Health Organization recommends 12 insecticides in IRS operations, including DDT and the pyrethroids cyfluthrin and deltamethrin. This public health use of small amounts of DDT is permitted under the Stockholm Convention, which prohibits its agricultural use. One problem with all forms of IRS is insecticide resistance. Mosquitoes affected by IRS tend to rest and live indoors, and due to the irritation caused by spraying, their descendants tend to rest and live outdoors, meaning that they are less affected by the IRS.

There are a number of other methods to reduce mosquito bites and slow the spread of malaria. Efforts to decrease mosquito larva by decreasing the availability of open water in which they develop or by adding substances to decrease their development is effective in some locations. Electronic mosquito repellent devices which make very high frequency sounds that are supposed to keep female mosquitoes away, do not have supporting evidence.

Other Methods

Community participation and health education strategies promoting awareness of malaria and the importance of control measures have been successfully used to reduce the incidence of malaria in some areas of the developing world. Recognizing the disease in the early stages can stop the disease from becoming fatal.

Education can also inform people to cover over areas of stagnant, still water, such as water tanks that are ideal breeding grounds for the parasite and mosquito, thus cutting down the risk of the transmission between people. This is generally used in urban areas where there are large centres of population in a confined space and transmission would be most likely in these areas. Intermittent preventive therapy is another intervention that has been used successfully to control malaria in pregnant women and infants, and in preschool children where transmission is seasonal.

Medications

There are a number of drugs that can help prevent malaria while travelling in areas where it exists. Most of these drugs are also sometimes used in treatment. Chloroquine may be used where the parasite is still sensitive. Because most *Plasmodium* is resistant to one or more medications, one of three medications—mefloquine (*Lariam*), doxycycline (available generically), or the combination of atovaquone and proguanil hydrochloride (*Malarone*)—is frequently needed. Doxycycline and the atovaquone and proguanil combination are the best tolerated; mefloquine is associated with death, suicide, and neurological and psychiatric symptoms.

The protective effect does not begin immediately, and people visiting areas where malaria exists usually start taking the drugs one to two weeks before arriving and continue taking them for four weeks after leaving (except for atovaquone/proguanil, which only needs to be started two days before and continued for seven days afterward). The use of preventative drugs is often not practical for those who live in areas where malaria exists, and their use is usually only in short-term visitors and travellers. This is due to the cost of the drugs, side effects from long-term use, and the difficulty in obtaining anti-malarial drugs outside of wealthy nations. The use of preventative drugs where malaria-bearing mosquitoes are present may encourage the development of partial resistance. An exception to this is during pregnancy when taking medication to prevent malaria has been found to improve the weight of the baby at birth and decrease the risk of anemia in the mother.

Treatment

Malaria is treated with antimalarial medications; the ones used depends on the type and severity of the disease. While medications against fever are commonly used, their effects on outcomes are not clear.

Uncomplicated malaria may be treated with oral medications. The most effective treatment for *P. falciparum* infection is the use of artemisinins in combination with other antimalarials (known as artemisinin-combination therapy, or ACT), which decreases resistance to any single drug component. These additional antimalarials include: amodiaquine, lumefantrine, mefloquine or sulfadoxine/pyrimethamine. Another recommended combination is dihydroartemisinin and piperaquine. ACT is about 90% effective when used to treat uncomplicated malaria. To treat malaria during pregnancy, the WHO recommends the use of quinine plus clindamycin early in the pregnancy (1st trimester), and ACT in later stages (2nd and 3rd trimesters). In the 2000s (decade), malaria with partial resistance to artemisins emerged in Southeast Asia.

Infection with *P. vivax*, *P. ovale* or *P. malariae* is usually treated without the need for hospitalization. Treatment of *P. vivax* requires both treatment of blood stages (with chloroquine or ACT) and clearance of liver forms with primaquine.

Recommended treatment for severe malaria is the intravenous use of antimalarial drugs. For severe malaria, artesunate is superior to quinine in both children and adults. Treatment of severe malaria involves supportive measures that are best done in a critical care unit. This includes the management of high fevers and the seizures that may result from it. It also includes monitoring for poor breathing effort, low blood sugar, and low blood potassium.

Resistance

Drug resistance poses a growing problem in 21st-century malaria treatment. Resistance is now common against all classes of antimalarial drugs save the artemisinins. Treatment of resistant strains became increasingly dependent on this class of drugs. The cost of artemisinins limits their use in the developing world. Malaria strains found on the Cambodia–Thailand border are resistant to combination therapies that include artemisinins, and may therefore be untreatable. Exposure of the parasite population to artemisinin monotherapies in subtherapeutic doses for over 30 years and the availability of substandard artemisinins likely drove the selection of the resistant phenotype. Resistance to artemisinin has been detected in Cambodia, Myanmar, Thailand, and Vietnam, and there has been emerging resistance in Laos.

Yellow Fever

Yellow fever, known historically as yellow jack or yellow plague, is an acute viral disease. In most cases, symptoms include fever, chills, loss of appetite, nausea, muscle pains particularly in the back, and headaches. Symptoms typically improve within five days. In some people within a day of improving, the fever comes back, abdominal pain occurs, and liver damage begins causing yellow skin. If this occurs, the risk of bleeding and kidney problems is also increased.

The disease is caused by the yellow fever virus and is spread by the bite of the female mosquito. It only infects humans, other primates, and several species of mosquitoes. In cities, it is primarily spread by mosquitoes of the *Aedes aegypti* species. The virus is an RNA virus of the genus *Flavivirus*. The disease may be difficult to tell apart from other illnesses, especially in the early stages. To confirm a suspected case, blood sample testing with polymerase chain reaction is required.

A safe and effective vaccine against yellow fever exists and some countries require vaccinations for travelers. Other efforts to prevent infection include reducing the population of the transmitting mosquito. In areas where yellow fever is common and vaccination is uncommon, early diagnosis of cases and immunization of large parts of the population is important to prevent outbreaks. Once infected, management is symptomatic with no specific measures effective against the virus. In those with severe disease, death occurs in about half of people without treatment.

Yellow fever causes 200,000 infections and 30,000 deaths every year, with nearly 90% of these occurring in Africa. Nearly a billion people live in an area of the world where the disease is common. It is common in tropical areas of South America and Africa, but not in Asia. Since the 1980s, the number of cases of yellow fever has been increasing. This is believed to be due to fewer people being immune, more people living in cities, people moving frequently, and changing climate. The disease originated in Africa, where it spread to South America through the slave trade in the 17th century. Since the 17th century, several major outbreaks of the disease have occurred in the Americas, Africa, and Europe. In the 18th and 19th centuries, yellow fever was seen as one of the most dangerous infectious diseases. The yellow fever virus was the first human virus discovered.

Signs and Symptoms

Yellow fever begins after an incubation period of three to six days. Most cases only cause a mild infection with fever, headache, chills, back pain, loss of appetite, nausea, and vomiting. In these cases, the infection lasts only three to four days.

In 15% of cases, however, sufferers enter a second, toxic phase of the disease with recurring fever, this time accompanied by jaundice due to liver damage, as well as abdominal pain. Bleeding in the mouth, the eyes, and the gastrointestinal tract will cause vomit containing blood, hence the Spanish name for yellow fever, *vomito negro* ("black vomit"). The toxic phase is fatal in about 20% of cases, making the overall fatality rate for the disease 3%. In severe epidemics, the mortality may exceed 50%.

Surviving the infection provides lifelong immunity, and normally there is no permanent organ damage.

Cause

Yellow fever is caused by the yellow fever virus, a 40- to 50-nm-wide enveloped RNA virus, the type species and namesake of the family Flaviviridae. It was the first illness shown to be transmissible by filtered human serum and transmitted by mosquitoes, by Walter Reed around 1900. The positive-sense, single-stranded RNA is around 11,000 nucleotides long and has a single open reading frame encoding a polyprotein. Host proteases cut this polyprotein into three structural (C, prM, E) and seven nonstructural proteins (NS1, NS2A, NS2B, NS3, NS4A, NS4B, NS5); the enumeration corresponds to the arrangement of the protein coding genes in the genome. Yellow fever belongs to the group of hemorrhagic fevers.

The viruses infect, amongst others, monocytes, macrophages, and dendritic cells. They attach to the cell surface via specific receptors and are taken up by an endosomal vesicle. Inside the endosome, the decreased pH induces the fusion of the endosomal membrane with the virus envelope. The capsid enters the cytosol, decays, and releases the genome. Receptor binding, as well as membrane fusion, are catalysed by the protein E, which changes its conformation at low pH, causing a rearrangement of the 90 homodimers to 60 homotrimers.

After entering the host cell, the viral genome is replicated in the rough endoplasmic reticulum (ER) and in the so-called vesicle packets. At first, an immature form of the virus particle is produced inside the ER, whose M-protein is not yet cleaved to its mature form and is therefore denoted as prM (precursor M) and forms a complex with protein E. The immature particles are processed in the Golgi apparatus by the host protein furin, which cleaves prM to M. This releases E from the complex which can now take its place in the mature, infectious virion.

Transmission

Yellow fever virus is mainly transmitted through the bite of the yellow fever mosquito *Aedes aegypti*, but other mosquitoes such as the tiger mosquito (*Aedes albopictus*) can also serve as a vector for this virus. Like other Arboviruses which are transmitted by mosquitoes, the yellow fever virus is taken up by a female mosquito when it ingests the blood of an infected human or other primate. Viruses reach the stomach of the mosquito, and if the virus concentration is high enough, the virions can infect epithelial cells and replicate there. From there, they reach the haemocoel (the blood system of mosquitoes) and from there the salivary glands. When the mosquito next sucks blood, it injects its saliva into the wound, and the virus reaches the bloodstream of the bitten person. Transovarial and transstadial transmission of the yellow fever virus within *A. aegypti*, that is, the transmission from a female mosquito to her eggs and then larvae, are indicated.

This infection of vectors without a previous blood meal seems to play a role in single, sudden breakouts of the disease.

Three epidemiologically different infectious cycles occur, in which the virus is transmitted from mosquitoes to humans or other primates. In the "urban cycle", only the yellow fever mosquito *A. aegypti* is involved. It is well adapted to urban areas and can also transmit other diseases, including dengue fever and chikungunya. The urban cycle is responsible for the major outbreaks of yellow fever that occur in Africa. Except in an outbreak in 1999 in Bolivia, this urban cycle no longer exists in South America.

Besides the urban cycle, both in Africa and South America, a sylvatic cycle (forest cycle or jungle cycle) is present, where *Aedes africanus* (in Africa) or mosquitoes of the genus *Haemagogus* and *Sabethes* (in South America) serve as vectors. In the jungle, the mosquitoes infect mainly non-human primates; the disease is mostly asymptomatic in African primates. In South America, the sylvatic cycle is currently the only way humans can infect each other, which explains the low incidence of yellow fever cases on the continent. People who become infected in the jungle can carry the virus to urban areas, where *A. aegypti* acts as a vector. Because of this sylvatic cycle, the yellow fever cannot be eradicated.

In Africa, a third infectious cycle known as "savannah cycle" or intermediate cycle, occurs between the jungle and urban cycles. Different mosquitoes of the genus *Aedes* are involved. In recent years, this has been the most common form of transmission of yellow fever in Africa.

Pathogenesis

After transmission from a mosquito, the viruses replicate in the lymph nodes and infect dendritic cells in particular. From there, they reach the liver and infect hepatocytes (probably indirectly via Kupffer cells), which leads to eosinophilic degradation of these cells and to the release of cytokines. Necrotic masses known as Councilman bodies appear in the cytoplasm of hepatocytes.

Fatality may occur when cytokine storm, shock, and multiple organ failure follow.

Diagnosis

Yellow fever is a clinical diagnosis, which often relies on the whereabouts of the diseased person during the incubation time. Mild courses of the disease can only be confirmed virologically. Since mild courses of yellow fever can also contribute significantly to regional outbreaks, every suspected case of yellow fever (involving symptoms of fever, pain, nausea and vomiting six to 10 days after leaving the affected area) is treated seriously. If yellow fever is suspected, the virus cannot be confirmed until six to 10 days after the illness. A direct confirmation can be obtained by reverse transcription polymerase chain reaction where the genome of the virus is amplified. Another direct approach is the isolation of the virus and its growth in cell culture using blood plasma; this can take one to four weeks.

Serologically, an enzyme linked immunosorbent assay during the acute phase of the disease using specific IgM against yellow fever or an increase in specific IgG-titer (compared to an earlier sample) can confirm yellow fever. Together with clinical symptoms, the detection of IgM or a fourfold increase in IgG-titer is considered sufficient indication for yellow fever. Since these tests can cross-react with other flaviviruses, like dengue virus, these indirect methods cannot conclusively prove yellow fever infection.

Liver biopsy can verify inflammation and necrosis of hepatocytes and detect viral antigens. Because of the bleeding tendency of yellow fever patients, a biopsy is only advisable *post mortem* to confirm the cause of death.

In a differential diagnosis, infections with yellow fever must be distinguished from other feverish illnesses like malaria. Other viral hemorrhagic fevers, such as Ebola virus, Lassa virus, Marburg virus, and Junin virus, must be excluded as cause.

Prevention

Personal prevention of yellow fever includes vaccination, as well as avoidance of mosquito bites in areas where yellow fever is endemic. Institutional measures for prevention of yellow fever include vaccination programmes and measures of controlling mosquitoes. Programmes for distribution of mosquito nets for use in homes are providing reductions in cases of both malaria and yellow fever.

Vaccination

Vaccination is recommended for those travelling to affected areas, because non-native people tend to suffer more severe illness when infected. Protection begins by the 10th day after vaccine administration in 95% of people, and lasts for at least 10 years. About 81% of people are still immune after 30 years. The attenuated live vaccine stem 17D was developed in 1937 by Max Theiler. The World Health Organization (WHO) recommends routine vaccinations for people living in affected areas between the ninth and 12th month after birth. Up to one in four people experience fever, aches, and local soreness and redness at the site of injection.

In rare cases (less than one in 200,000 to 300,000), the vaccination can cause yellow fever vaccine-associated viscerotropic disease, which is fatal in 60% of cases. It is probably due to the genetic morphology of the immune system. Another possible side effect is an infection of the nervous system, which occurs in one in 200,000 to 300,000 cases, causing yellow fever vaccine-associated neurotropic disease, which can lead to meningoencephalitis and is fatal in less than 5% of cases.

In 2009, the largest mass vaccination against yellow fever began in West Africa, specifically Benin, Liberia, and Sierra Leone. When it is completed in 2015, more than 12 million people will have been vaccinated against the disease. According to the WHO, the mass vaccination cannot eliminate yellow fever because of the vast number of infected mosquitoes in urban areas of the target countries, but it will significantly reduce the number of people infected. The WHO plans to continue the vaccination campaign in another five African countries — the Central African Republic, Ghana, Guinea, Côte d'Ivoire, and Nigeria &mdash ;and stated that about 160 million people in the continent could be at risk unless the organization acquires additional funding to support widespread vaccinations.

In 2013, the WHO stated, "a single dose of vaccination is sufficient to confer life-long immunity against yellow fever disease."

Compulsory Vaccination

Some countries in Asia are theoretically in danger of yellow fever epidemics (mosquitoes with the capability to transmit yellow fever and susceptible monkeys are present), although the disease does not yet occur there. To prevent introduction of the virus, some countries demand previous vaccination of foreign visitors if they have passed through yellow fever areas. Vaccination has to be proven in a vaccination certificate which is valid 10 days after the vaccination and lasts for 10 years. A list of the countries that require yellow fever vaccination is published by the WHO. If the vaccination cannot be conducted for some reasons, dispensation may be possible. In this case, an exemption certificate issued by a WHO-approved vaccination centre is required. Although 32 of 44 countries where yellow fever occurs endemically do have vaccination programmes, in many of these countries, less than 50% of their population is vaccinated.

Vector Control

Control of the yellow fever mosquito *A. aegypti* is of major importance, especially because the same mosquito can also transmit dengue fever and chikungunya disease. *A. aegypti* breeds preferentially in water, for example in installations by inhabitants of areas with precarious drinking water supply, or in domestic waste; especially tires, cans, and plastic bottles. These conditions are common in urban areas in developing countries.

Two main strategies are employed to reduce mosquito populations. One approach is to kill the developing larvae. Measures are taken to reduce the water accumulations in which the larva develops. Larvicides are used, as well as larvae-eating fish and copepods, which reduce the number of larvae. For many years, copepods of the genus *Mesocyclops* have been used in Vietnam for preventing dengue fever. It eradicated the mosquito vector in several areas. Similar efforts may be effective against yellow fever. Pyriproxyfen is recommended as a chemical larvicide, mainly because it is safe for humans and effective even in small doses.

The second strategy is to reduce populations of the adult yellow fever mosquito. Lethal ovitraps can reduce *Aedes* populations, but with a decreased amount of pesticide because it targets the mosquitoes directly. Curtains and lids of water tanks can be sprayed with insecticides, but application inside houses is not recommended by the WHO. Insecticide-treated mosquito nets are effective, just as they are against the *Anopheles* mosquito that carries malaria.

Treatment

As for other flavivirus infections, no cure is known for yellow fever. Hospitalization is advisable and intensive care may be necessary because of rapid deterioration in some cases. Different methods for acute treatment of the disease have been shown to not be very successful; passive immunisation after emergence of symptoms is probably without effect. Ribavirin and other antiviral drugs, as well as treatment with interferons, do not have a positive effect in patients. A symptomatic treatment includes rehydration and pain relief with drugs such as paracetamol (acetaminophen in the United States). Acetylsalicylic acid (aspirin) should not be given because of its anticoagulant effect, which can be devastating in the case of internal bleeding that can occur with yellow fever.

Dengue Fever

Dengue fever, also known as breakbone fever, is a mosquito-borne tropical disease caused by the dengue virus. Symptoms include fever, headache, muscle and joint pains, and a characteristic skin rash that is similar to measles. In a small proportion of cases the disease develops into the life-threatening dengue hemorrhagic fever, resulting in bleeding, low levels of blood platelets and blood plasma leakage, or into dengue shock syndrome, where dangerously low blood pressure occurs.

Dengue is transmitted by several species of mosquito within the genus *Aedes*, principally *A. aegypti*. The virus has five different types; infection with one type usually gives lifelong immunity to that type, but only short-term immunity to the others. Subsequent infection with a different type increases the risk of severe complications. As there is no commercially available vaccine, prevention is sought by reducing the habitat and the number of mosquitoes and limiting exposure to bites.

Treatment of acute dengue is supportive, using either oral or intravenous rehydration for mild or moderate disease, and intravenous fluids and blood transfusion for more severe cases. The number of cases of dengue fever has increased dramatically since the 1960s, with between 50 and 528 million people infected yearly. Early descriptions of the condition date from 1779, and its viral cause and the transmission were figured out in the early 20th century. Dengue has become a global problem since the Second World War and is endemic in more than 110 countries. Apart from eliminating the mosquitoes, work is ongoing on a vaccine, as well as medication targeted directly at the virus.

Signs and Symptoms

Typically, people infected with dengue virus are asymptomatic (80%) or only have mild symptoms such as an uncomplicated fever. Others have more severe illness (5%), and in a small proportion it is life-threatening. The incubation period (time between exposure and onset of symptoms) ranges from 3 to 14 days, but most often it is 4 to 7 days. Therefore, travellers returning from endemic areas are unlikely to have dengue if fever or other symptoms start more than 14 days after arriving home. Children often experience symptoms similar to those of the common cold and gastroenteritis (vomiting and diarrhea) and have a greater risk of severe complications, though initial symptoms are generally mild but include high fever.

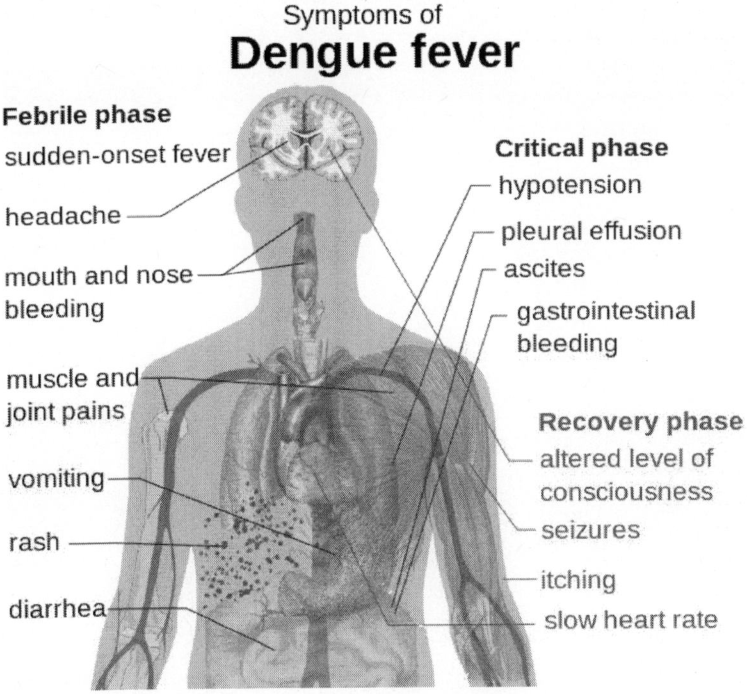

Figure: *Schematic depiction of the symptoms of dengue fever*

Clinical Course

The characteristic symptoms of dengue are sudden-onset fever, headache (typically located behind the eyes), muscle and joint pains, and a rash. The alternative name for dengue, "breakbone fever", comes from the associated muscle and joint pains.

The course of infection is divided into three phases: febrile, critical, and recovery.

The febrile phase involves high fever, potentially over 40 °C (104 °F), and is associated with generalized pain and a headache; this usually lasts two to seven days. Nausea and vomiting may also occur. A rash occurs in 50–80% of those with symptoms in the first or second day of symptoms as flushed skin, or later in the course of illness (days 4–7), as a measles-like rash.

A rash described as "islands of white in a sea of red" has also been described. Some petechiae (small red spots that do not disappear when the skin is pressed, which are caused by broken capillaries) can appear at this point, as may some mild bleeding from the mucous membranes of the mouth and nose. The fever itself is classically biphasic or saddleback in nature, breaking and then returning for one or two days.

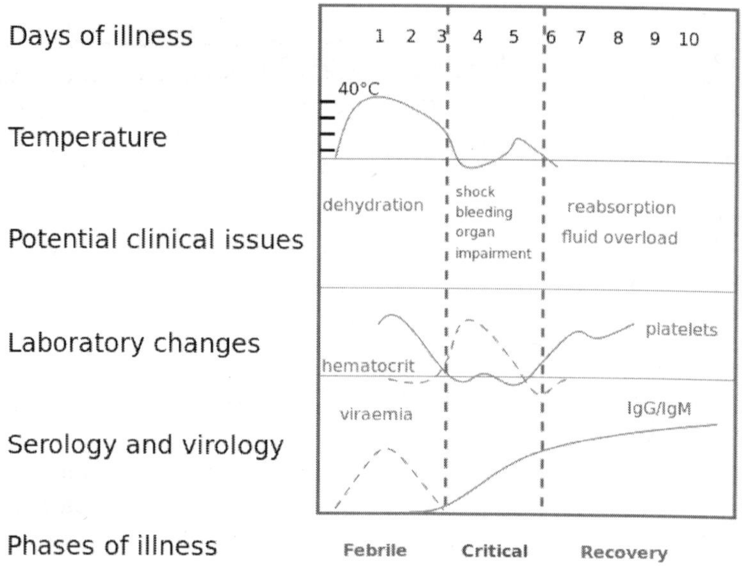

Figure: *Clinical course of dengue fever*

In some people, the disease proceeds to a critical phase as fever resolves. During this period there is leakage of plasma from the blood vessels which typically lasts one to two days. This may result in fluid accumulation in the chest and abdominal cavity as well as depletion of fluid from the circulation and decreased blood supply to vital organs. There may also be organ dysfunction and severe bleeding, typically from the gastrointestinal tract. Shock (dengue shock syndrome) and hemorrhage (dengue hemorrhagic fever) occur in less than 5% of all cases of dengue, however those who have previously been infected with other serotypes of dengue virus ("secondary infection") are at an increased risk. This critical phase, while rare, occurs relatively more commonly in children and young adults.he recovery phase occurs next, with resorption of the leaked fluid into the bloodstream. This usually lasts two to three days. The improvement is often striking, and can be accompanied with severe itching and a slow heart rate. Another rash may occur with either a maculopapular or a vasculitic appearance, which is followed by peeling of the skin. During this stage, a fluid overload state may occur; if it affects the brain, it may cause a reduced level of consciousness or seizures. A feeling of fatigue may last for weeks in adults.

Associated Problems

Dengue can occasionally affect several other body systems, either in isolation or along with the classic dengue symptoms. A decreased level of consciousness occurs in 0.5–6% of severe cases, which is attributable either to inflammation of the brain by the virus or indirectly as a result of impairment of vital organs, for example, the liver.

Other neurological disorders have been reported in the context of dengue, such as transverse myelitis and Guillain-Barré syndrome. Infection of the heart and acute liver failure are among the rarer complications.

Cause

Virology

Dengue fever virus (DENV) is an RNA virus of the family *Flaviviridae*; genus *Flavivirus*. Other members of the same genus include yellow fever virus, West Nile virus, St. Louis encephalitis virus, Japanese encephalitis virus, tick-borne encephalitis virus, Kyasanur forest disease virus, and Omsk hemorrhagic fever virus. Most are transmitted by arthropods (mosquitoes or ticks), and are therefore also referred to as arboviruses (*ar*thropod-*bo*rne viruses).

The dengue virus genome (genetic material) contains about 11,000 nucleotide bases, which code for the three different types of protein molecules (C, prM and E) that form the virus particle and seven other types of protein molecules (NS1, NS2a, NS2b, NS3, NS4a, NS4b, NS5) that are only found in infected host cells and are required for replication of the virus. There are five strains of the virus, called serotypes, of which the first four are referred to as DENV-1, DENV-2, DENV-3 and DENV-4. The fifth type was announced in 2013. The distinctions between the serotypes are based on their antigenicity.

Transmission

Dengue virus is primarily transmitted by *Aedes* mosquitoes, particularly *A. aegypti*. These mosquitoes usually live between the latitudes of 35° North and 35° South below an elevation of 1,000 metres (3,300 ft). They typically bite during the day, particularly in the early morning and in the evening, but they are able to bite and thus spread infection at any time of day all during the year. Other *Aedes* species that transmit the disease include *A. albopictus*, *A. polynesiensis* and *A. scutellaris*. Humans are the primary host of the virus, but it also circulates in nonhuman primates. An infection can be acquired via a single bite. A female mosquito that takes a blood meal from a person infected with dengue fever, during the initial 2–10 day febrile period, becomes itself infected with the virus in the cells lining its gut. About 8–10 days later, the virus spreads to other tissues including the mosquito's salivary glands and is subsequently released into its saliva. The virus seems to have no detrimental effect on the mosquito, which remains infected for life. *Aedes aegypti* is particularly involved, as it prefers to lay its eggs in artificial water containers, to live in close proximity to humans, and to feed on people rather than other vertebrates.

Dengue can also be transmitted via infected blood products and through organ donation. In countries such as Singapore, where dengue is endemic, the risk is estimated to be between 1.6 and 6 per 10,000 transfusions. Vertical transmission (from mother to child) during pregnancy or at birth has been reported. Other person-to-person modes of transmission have also been reported, but are very unusual. The genetic variation in dengue viruses is region specific, suggestive that establishment into new territories is relatively infrequent, despite dengue emerging in new regions in recent decades.

Predisposition

Severe disease is more common in babies and young children, and in contrast to many other infections it is more common in children that are relatively well nourished. Other risk factors for severe disease include female sex, high body mass index, and viral load. While each serotype can cause the full spectrum of disease, virus strain is a risk factor. Infection with one serotype is thought to produce lifelong immunity to that type, but only short-term protection against the other three. The risk of severe disease from secondary infection increases if someone previously exposed to serotype DENV-1 contracts serotype DENV-2 or DENV-3, or if someone previously exposed to DENV-3 acquires DENV-2. Dengue can be life-threatening in people with chronic diseases such as diabetes and asthma.

Polymorphisms (normal variations) in particular genes have been linked with an increased risk of severe dengue complications. Examples include the genes coding for the proteins known as TNFá, mannan-binding lectin, CTLA4, TGFâ, DC-SIGN, PLCE1, and particular forms of human leukocyte antigen from gene variations of HLA-B. A common genetic abnormality, especially in Africans, known as glucose-6-phosphate dehydrogenase deficiency, appears to increase the risk. Polymorphisms in the genes for the vitamin D receptor and FcãR seem to offer protection against severe disease in secondary dengue infection.

Mechanism

When a mosquito carrying dengue virus bites a person, the virus enters the skin together with the mosquito's saliva. It binds to and enters white blood cells, and reproduces inside the cells while they move throughout the body. The white blood cells respond by producing a number of signalling proteins, such as cytokines and interferons, which are responsible for many of the symptoms, such as the fever, the flu-like symptoms and the severe pains. In severe infection, the virus production inside the body is greatly increased, and many more organs (such as the liver and the bone marrow) can be affected. Fluid from the bloodstream leaks through the wall of small blood vessels into body cavities due to capillary permeability. As a result, less blood circulates in the blood vessels, and the blood pressure becomes so low that it cannot supply sufficient blood to vital organs. Furthermore, dysfunction of the bone marrow due to infection of the stromal cells leads to reduced numbers of platelets, which are necessary for effective blood clotting; this increases the risk of bleeding, the other major complication of dengue fever.

Viral Replication

Once inside the skin, dengue virus binds to Langerhans cells (a population of dendritic cells in the skin that identifies pathogens). The virus enters the cells through binding between viral proteins and membrane proteins on the Langerhans cell, specifically the C-type lectins called DC-SIGN, mannose receptor and CLEC5A. DC-SIGN, a non-specific receptor for foreign material on dendritic cells, seems to be the main point of entry. The dendritic cell moves to the nearest lymph node. Meanwhile, the virus genome is translated in membrane-bound vesicles on the cell's endoplasmic reticulum, where the cell's protein synthesis apparatus produces new viral proteins that replicate the viral RNA and begin to form viral particles. Immature virus particles are transported to the Golgi apparatus, the part of the cell where some of the proteins receive necessary sugar chains (glycoproteins). The now mature new viruses bud on the surface of the infected cell and are released by exocytosis. They are then able to enter other white blood cells, such as monocytes and macrophages.

The initial reaction of infected cells is to produce interferon, a cytokine that raises a number of defences against viral infection through the innate immune system by augmenting the production of a large group of proteins mediated by the JAK-STAT pathway. Some serotypes of dengue virus appear to have mechanisms to slow down this process. Interferon also activates the adaptive immune system, which leads to the generation of antibodies against the virus as well as T cells that directly attack any cell infected with the virus. Various antibodies are generated; some bind closely to the viral proteins and target them for phagocytosis (ingestion by specialized cells and destruction), but some bind the virus less well and appear instead to deliver the virus into a part of the phagocytes where it is not destroyed but is able to replicate further.

Severe Disease

It is not entirely clear why secondary infection with a different strain of dengue virus places people at risk of dengue hemorrhagic fever and dengue shock syndrome. The most widely accepted hypothesis is that of antibody-dependent enhancement (ADE). The exact mechanism behind ADE is unclear. It may be caused by poor binding of non-neutralizing antibodies and delivery into the wrong compartment of white blood cells that have ingested the virus for destruction. There is a suspicion that ADE is not the only mechanism underlying severe dengue-related complications, and various lines of research have implied a role for T cells and soluble factors such as cytokines and the complement system.

Severe disease is marked by the problems of capillary permeability (an allowance of fluid and protein normally contained within blood to pass) and disordered blood clotting. These changes appear associated with a disordered state of the endothelial glycocalyx, which acts as a molecular filter of blood components. Leaky capillaries (and the critical phase) are thought to be caused by an immune system response. Other processes of interest include infected cells that become necrotic—which affect both coagulation and fibrinolysis (the opposing systems of blood clotting and clot degradation)—and low platelets in the blood, also a factor in normal clotting.

Diagnosis

The diagnosis of dengue is typically made clinically, on the basis of reported symptoms and physical examination; this applies especially in endemic areas. However, early disease can be difficult to differentiate from other viral infections. A probable diagnosis is based on the findings of fever plus two of the following: nausea and vomiting, rash, generalized pains, low white blood cell count, positive tourniquet test, or any warning sign in someone who lives in an endemic area. Warning signs typically occur before the onset of severe dengue. The tourniquet test, which is particularly useful in settings where no laboratory investigations are readily available, involves the application of a blood pressure cuff at between the diastolic and systolic pressure for five minutes, followed by the counting of any petechial hemorrhages; a higher number makes a diagnosis of dengue more likely with the cut off being more than 10 to 20 per 1 inch^2 (6.25 cm^2).

The diagnosis should be considered in anyone who develops a fever within two weeks of being in the tropics or subtropics. It can be difficult to distinguish dengue fever and chikungunya, a similar viral infection that shares many symptoms and occurs in similar parts of the world to dengue. Often, investigations are performed to exclude other conditions that cause similar symptoms, such as malaria, leptospirosis, viral hemorrhagic fever, typhoid fever, meningococcal disease, measles, and influenza.

The earliest change detectable on laboratory investigations is a low white blood cell count, which may then be followed by low platelets and metabolic acidosis. A moderately elevated level of aminotransferase (AST and ALT) from the liver is commonly associated with low platelets and white blood cells. In severe disease, plasma leakage results in hemoconcentration (as indicated by a rising hematocrit) and hypoalbuminemia. Pleural effusions or ascites can be detected by physical examination when large, but the demonstration of fluid on ultrasound may assist in the early identification of dengue shock syndrome. The use of ultrasound is limited by lack of availability in many settings. Dengue shock syndrome is present if pulse pressure drops to d" 20 mm Hg along with peripheral vascular collapse. Peripheral vascular collapse is determined in children via delayed capillary refill, rapid heart rate, or cold extremities. While warning signs are an important aspect for early detection of potential serious disease, the evidence for any specific clinical or laboratory marker is weak.

Classification

The World Health Organization's 2009 classification divides dengue fever into two groups: uncomplicated and severe. This replaces the 1997 WHO classification, which needed to be simplified as it had been found to be too restrictive, though the older classification is still widely used including by the World Health Organization's Regional Office for South-East Asia as of 2011. Severe dengue is defined as that associated with severe bleeding, severe organ dysfunction, or severe plasma leakage while all other cases are uncomplicated. The 1997 classification divided dengue into undifferentiated fever, dengue fever, and dengue hemorrhagic fever. Dengue hemorrhagic fever was subdivided further into grades I–IV. Grade I is the presence only of easy bruising or a positive tourniquet test in someone with fever, grade II is the presence of spontaneous bleeding into the skin and elsewhere, grade III is the clinical evidence of shock, and grade IV is shock so severe that blood pressure and pulse cannot be detected. Grades III and IV are referred to as "dengue shock syndrome".

Laboratory Tests

The diagnosis of dengue fever may be confirmed by microbiological laboratory testing. This can be done by virus isolation in cell cultures, nucleic acid detection by PCR, viral antigen detection (such as for NS1) or specific antibodies (serology). Virus isolation and nucleic acid detection are more accurate than antigen detection, but these tests are not widely available due to their greater cost. Detection of NS1 during the febrile phase of a primary infection may be greater than 90% sensitive however is only 60–80% in subsequent infections. All tests may be negative in the early stages of the disease. PCR and viral antigen detection are more accurate in the first seven days. In 2012 a PCR test was introduced that can run on equipment used to diagnose influenza; this is likely to improve access to PCR-based diagnosis.

These laboratory tests are only of diagnostic value during the acute phase of the illness with the exception of serology. Tests for dengue virus-specific antibodies, types IgG and IgM, can be useful in confirming a diagnosis in the later stages of the infection. Both IgG and IgM are produced after 5–7 days. The highest levels (titres) of IgM are detected following a primary infection, but IgM is also produced in reinfection. IgM becomes undetectable 30–90 days after a primary infection, but earlier following re-infections. IgG, by contrast, remains detectable for over 60 years and, in the absence of symptoms, is a useful indicator of past infection. After a primary infection IgG reaches peak levels in the blood after 14–21 days. In subsequent re-infections, levels peak earlier and the titres are usually higher. Both IgG and IgM provide protective immunity to the infecting serotype of the virus. In testing for IgG and IgM antibodies there may be cross-reactivity with other flaviviruses which may result in a false positive after recent infections or vaccinations with yellow fever virus or Japanese encephalitis. The detection of IgG alone is not considered diagnostic unless blood samples are collected 14 days apart and a greater than fourfold increase in levels of specific IgG is detected. In a person with symptoms, the detection of IgM is considered diagnostic.

Prevention

There are no approved vaccines for the dengue virus. Prevention thus depends on control of and protection from the bites of the mosquito that transmits it. The World Health Organization recommends an Integrated Vector Control programme consisting of five elements:

1. Advocacy, social mobilization and legislation to ensure that public health bodies and communities are strengthened;

2. Collaboration between the health and other sectors (public and private);
3. An integrated approach to disease control to maximize use of resources;
4. Evidence-based decision making to ensure any interventions are targeted appropriately; and
5. Capacity-building to ensure an adequate response to the local situation.

The primary method of controlling *A. aegypti* is by eliminating its habitats. This is done by getting rid of open sources of water, or if this is not possible, by adding insecticides or biological control agents to these areas. Generalized spraying with organophosphate or pyrethroid insecticides, while sometimes done, is not thought to be effective. Reducing open collections of water through environmental modification is the preferred method of control, given the concerns of negative health effects from insecticides and greater logistical difficulties with control agents. People can prevent mosquito bites by wearing clothing that fully covers the skin, using mosquito netting while resting, and/or the application of insect repellent (DEET being the most effective). However, these methods appear not to be sufficiently effective, as the frequency of outbreaks appears to be increasing in some areas, probably due to urbanization increasing the habitat of *A. aegypti*. The range of the disease appears to be expanding possibly due to climate change.

Management

There are no specific antiviral drugs for dengue, however maintaining proper fluid balance is important. Treatment depends on the symptoms. Those who are able to drink, are passing urine, have no "warning signs" and are otherwise healthy can be managed at home with daily follow up and oral rehydration therapy. Those who have other health problems, have "warning signs" or who cannot manage regular follow up should be cared for in hospital. In those with severe dengue care should be provided in an area where there is access to an intensive care unit.

Intravenous hydration, if required, is typically only needed for one or two days. The rate of fluid administration is titrated to a urinary output of 0.5–1 mL/kg/h, stable vital signs and normalization of hematocrit. The smallest amount of fluid required to achieve this is recommended. Invasive medical procedures such as nasogastric intubation, intramuscular injections and arterial punctures are avoided, in view of the bleeding risk. Paracetamol (acetaminophen) is used for fever and discomfort while NSAIDs such as ibuprofen and aspirin are avoided as they might aggravate the risk of bleeding. Blood transfusion is initiated early in people presenting with unstable vital signs in the face of a *decreasing hematocrit*, rather than waiting for the hemoglobin concentration to decrease to some predetermined "transfusion trigger" level. Packed red blood cells or whole blood are recommended, while platelets and fresh frozen plasma are usually not. There is not enough evidence to determine if corticosteroids have a positive or negative effect in dengue fever. During the recovery phase intravenous fluids are discontinued to prevent a state of fluid overload. If fluid overload occurs and vital signs are stable, stopping further fluid may be all that is needed. If a person is outside of the critical phase, a loop diuretic such as furosemide may be used to eliminate excess fluid from the circulation.

Plague

Plague is a deadly infectious disease that is caused by the enterobacteria *Yersinia pestis*, named after the French-Swiss bacteriologist Alexandre Yersin. Until June 2007, plague was one of the three epidemic diseases specifically reportable to the World Health Organization (the other two being cholera and yellow fever).

Depending on lung infection, or sanitary conditions, plague can be spread in the air, by direct contact, or by contaminated undercooked food or materials. The symptoms of plague depend on the concentrated areas of infection in each person: bubonic plague in lymph nodes, septicemic plague in blood vessels, pneumonic plague in lungs, and so on. It is treatable if detected early. Plague is still endemic in some parts of the world.

Name

The epidemiological use of the term *"plague"* is currently applied to bacterial infections that cause *buboes*, although historically the medical use of the term "plague" has been applied to pandemic infections in general. Plague is often synonymous with "bubonic plague", but this describes just one of its manifestations. Other names have been used to describe this disease, such as "The Black Plague" and "The Black Death"; the latter is now used primarily by scholars to describe the second, and most devastating, pandemic of the disease.

The etymology of the word *"plague"* is believed to come from the Latin word *plâga* ("blow, wound") and *plangere* ("to strike, or to strike down"), cf. German *Plage* ("infestation").

Chapter 7

Epidemiology and Distribution

Infection and Transmission

Transmission of *Y. pestis* to an uninfected individual is possible by any of the following means.

- droplet contact – coughing or sneezing on another person
- direct physical contact – touching an infected person, including sexual contact
- indirect contact – usually by touching soil contamination or a contaminated surface
- airborne transmission – if the microorganism can remain in the air for long periods
- fecal-oral transmission – usually from contaminated food or water sources
- vector borne transmission – carried by insects or other animals.

Yersinia pestis circulates in animal reservoirs, particularly in rodents, in the natural foci of infection found on all continents except Australia. The natural foci of plague are situated in a broad belt in the tropical and sub–tropical latitudes and the warmer parts of the temperate latitudes around the globe, between the parallels 55 degrees North and 40 degrees South. Contrary to popular belief, rats did not directly start the spread of the bubonic plague. It is mainly a disease in the fleas (*Xenopsylla cheopis*) that infested the rats, making the rats themselves the first victims of the plague. Infection in a human occurs when a person is bitten by a flea that has been infected by biting a rodent that itself has been infected by the bite of a flea carrying the disease. The bacteria multiply inside the flea, sticking together to form a plug that blocks its stomach and causes it to starve. The flea then bites a host and continues to feed, even though it cannot quell its hunger, and consequently the flea vomits blood tainted with the bacteria back into the bite wound. The bubonic plague bacterium then infects a new victim, and the flea eventually dies from starvation. Serious outbreaks of plague are usually started by other disease outbreaks in rodents, or a rise in the rodent population. In 1894, two bacteriologists, Alexandre Yersin of France and Kitasato Shibasaburô of Japan, independently isolated the bacterium in Hong Kong responsible for the Third Pandemic. Though both investigators reported their findings, a series of confusing and contradictory statements by Kitasato eventually led to the acceptance of Yersin as the primary discoverer of the organism. Yersin named it *Pasteurella pestis* in honour of the Pasteur Institute, where he worked, but in 1967 it was moved to a new genus, renamed *Yersinia pestis* in honour of Yersin. Yersin also noted that rats were affected by plague not only during plague epidemics but also often preceding such epidemics in humans, and that plague was regarded by many locals as a disease of rats: villagers in China and India asserted that, when large numbers of rats were found dead, plague outbreaks soon followed.

In 1898, the French scientist Paul-Louis Simond (who had also come to China to battle the Third Pandemic) established the rat-flea vector that drives the disease. He had noted that persons who became ill did not have to be in close contact with each other to acquire the disease. In Yunnan, China, inhabitants would flee from their homes as soon as they saw dead rats, and on the island of Formosa (Taiwan), residents considered the handling of dead rats heightened the risks of developing plague. These observations led him to suspect that the flea might be an intermediary factor in the transmission of plague, since people acquired plague only if they were in contact with recently dead rats, who had died less than 24 hours before. In a now classic experiment, Simond demonstrated how a healthy rat died of plague, after infected fleas had jumped to it, from a rat which had recently died of the plague.

Plague Immunization

Since human plague is rare in most parts of the world, routine vaccination is not needed other than for those at particularly high risk of exposure, nor for people living in areas with enzootic plague, such as the western United States. It is not even indicated for most travellers to countries with known recent reported cases, particularly if their travel is limited to urban areas with modern hotels. The CDC thus only recommends vaccination for: (1) all laboratory and field personnel who are working with *Y. pestis* organisms resistant to antimicrobials; (2) people engaged in aerosol experiments with *Y. pestis*; and (3) people engaged in field operations in areas with enzootic plague where preventing exposure is not possible (such as some disaster areas).

A systematic review by the Cochrane Collaboration found no studies of sufficient quality to make any statement on the efficacy of the vaccine.

Pathology

Bubonic Plague

When a flea bites a human and contaminates the wound with regurgitated blood, the plague carrying bacteria are passed into the tissue. *Y. pestis* can reproduce inside cells, so even if phagocytosed, they can still survive. Once in the body, the bacteria can enter the lymphatic system, which drains interstitial fluid. Plague bacteria secrete several toxins, one of which is known to cause dangerous beta-adrenergic blockade.

Y. pestis spreads through the lymphatics of the infected human until it reaches a lymph node, where it stimulates severe haemorrhagic inflammation that causes the lymph nodes to expand. The expansion of lymph nodes is the cause of the characteristic "bubo" associated with the disease.

If the lymph node is overwhelmed, the infection can pass into the bloodstream, causing *secondary septicemic plague* and if the lungs are seeded, it can cause *secondary pneumonic plague.*

Septicemic Plague

Lymphatics ultimately drain into the bloodstream, so the plague bacteria may enter the blood and travel to almost any part of the body. In septicemic plague, bacterial endotoxins cause disseminated intravascular coagulation (DIC), causing tiny clots throughout the body and possibly ischaemic necrosis (tissue death due to lack of circulation/ perfusion to that tissue) from the clots. DIC results in depletion of the body's clotting resources, so that it can no longer control bleeding. Consequently, there is bleeding into the skin and other organs, which can cause red and/or black patchy rash and hemoptysis/hematemesis (coughing up/ vomiting of blood). There are bumps on the skin that look somewhat like insect bites; these are usually red, and sometimes white in the centre. Untreated, septicemic plague is usually fatal. Early treatment with antibiotics reduces the mortality rate to between 4 and 15 percent. People who die from this form of plague often die on the same day symptoms first appear.

Pneumonic Plague

The pneumonic form of plague arises from infection of the lungs. It causes coughing and sneezing and thereby produces airborne droplets that contain bacterial cells and are likely to infect anyone inhaling them. The incubation period for pneumonic plague is short, usually two to four days, but sometimes just a few hours. The initial signs are indistinguishable from several other respiratory illnesses; they include headache, weakness, and hemoptysis or hematemesis (spitting or vomiting of blood). The course of the disease is rapid; unless diagnosed and treated soon enough, typically within a few hours, death may follow in one to six days; in untreated cases mortality is nearly 100%.

Pharyngeal Plague

This is an uncommon form of plague that resembles tonsillitis found in cases of close contact of patients with other forms of plague.

Meningeal Plague

This form of plague occurs when bacteria cross the blood-brain barrier, leading to infectious meningitis.

Other Clinical Forms

There are a few other rare manifestations of plague, including asymptomatic plague and abortive plague. *Cellulocutaneous plague* sometimes results in infection of the skin and soft tissue, often around the bite site of a flea.

Treatments

Waldemar Haffkine, a doctor who worked in Bombay, India, was the first to invent and test a plague vaccine against bubonic plague in 1897.

If diagnosed in time the various forms of plague are usually highly responsive to antibiotic therapy. The antibiotics often used are streptomycin, chloramphenicol and tetracycline. Amongst the newer generation of antibiotics, gentamicin and doxycycline have proven effective in monotherapeutic treatment of plague.

History

Antiquity: The earliest account describing a possible plague epidemic is found in I Samuel 5:6 of the Hebrew Bible (Tanakh). In this account, the Philistines of Ashdod were stricken with a plague for the crime of stealing the Ark of the Covenant from the Children of Israel. The word "tumors" is used in most English translations to describe the sores that came upon the Philistines. The account indicates that the Philistine city and its political territory were stricken with a "ravaging of mice" and a plague, bringing death to a large segment of the population.

In the second year of the Peloponnesian War (430 BC), Thucydides described an epidemic disease which was said to have begun in Ethiopia, passed through Egypt and Libya, then come to the Greek world. In the Plague of Athens, the city lost possibly one third of its population, including Pericles. Modern historians disagree on whether the plague was a critical factor in the loss of the war. Although this epidemic has long been considered an outbreak of plague, many modern scholars believe that typhus, smallpox, or measles may better fit the surviving descriptions. A recent study of DNA found in the dental pulp of plague victims suggests that typhoid was actually responsible.

In the first century AD, Rufus of Ephesus, a Greek anatomist, refers to an outbreak of plague in Libya, Egypt, and Syria. He records that Alexandrian doctors named Dioscorides and Posidonius described symptoms including acute fever, pain, agitation, and delirium. Buboes—large, hard, and non-suppurating—developed behind the knees, around the elbows, and "in the usual places." The death toll of those infected was very high. Rufus also wrote that similar buboes were reported by a Dionysius Curtus, who may have practiced medicine in Alexandria in the third century BC. If this is correct, the eastern Mediterranean world may have been familiar with bubonic plague at that early date.

In the second century, the Antonine Plague, named after Marcus Aurelius' family name of Antoninus and also known as the Plague of Galen, who had first hand knowledge of the disease, may in fact have been smallpox. Galen was in Rome when it struck in 166 AD, and was also present in the winter of 168–69 during an outbreak among troops stationed at Aquileia; he had experience with the epidemic, referring to it as very long lasting, and describes its symptoms and his treatment of it. Unfortunately, his references are scattered and brief. According to Barthold Georg Niebuhr "this pestilence must have raged with incredible fury; it carried off innumerable victims. The ancient world never recovered from the blow inflected upon it by the plague which visited it in the reign of M. Aurelius." The mortality rate of the plague was 7–10 percent; the outbreak in 165–6–168 would have caused approximately 3.5 to 5 million deaths. Otto Seek believes that over half the population of the empire perished. J. F. Gilliam believes that the Antonine plague probably caused more deaths than any other epidemic during the empire before the mid-3rd century.

Medieval and Post-medieval Pandemics

Local outbreaks of the plague are grouped into three plague pandemics, whereby the respective start and end dates and the assignment of some outbreaks to either pandemic are still subject to discussion. According to Joseph P. Byrne from Belmont University, the pandemics were:

- the first plague pandemic from 541 to ~750, spreading from Egypt to the Mediterranean (starting with the Plague of Justinian) and northwestern Europe
- the second plague pandemic from ~1345 to ~1840, spreading from Central Asia to the Mediterranean and Europe (starting with the Black Death), and probably also to China
- the third plague pandemic from 1866 to the 1960s, spreading from China to various places around the world, notably India and the West Coast of the United States.

However, the late medieval Black Death is sometimes seen not as the start of the second, but as the end of the first pandemic – in that case, the second pandemic's start would be 1361; also vary the end dates of the second pandemic given in literature, e.g. ~1890 instead of ~1840.

First Pandemic: Early Middle Ages (Plague of Justinian)

The Plague of Justinian in AD 541–542 is the first known attack on record, and marks the first firmly recorded pattern of bubonic plague. This disease is thought to have originated in China. It then spread to Africa from where the huge city of Constantinople imported massive amounts of grain, mostly from Egypt, to feed its citizens. The grain ships were the source of contagion for the city, with massive public granaries nurturing the rat and flea population. At its peak the plague was killing 10,000 people in Constantinople every day and ultimately destroyed perhaps 40% of the city's inhabitants. It went on to destroy up to a quarter of the human population of the eastern Mediterranean.

In AD 588 a second major wave of plague spread through the Mediterranean into what is now France. It is estimated that the Plague of Justinian killed as many as 100 million people across the world. It caused Europe's population to drop by around 50% between 541 and 700. It also may have contributed to the success of the Arab conquests. An outbreak of it in the AD 560s was described in AD 790 as causing "swellings in the glands ... in the manner of a nut or date" in the groin "and in other rather delicate places followed by an unbearable fever". While the swellings in this description have been identified by some as buboes, there is some contention as to whether the pandemic should be attributed to the bubonic plague, *Yersinia pestis*, known in modern times.

Second Pandemic: from 14th Century (Black Death) to 19th Century

From 1347 to 1351, the Black Death, a massive and deadly pandemic originating in China, spread along the Silk Road and swept through Asia, Europe and Africa. It may have reduced the world's population from 450 million to between 350 and 375 million. China lost around half of its population, from around 123 million to around 65 million; Europe around 1/3 of its population, from about 75 million to about 50 million; and Africa approximately 1/8 of its population, from around 80 million to 70 million (mortality rates tended to be correlated with population density so Africa, being less dense overall, had the lowest death rate). This makes the Black Death the largest death toll from any known non-viral epidemic. Although accurate statistical data does not exist, it is thought that 1.4 million died in England (1/3 of England's 4.2 million people), while an even higher percentage of Italy's population was likely wiped out. On the other hand, Northeastern Germany, Bohemia, Poland and Hungary are believed to have suffered less, and there are no estimates available for Russia or the Balkans. It is conceivable that Russia may not have been as affected due to its very cold climate and large size, hence often less close contact with the contagion.

The plague repeatedly returned to haunt Europe and the Mediterranean throughout the 14th to 17th centuries. According to Biraben, plague was present somewhere in Europe in every year between 1346 and 1671. The Second Pandemic was particularly widespread in the following years: 1360–1363; 1374; 1400; 1438–1439; 1456–1457; 1464–1466; 1481–1485; 1500–1503; 1518–1531; 1544–1548; 1563–1566; 1573–1588; 1596–1599; 1602–1611; 1623–1640; 1644–1654; and 1664–1667; subsequent outbreaks, though severe, marked the retreat from most of Europe (18th century) and northern Africa (19th century). According to Geoffrey Parker, "France alone lost almost a million people to plague in the epidemic of 1628–31."

In England, in the absence of census figures, historians propose a range of pre-incident population figures from as high as 7 million to as low as 4 million in 1300, and a postincident population figure as low as 2 million. By the end of 1350, the Black Death subsided, but it never really died out in England. Over the next few hundred years, further outbreaks occurred in 1361–62, 1369, 1379–83, 1389–93, and throughout the first half of the 15th century. An outbreak in 1471 took as much as 10–15% of the population, while the death rate of the plague of 1479–80 could have been as high as 20%. The most general outbreaks in Tudor and Stuart England seem to have begun in 1498, 1535, 1543, 1563, 1589, 1603, 1625, and 1636, and ended with the Great Plague of London in 1665.

In 1466, perhaps 40,000 people died of plague in Paris. During the 16th and 17th centuries, plague visited Paris for almost one year out of three. The Black Death ravaged Europe for three years before it continued on into Russia, where the disease hit somewhere once every five or six years from 1350 to 1490. Plague epidemics ravaged London in 1563, 1593, 1603, 1625, 1636, and 1665, reducing its population by 10 to 30% during those years. Over 10% of Amsterdam's population died in 1623–1625, and again in 1635–1636, 1655, and 1664. There were 22 outbreaks of plague in Venice between 1361 and 1528. The plague of 1576–1577 killed 50,000 in Venice, almost a third of the population. Late outbreaks in central Europe included the Italian Plague of 1629–1631, which is associated with troop movements during the Thirty Years' War, and the Great Plague of Vienna in 1679. Over 60% of Norway's population died from 1348 to 1350. The last plague outbreak ravaged Oslo in 1654.

In the first half of the 17th century, a plague claimed some 1.7 million victims in Italy, or about 14% of the population. In 1656, the plague killed about half of Naples' 300,000 inhabitants. More than 1.25 million deaths resulted from the extreme incidence of plague in 17th-century Spain. The plague of 1649 probably reduced the population of Seville by half. In 1709–1713, a plague epidemic that followed the Great Northern War (1700–1721, Sweden v. Russia and allies) killed about 100,000 in Sweden, and 300,000 in Prussia. The plague killed two-thirds of the inhabitants of Helsinki, and claimed a third of Stockholm's population. Western Europe's last major epidemic occurred in 1720 in Marseilles, in Central Europe the last major outbreaks happened during the plague during the Great Northern War, and in Eastern Europe during the Russian plague of 1770-1772

The Black Death ravaged much of the Islamic world. Plague was present in at least one location in the Islamic world virtually every year between 1500 and 1850. Plague repeatedly struck the cities of North Africa. Algiers lost 30,000–50,000 to it in 1620–21, and again in 1654–57, 1665, 1691, and 1740–42. Plague remained a major event in

Ottoman society until the second quarter of the 19th century. Between 1701 and 1750, 37 larger and smaller epidemics were recorded in Constantinople, and 31 between 1751 and 1800. Baghdad has suffered severely from visitations of the plague, and sometimes two-thirds of its population has been wiped out.

Nature of the Black Death

In the early 20th century, following the identification by Yersin and Kitasato of the plague bacterium that caused the late 19th and early 20th century Asian bubonic plague (the Third Pandemic), most scientists and historians came to believe that the Black Death was an incidence of this plague, with a strong presence of the more contagious pneumonic and septicemic varieties increasing the pace of infection, spreading the disease deep into inland areas of the continents.

Some modern researchers have argued that the disease was more likely to have been viral, pointing to the absence of rats from some parts of Europe that were badly affected and to the conviction of people at the time that the disease was spread by direct human contact. According to the accounts of the time the Black Death was extremely virulent, unlike the 19th and early 20th century bubonic plague. Samuel K. Cohn has made a comprehensive attempt to rebut the bubonic plague theory. Researchers have offered a mathematical model based on the changing demography of Europe from AD 1000 to 1800 demonstrating how plague epidemics, 1347 to 1670, could have provided the selection pressure that raised the frequency of a mutation to the level seen today that prevent HIV from entering macrophages and CD4+ T cells that carry the mutation (the average frequency of this allele is 10% in European populations). It is suggested that the original single mutation appeared over 2,500 years ago and that persistent epidemics of a haemorrhagic fever struck at the early classical civilizations.

However recent research published in the open-access scientific journal *PloS Pathogens* in October 2010 presented conclusive evidence that two previously unknown clades (variant strains) of *Y. pestis* were responsible for the Black Death. A multinational team conducted new surveys that used both ancient DNA analyses and protein-specific detection to find DNA and protein signatures specific for *Y. pestis* in human skeletons from widely distributed mass graves in northern, central and southern Europe that were associated archaeologically with the Black Death and subsequent resurgences. The authors concluded that this research, together with prior analyses from the south of France and Germany,

> *"... ends the debate about the etiology of the Black Death, and unambiguously demonstrates that* Y. pestis *was the causative agent of the epidemic plague that devastated Europe during the Middle Ages."*

The study also identified two previously unknown but related strains of *Y. pestis* that were associated with distinct medieval mass graves. These were found to be ancestral to modern isolates of the present-day *Y. pestis* strains 'Orientalis' and 'Medievalis', suggesting that these variant strains (which are now presumed to be extinct) may have entered Europe in two waves. Surveys of plague pit remains in France and England indicate that the first variant entered Europe through the port of Marseille around November 1347 and spread through France over the next two years, eventually reaching England in the spring of 1349, where it spread through the country in three successive epidemics.

Surveys of plague pit remains from the Netherlands town of Bergen op Zoom showed evidence of a second *Y. pestis* genotype which differed from that found in Britain and France and this second strain is now thought to have been responsible for the pandemic that spread through the Low Countries from 1350. This discovery implies that Bergen op Zoom (and possibly other parts of the southern Netherlands) was not directly infected from England or France c. AD 1349, and the researchers have suggested that a second wave of plague infection, distinct from that which occurred in Britain and France, may have been carried to the Low Countries from Norway, the Hanseatic cities, or another site.

Third Pandemic: 19th and 20th Centuries

The Third Pandemic began in China's Yunnan province in 1855, spreading plague to all inhabited continents and ultimately killing more than 12 million people in India and China alone. Casualty patterns indicate that waves of this pandemic may have come from two different sources. The first was primarily bubonic and was carried around the world through ocean-going trade, transporting infected persons, rats, and cargoes harbouring fleas. The second, more virulent strain was primarily pneumonic in character, with a strong person-to-person contagion. This strain was largely confined to Manchuria and Mongolia. Researchers during the "Third Pandemic" identified plague vectors and the plague bacterium, leading in time to modern treatment methods.

Plague occurred in Russia in 1877–1889 in rural areas near the Ural Mountains and the Caspian Sea. Efforts in hygiene and patient isolation reduced the spread of the disease, with approximately 420 deaths in the region. Significantly, the region of Vetlianka in this area is near a population of the bobak marmot, a small rodent considered a very dangerous plague reservoir. The last significant Russian outbreak of Plague was in Siberia in 1910 after sudden demand for marmot skins (a substitute for sable) increased the price by 400 percent. The traditional hunters would not hunt a sick Marmot and it was taboo to eat the fat from under the arm (the axillary lymphatic gland that often harboured the plague) so outbreaks tended to be confined to single individuals. The price increase, however, attracted thousands of Chinese hunters from Manchuria who not only caught the sick animals but also ate the fat, which was considered a delicacy. The plague spread from the hunting grounds to the terminus of the Chinese Eastern Railway and then followed the track for 2,700 km. The plague lasted 7 months and killed 60,000 people.

The bubonic plague continued to circulate through different ports globally for the next fifty years; however, it was primarily found in Southeast Asia. An epidemic in Hong Kong in 1894 had particularly high death rates, 90%. As late as 1897, medical authorities in the European powers organized a conference in Venice, seeking ways to keep the plague out of Europe. Mumbai plague epidemic struck the city of Bombay (Mumbai) in 1896. The disease reached the Territory of Hawaii in December 1899, and the Board of Health's decision to initiate controlled burns of select buildings in Honolulu's Chinatown turned into an uncontrolled fire which led to the inadvertent burning of most of Chinatown on January 20, 1900. Shortly thereafter, plague reached the continental US, initiating the San Francisco plague of 1900–1904. Plague persisted in Hawaii on the outer islands of Maui and Hawaii (The Big Island) until it was finally eradicated in 1959.

Although the outbreak that began in China in 1855 is conventionally known as the Third Pandemic, it is unclear whether there have been fewer, or more, than three major outbreaks of bubonic plague. Most modern outbreaks of bubonic plague amongst humans have been preceded by a striking, high mortality amongst rats, yet this phenomenon is absent from descriptions of some earlier plagues, especially the Black Death. The buboes, or swellings in the groin, that are especially characteristic of bubonic plague, are a feature of other diseases as well.

Research done by a team of biologists from the Institute of Pasteur in Paris and Johannes Gutenberg University Mainz in Germany by analysing the DNA and proteins from plague pits was published in October 2010, reported beyond doubt that all 'the three major plagues' were due to at least two previously unknown strains of *Yersinia pestis* and originated from China. A team of medical geneticists led by Mark Achtman of University College Cork in Ireland reconstructed a family tree of the bacterium and concluded in an online issue of Nature Genetics published on 31 October 2010 that all three of the great waves of plague originated from China.

Plague as a Biological Weapon

Plague has a long history as a biological weapon. Historical accounts from ancient China and medieval Europe detail the use of infected animal carcasses, such as cows or horses, and human carcasses, by the Xiongnu/Huns, Mongols, Turks, and other groups, to contaminate enemy water supplies. Han Dynasty General Huo Qubing is recorded to have died of such a contamination while engaging in warfare against the Xiongnu. Plague victims were also reported to have been tossed by catapult into cities under siege.

In 1347, the Genoese possession of Caffa, a great trade emporium on the Crimean peninsula, came under siege by an army of Mongol warriors of the Golden Horde under the command of Janibeg. After a protracted siege during which the Mongol army was reportedly withering from the disease, they decided to use the infected corpses as a biological weapon. The corpses were catapulted over the city walls, infecting the inhabitants. The Genoese traders fled, transferring the plague (Black Death) via their ships into the south of Europe, whence it rapidly spread. During World War II, the Japanese Army developed weaponised plague, based on the breeding and release of large numbers of fleas. During the Japanese occupation of Manchuria, Unit 731 deliberately infected Chinese, Korean, and Manchurian civilians and prisoners of war with the plague bacterium. These subjects, termed "maruta", or "logs", were then studied by dissection, others by vivisection while still conscious. Members of the unit such as Shiro Ishii were exonerated from the Tokyo tribunal by Douglas MacArthur but 12 of them were prosecuted in the Khabarovsk War Crime Trials in 1949 during which some admitted having spread bubonic plague within a 36-km radius around the city of Changde.

Ishii innovated bombs containing live mice and fleas, with very small explosive loads, to deliver the weaponized microbes, overcoming the problem of the explosive killing the infected animal and insect by the use of a ceramic, rather than metal, casing for the warhead. While no records survive of the actual usage of the ceramic shells, prototypes exist and are believed to have been used in experiments during WWII.

After World War II, both the United States and the Soviet Union developed means of weaponising pneumonic plague. Experiments included various delivery methods, vacuum drying, sizing the bacterium, developing strains resistant to antibiotics, combining the bacterium with other diseases (such as diphtheria), and genetic engineering. Scientists who worked in USSR bio-weapons programmes have stated that the Soviet effort was formidable and that large stocks of weaponised plague bacteria were produced. Information on many of the Soviet projects is largely unavailable. Aerosolized pneumonic plague remains the most significant threat. The plague can be easily treated with antibiotics, thus a widespread epidemic is highly unlikely in developed countries.

1994 Epidemic in Surat, India

In 1994, there was a pneumonic plague epidemic in Surat, India that resulted in 52 deaths and in a large internal migration of about 300,000 residents, who fled fearing quarantine.

A combination of heavy monsoon rain and clogged sewers led to massive flooding which resulted in unhygienic conditions and a number of uncleared animal carcasses. It is believed that this situation precipitated the epidemic. There was widespread fear that the sudden rush of people from this area might spread the epidemic to other parts of India and the world, but that scenario was averted, probably as a result of effective public health response mounted by the Indian health authorities. Some countries, especially those in the nearby Gulf region, took the step of cancelling some flights and putting a pause on shipments from India.

Much like the Black Death that spread through medieval Europe, some questions still remain unanswered about the 1994 epidemic in Surat. Initial questions about whether it was an epidemic of plague arose because the Indian health authorities were unable to culture *Yersinia pestis*, but this could have been due to poor laboratory procedures. Yet, there are several lines of evidence strongly suggesting that it was a plague epidemic: blood tests for Yersinia were positive, a number of individuals showed antibodies against Yersinia and the clinical symptoms displayed by the affected were all consistent with the disease being plague.

Housefly

The housefly (also house fly, house-fly or common housefly), *Musca domestica*, is a fly of the suborder Cyclorrhapha. It is the most common of all domestic flies, accounting for about 91% of all flies in human habitations, and indeed one of the most widely distributed insects, found all over the world. It is considered a pest that can carry serious diseases.

Physical Description

The adults are about 5–8 mm long. Their thorax is gray or sometimes even black, with four longitudinal dark lines on the back. The whole body is covered with hair-like projections. The females are slightly larger than the males, and have a much larger space between their red compound eyes. The mass of pupae can range from about 8 to 20 mg under different conditions.

Like other Diptera (meaning "two-winged"), houseflies have only one pair of wings; the hind pair is reduced to small halteres that aid in flight stability. Characteristically, the media vein (M1+2 or fourth long vein of the wing) shows a sharp upward bend.

Species that appear similar to the housefly include:

- The lesser house fly, *Fannia canicularis*, is somewhat smaller, more slender, and the media vein is straight.
- The stable fly, *Stomoxys calcitrans*, has piercing mouthparts and the media vein is only slightly curved.

Life Cycle

Each female fly can lay approximately 9,000 eggs in a lifetime, in several batches of about 75 to 150. The eggs are white and are about 1.2 mm in length. Within a day, larvae (maggots) hatch from the eggs; they live and feed on (usually dead and decaying) organic material, such as garbage, carrion or feces. They are pale-whitish, 3–9 mm long, thinner at the mouth end, and have no legs. Their life cycle ranges from 14 hours to 36 hours.

Figure: *The male mounts the female from behind*

At the end of their third instar, the maggots crawl to a dry, cool place and transform into pupae, coloured reddish or brown and about 8 mm long. The adult flies then emerge from the pupae. (This whole cycle is known as complete metamorphosis.) The adults live from two weeks to a month in the wild, or longer in benign laboratory conditions. Having emerged from the pupae, the flies cease to grow; small flies are not necessarily young flies, but are instead the result of getting insufficient food during the larval stage.

Some 36 hours after having emerged from the pupa, the female is receptive for mating. The male mounts her from behind to inject sperm. Copulation takes a few seconds to a couple of minutes. Normally, the female mates only once, storing the sperm to use it repeatedly for laying several sets of eggs.

Figure: *Two houseflies mating.*

Figure: *Housefly pupae are killed by parasitic wasp larvae. Each pupa has one hole through which a single adult wasp emerged; feeding occurs during the wasp's larval stage.*

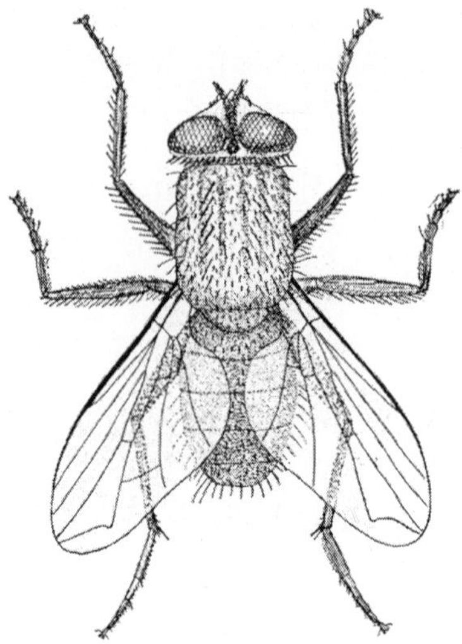

Figure: *Illustration of a housefly*

The flies depend on warm temperatures; generally, the warmer the temperature, the faster the flies will develop.

Aging

Because the somatic tissue of the housefly consists of long-lived post-mitotic cells, it can be used as an informative model system for understanding cumulative age-related cellular alterations. Agarwal and Sohal studied the level of the oxidative DNA damage 8-hydroxydeoxyguanosine (8-OHdG) in houseflies. They found that the level of 8-OHdG increased with age of the flies. They also found an inverse association of 8-OHdG level with life expectancy of the flies. They concluded that their results support the hypothesis that oxidative molecular damage is a causal factor in senescence (aging). These findings are in accord with the general view that oxidative DNA damage, particularly in post-mitotic tissues, is a principal cause of aging.

Sex Determination

The housefly is an object of biological research, mainly because of one remarkable quality: the sex determination mechanism. Although a wide variety of sex determination mechanisms exist in nature (e.g. male and female heterogamy, haplodiploidy, environmental factors), the way sex is determined is usually fixed within one species. However, the housefly exhibits many different mechanisms for sex determination, such as male heterogamy (like most insects and mammals), female heterogamy (like birds) and maternal control over offspring sex. This makes the housefly one of the most suitable species to study the evolution of sex determination.

Evolution

Even though the order of flies (Diptera) is much older, true houseflies are believed to have evolved in the beginning of the Cenozoic era, some 65 million years ago. They are thought to have originated in the southern Palearctic region, particularly the Middle East. Because of their close, commensal relationship with humans, they probably owe their worldwide dispersal to co-migration with humans.

Relationship with Humans

In colder climates, houseflies survive only with humans. They have a tendency to aggregate and are difficult to dispose of. They are capable of carrying over 100 pathogens, such as those causing typhoid, cholera, salmonellosis, bacillary dysentery, tuberculosis, anthrax, ophthalmia, and parasitic worms. Some strains have become immune to most common insecticides.

House flies feed on liquid or semiliquid substances beside solid material which has been softened by saliva or vomit. Because of their large intake of food, they deposit feces constantly, one of the factors that makes the insect a dangerous carrier of pathogens. Although they are domestic flies, usually confined to human habitations, they can fly for several miles from the breeding place. They are active only in daytime, and rest at night, e.g., at the corners of rooms, ceiling hangings, cellars, and barns, where they can survive the coldest winters by hibernation, and when spring arrives, adult flies are seen only a few days after the first thaw.

As a Transmitter of Disease

Mechanical transmission of organisms on its hairs, mouthparts, vomitus and feces:

- parasitic diseases: cysts of protozoa e.g. *Entamoeba histolytica, Giardia lamblia* and eggs of helminths, e.g., *Ascaris lumbricoides, Trichuris trichiura, Hymenolepis nana, Enterobius vermicularis.*
- bacterial diseases: typhoid, cholera, dysentery, pyogenic cocci, etc. House flies have been demonstrated to be vectors of *Campylobacter* and *E. coli* O157:H7 using PCR. House flies can be monitored for bacterial pathogens using filter paper spot cards and PCR
- Viruses: enteroviruses: poliomyelitis, viral hepatitis (A & E)..etc.

Potential in Waste Management

The ability of housefly larvae to feed and develop in a wide range of decaying organic matter is important for recycling of nutrients in nature. Research suggests that this adaptation may be exploited to combat ever-increasing amounts of waste. Housefly larvae can be mass-reared in a controlled manner in animal manure, thus reducing the bulk of waste and minimizing environmental risks of its disposal. Harvested maggots may be used as feed for animal nutrition.

Cholera

Cholera is an infection of the small intestine caused by the bacterium *Vibrio cholerae*. The main symptoms are watery diarrhea and vomiting. This may result in dehydration and in severe cases grayish-bluish skin. Transmission occurs primarily by drinking water or eating food that has been contaminated by the feces (waste product) of an infected person, including one with no apparent symptoms.

The severity of the diarrhea and vomiting can lead to rapid dehydration and electrolyte imbalance, and death in some cases. The primary treatment is oral rehydration therapy, typically with oral rehydration solution, to replace water and electrolytes. If this is not tolerated or does not provide improvement fast enough, intravenous fluids can also be used. Antibacterial drugs are beneficial in those with severe disease to shorten its duration and severity.

Worldwide, it affects 3–5 million people and causes 100,000–130,000 deaths a year as of 2010. Cholera was one of the earliest infections to be studied by epidemiological methods.

Signs and Symptoms

The primary symptoms of cholera are profuse diarrhea and vomiting of clear fluid. These symptoms usually start suddenly, half a day to five days after ingestion of the bacteria. The diarrhea is frequently described as "rice water" in nature and may have a fishy odour. An untreated person with cholera may produce 10 to 20 litres (3 to 5 US gal) of diarrhea a day. Severe cholera kills about half of affected individuals. Estimates of the ratio of asymptomatic to symptomatic infections have ranged from 3 to 100. Cholera has been nicknamed the "blue death" because a person's skin may turn bluish-gray from extreme loss of fluids.If the severe diarrhea is not treated, it can result in life-threatening dehydration and electrolyte imbalances.

Fever is rare and should raise suspicion for secondary infection. Patients can be lethargic, and might have sunken eyes, dry mouth, cold clammy skin, decreased skin turgor, or wrinkled hands and feet. Kussmaul breathing, a deep and laboured breathing pattern, can occur because of acidosis from stool bicarbonate losses and lactic acidosis associated with poor perfusion. Blood pressure drops due to dehydration, peripheral pulse is rapid and thready, and urine output decreases with time. Muscle cramping and weakness, altered consciousness, seizures, or even coma due to electrolyte losses and ion shifts are common, especially in children.

Cause

Transmission is mostly from the fecal contamination of food and water caused by poor sanitation.

Susceptibility

About 100 million bacteria must typically be ingested to cause cholera in a normal healthy adult. This dose, however, is less in those with lowered gastric acidity (for instance those using proton pump inhibitors). Children are also more susceptible, with two- to four-year-olds having the highest rates of infection. Individuals' susceptibility to cholera is also affected by their blood type, with those with type O blood being the most susceptible. Persons with lowered immunity, such as persons with AIDS or children who are malnourished, are more likely to experience a severe case if they become infected. Any individual, even a healthy adult in middle age, can experience a severe case, and each person's case should be measured by the loss of fluids, preferably in consultation with a professional health care provider.

The cystic fibrosis genetic mutation in humans has been said to maintain a selective advantage: heterozygous carriers of the mutation (who are thus not affected by cystic fibrosis) are more resistant to *V. cholerae* infections. In this model, the genetic deficiency in the cystic fibrosis transmembrane conductance regulator channel proteins interferes with bacteria binding to the gastrointestinal epithelium, thus reducing the effects of an infection.

Transmission

Cholera is typically transmitted by either contaminated food or water. In the developed world, seafood is the usual cause, while in the developing world it is more often water. Most cholera cases in developed countries are a result of transmission by food. This occurs when people harvest oysters in waters infected with sewage, as *Vibrio cholerae* accumulates in zooplankton and the oysters eat the zooplankton. Cholera has been found in two animal populations: shellfish and plankton.

People infected with cholera often have diarrhea, and if this highly liquid stool, colloquially referred to as "rice-water", contaminates water used by others, disease transmission may occur. The source of the contamination is typically other cholera sufferers when their untreated diarrheal discharge is allowed to get into waterways, groundwater or drinking water supplies. Drinking any infected water and eating any foods washed in the water, as well as shellfish living in the affected waterway, can cause a person to contract an infection. Cholera is rarely spread directly from person to person. Both toxic and nontoxic strains exist. Nontoxic strains can acquire toxicity through a temperate bacteriophage. Coastal cholera outbreaks typically follow zooplankton blooms, thus making cholera a zoonotic disease.

Mechanism

When consumed, most bacteria do not survive the acidic conditions of the human stomach. The few surviving bacteria conserve their energy and stored nutrients during the passage through the stomach by shutting down much protein production. When the surviving bacteria exit the stomach and reach the small intestine, they need to propel themselves through the thick mucus that lines the small intestine to get to the intestinal walls where they can thrive. *V. cholerae* bacteria start up production of the hollow cylindrical protein flagellin to make flagella, the cork-screw helical fibres they rotate to propel themselves through the mucus of the small intestine.

Once the cholera bacteria reach the intestinal wall they no longer need the flagella to move. The bacteria stop producing the protein flagellin to conserve energy and nutrients by changing the mix of proteins which they express in response to the changed chemical surroundings. On reaching the intestinal wall, *V. cholerae* start producing the toxic proteins that give the infected person a watery diarrhea. This carries the multiplying new generations of *V. cholerae* bacteria out into the drinking water of the next host if proper sanitation measures are not in place.

The cholera toxin (CTX or CT) is an oligomeric complex made up of six protein subunits: a single copy of the A subunit (part A), and five copies of the B subunit (part B), connected by a disulfide bond. The five B subunits form a five-membered ring that binds to GM1 gangliosides on the surface of the intestinal epithelium cells. The A1 portion of the A subunit is an enzyme that ADP-ribosylates G proteins, while the A2 chain fits into the central pore of the B subunit ring. Upon binding, the complex is taken into the cell via receptor-mediated endocytosis. Once inside the cell, the disulfide bond is reduced, and the A1 subunit is freed to bind with a human partner protein called ADP-ribosylation factor 6 (Arf6). Binding exposes its active site, allowing it to permanently ribosylate the Gs alpha subunit of the heterotrimeric G protein.

This results in constitutive cAMP production, which in turn leads to secretion of H_2O, Na^+, K^+, Cl^-, and HCO_3^- into the lumen of the small intestine and rapid dehydration. The gene encoding the cholera toxin was introduced into *V. cholerae* by horizontal gene transfer. Virulent strains of *V. cholerae* carry a variant of temperate bacteriophage called CTXf or CTXö.

Microbiologists have studied the genetic mechanisms by which the *V. cholerae* bacteria turn off the production of some proteins and turn on the production of other proteins as they respond to the series of chemical environments they encounter, passing through the stomach, through the mucous layer of the small intestine, and on to the intestinal wall. Of particular interest have been the genetic mechanisms by which cholera bacteria turn on the protein production of the toxins that interact with host cell mechanisms to pump chloride ions into the small intestine, creating an ionic pressure which prevents sodium ions from entering the cell.

The chloride and sodium ions create a salt-water environment in the small intestines, which through osmosis can pull up to six litres of water per day through the intestinal cells, creating the massive amounts of diarrhea. The host can become rapidly dehydrated if an appropriate mixture of dilute salt water and sugar is not taken to replace the blood's water and salts lost in the diarrhea.

By inserting separate, successive sections of *V. cholerae* DNA into the DNA of other bacteria, such as *E. coli* that would not naturally produce the protein toxins, researchers have investigated the mechanisms by which *V. cholerae* responds to the changing chemical environments of the stomach, mucous layers, and intestinal wall. Researchers have discovered a complex cascade of regulatory proteins controls expression of *V. cholerae* virulence determinants. In responding to the chemical environment at the intestinal wall, the *V. cholerae* bacteria produce the TcpP/TcpH proteins, which, together with the ToxR/ToxS proteins, activate the expression of the ToxT regulatory protein. ToxT then directly activates expression of virulence genes that produce the toxins, causing diarrhea in the infected person and allowing the bacteria to colonize the intestine. Current research aims at discovering "the signal that makes the cholera bacteria stop swimming and start to colonize (that is, adhere to the cells of) the small intestine."

Genetic Structure

Amplified fragment length polymorphism fingerprinting of the pandemic isolates of *V. cholerae* has revealed variation in the genetic structure. Two clusters have been identified: Cluster I and Cluster II. For the most part, Cluster I consists of strains from the 1960s and 1970s, while Cluster II largely contains strains from the 1980s and 1990s, based on the change in the clone structure. This grouping of strains is best seen in the strains from the African continent.

Diagnosis

A rapid dipstick test is available to determine the presence of *V. cholerae*. In those samples that test positive, further testing should be done to determine antibiotic resistance. In epidemic situations, a clinical diagnosis may be made by taking a patient history and doing a brief examination. Treatment is usually started without or before confirmation by laboratory analysis.

Stool and swab samples collected in the acute stage of the disease, before antibiotics have been administered, are the most useful specimens for laboratory diagnosis. If an epidemic of cholera is suspected, the most common causative agent is *V. cholerae* O1. If *V. cholerae* serogroup O1 is not isolated, the laboratory should test for *V. cholerae* O139. However, if neither of these organisms is isolated, it is necessary to send stool specimens to a reference laboratory.

Infection with *V. cholerae* O139 should be reported and handled in the same manner as that caused by *V. cholerae* O1. The associated diarrheal illness should be referred to as cholera and must be reported in the United States.

Prevention

The World Health Organization recommends focusing on prevention, preparedness, and response to combat the spread of cholera. They also stress the importance of an effective surveillance system. Governments can play a role in all of these areas, and in preventing cholera or indirectly facilitating its spread.

Although cholera may be life-threatening, prevention of the disease is normally straightforward if proper sanitation practices are followed. In developed countries, due to nearly universal advanced water treatment and sanitation practices, cholera is no longer a major health threat. The last major outbreak of cholera in the United States occurred in 1910–1911. Effective sanitation practices, if instituted and adhered to in time, are usually sufficient to stop an epidemic. There are several points along the cholera transmission path at which its spread may be halted:

- Sterilization: Proper disposal and treatment of infected fecal waste water produced by cholera victims and all contaminated materials (e.g. clothing, bedding, etc.) are essential. All materials that come in contact with cholera patients should be sanitized by washing in hot water, using chlorine bleach if possible. Hands that touch cholera patients or their clothing, bedding, etc., should be thoroughly cleaned and disinfected with chlorinated water or other effective antimicrobial agents.
- Sewage: antibacterial treatment of general sewage by chlorine, ozone, ultraviolet light or other effective treatment before it enters the waterways or underground water supplies helps prevent undiagnosed patients from inadvertently spreading the disease.
- Sources: Warnings about possible cholera contamination should be posted around contaminated water sources with directions on how to decontaminate the water (boiling, chlorination etc.) for possible use.
- Water purification: All water used for drinking, washing, or cooking should be sterilized by either boiling, chlorination, ozone water treatment, ultraviolet light sterilization (e.g. by solar water disinfection), or antimicrobial filtration in any area where cholera may be present. Chlorination and boiling are often the least expensive and most effective means of halting transmission. Cloth filters or sari filtration, though very basic, have significantly reduced the occurrence of cholera when used in poor villages in Bangladesh that rely on untreated surface water. Better antimicrobial filters, like those present in advanced individual water treatment hiking kits, are most effective. Public health education and adherence to appropriate sanitation practices are of primary importance to help prevent and control transmission of cholera and other diseases.

Surveillance

Surveillance and prompt reporting allow for containing cholera epidemics rapidly. Cholera exists as a seasonal disease in many endemic countries, occurring annually mostly during rainy seasons. Surveillance systems can provide early alerts to outbreaks, therefore leading to coordinated response and assist in preparation of preparedness plans. Efficient surveillance systems can also improve the risk assessment for potential cholera outbreaks. Understanding the seasonality and location of outbreaks provides guidance for improving cholera control activities for the most vulnerable. For prevention to be effective, it is important that cases be reported to national health authorities.

Vaccine

A number of safe and effective oral vaccines for cholera are available. Dukoral, an orally administered, inactivated whole cell vaccine, has an overall efficacy of about 52% during the first year after being given and 62% in the second year, with minimal side effects. It is available in over 60 countries. However, it is not currently recommended by the Centres for Disease Control and Prevention (CDC) for most people travelling from the United States to endemic countries. One injectable vaccine was found to be effective for two to three years. The protective efficacy was 28% lower in children less than 5 years old. However, as of 2010, it has limited availability. Work is under way to investigate the role of mass vaccination. The World Health Organization (WHO) recommends immunization of high-risk groups, such as children and people with HIV, in countries where this disease is endemic. If people are immunized broadly, herd immunity results, with a decrease in the amount of contamination in the environment.

Sari Filtration

An effective and relatively cheap method to prevent the transmission of cholera is the use of a folded *sari* (a long cloth garment) to filter drinking water. In Bangladesh this practice was found to decrease rates of cholera by nearly half. It involves folding a *sari* four to eight times. Between uses the cloth should be rinsed in clean water and dried in the sun to kill any bacteria on it. A nylon cloth appears to work as well.

Treatment

Continued eating speeds the recovery of normal intestinal function. The World Health Organization recommends this generally for cases of diarrhea no matter what the underlying cause. A CDC training manual specifically for cholera states: "Continue to breastfeed your baby if the baby has watery diarrhea, even when travelling to get treatment. Adults and older children should continue to eat frequently."

Fluids

The most common error in caring for patients with cholera is to underestimate the speed and volume of fluids required. In most cases, cholera can be successfully treated with oral rehydration therapy (ORT), which is highly effective, safe, and simple to administer. Rice-based solutions are preferred to glucose-based ones due to greater efficiency.

In severe cases with significant dehydration, intravenous rehydration may be necessary. Ringer's lactate is the preferred solution, often with added potassium. Large volumes and continued replacement until diarrhea has subsided may be needed. Ten percent of a person's body weight in fluid may need to be given in the first two to four hours. This method was first tried on a mass scale during the Bangladesh Liberation War, and was found to have much success.

If commercially produced oral rehydration solutions are too expensive or difficult to obtain, solutions can be made. One such recipe calls for 1 liter of boiled water, 1/2 teaspoon of salt, 6 teaspoons of sugar, and added mashed banana for potassium and to improve taste.

Electrolytes

As there frequently is initially acidosis, the potassium level may be normal, even though large losses have occurred. As the dehydration is corrected, potassium levels may decrease rapidly, and thus need to be replaced. This may be done by eating foods high in potassium like bananas or green coconut water.

Antibiotics

Antibiotic treatments for one to three days shorten the course of the disease and reduce the severity of the symptoms. Use of antibiotics also reduces fluid requirements. People will recover without them, however, if sufficient hydration is maintained. The World Health Organization only recommends antibiotics in those with severe dehydration.

Doxycycline is typically used first line, although some strains of *V. cholerae* have shown resistance. Testing for resistance during an outbreak can help determine appropriate future choices. Other antibiotics proven to be effective include cotrimoxazole, erythromycin, tetracycline, chloramphenicol, and furazolidone. Fluoroquinolones, such as ciprofloxacin, also may be used, but resistance has been reported.

In many areas of the world, antibiotic resistance is increasing. In Bangladesh, for example, most cases are resistant to tetracycline, trimethoprim-sulfamethoxazole, and erythromycin. Rapid diagnostic assay methods are available for the identification of multiple drug-resistant cases. New generation antimicrobials have been discovered which are effective against in *in vitro* studies.

Zinc Supplementation

In Bangladesh zinc supplementation reduced the duration and severity of diarrhea in children with cholera when given with antibiotics and rehydration therapy as needed. It reduced the length of disease by eight hours and the amount of diarrheal stool by 10%. Supplementation appears to be also effective in both treating and preventing infectious diarrhea due to other causes among children in the developing world.

Prognosis

If people with cholera are treated quickly and properly, the mortality rate is less than 1%; however, with untreated cholera, the mortality rate rises to 50–60%. For certain genetic strains of cholera, such as the one present during the 2010 epidemic in Haiti and the 2004 outbreak in India, death can occur within two hours of becoming ill.

Dysentery

Dysentery is diarrhea which contains blood. Other symptoms may include fever, abdominal pain, and rectal tenesmus (a feeling of incomplete defecation).

It is caused by any kind of infection. It is a type of gastroenteritis. The mechanism is an inflammatory disorder of the intestine, especially of the colon.

Signs and Symptoms

In developed countries, the most common form of dysentery is bacillary dysentery which is typically a mild illness, causing symptoms normally consisting of mild stomach pains and frequent passage of stool or diarrhea. Symptoms normally present themselves after one to three days and are usually no longer present after a week.

The frequency of urges to defecate, the large volume of liquid feces passed, and the presence of mucus, pus and blood depends on the pathogen that is causing the disease. Temporary lactose intolerance can occur. In some caustic occasions severe abdominal pain, fever, shock, and delirium can all be symptoms.

In extreme cases, dysentery patients may pass over one litre of fluid per hour. More often, individuals will complain of nausea, abdominal pain, and frequent watery and usually foul-smelling diarrhea, accompanied by mucus and blood, rectal pain, and fever. Vomiting, rapid weight-loss, and generalized muscle aches sometimes also accompany dysentery.

On rare occasions, the amoebic parasite will invade the body through the bloodstream and spread beyond the intestines. In such cases, it may more seriously infect other organs such as the brain, lungs, and the liver.

Mechanism

Dysentery results from viral infections, bacterial infections, or parasitic infestations. These pathogens typically reach the large intestine after entering orally, through ingestion of contaminated food or water, oral contact with contaminated objects or hands, and so on.

Each specific pathogen has its own mechanism or pathogenesis, but in general the result is damage to the intestinal lining, leading to the inflammatory immune response. This can cause elevated temperature, painful spasms of the intestinal muscles (cramping), swelling due to water leaking from capillaries of the intestine (edema), and further tissue damage by the body's immune cells and the chemicals, called cytokines, they release to fight the infection. The result can be impaired nutrient absorption, excessive water and mineral loss through the stools due to breakdown of the control mechanisms in the intestinal tissue that normally remove water from the stools, and in severe cases the entry of pathogenic organisms into the bloodstream.

Some microorganisms – for example, bacteria of the genus *Shigella* – secrete substances known as cytotoxins, which kill and damage intestinal tissue on contact. Viruses directly attack the intestinal cells, taking over their metabolic machinery to make copies of themselves, which leads to cell death.

Definitions of *dysentery* can vary by region and by medical speciality. The U. S. Centres for Disease Control and Prevention (CDC) limits its definition to "diarrhea with visible blood." Others define the term more broadly. These differences in definition must be taken into account when defining mechanisms. For example, using the CDC definition requires that intestinal tissue be so severely damaged that blood vessels have ruptured, allowing visible quantities of blood to be lost with defecation. Other definitions require less specific damage.

Amoebic Dysentery

Dysentery may be caused by amoebiasis, an infection by the amoeba *Entamoeba histolytica*, and is then known as amoebic dysentery. Proper treatment of the underlying infection of amoebic dysentery is important; insufficiently treated amoebiasis can lie dormant for years and then lead to severe, potentially fatal, complications. *Entamoeba histolytica* is mainly found in tropical areas. When the amoebas inside the bowel of an infected person are ready to leave the body, they group together and form a shell that surrounds and protects them. This group of amoebas is known as a cyst. The cyst passes out of the person's body in the feces and can survive outside the body. If hygiene standards are poor; for example, if the person does not dispose of the feces hygienically, it can contaminate the surroundings, such as nearby food and water. If another person then eats or drinks food or water that has been contaminated with feces containing the cyst, that person will also become infected with the amoeba. Amoebic dysentery is particularly common in parts of the world where human feces are used as fertilizer. After entering the person's body through the mouth, the cyst will travel down into the stomach. The amoebas inside the cyst are protected from the stomach's digestive acid. From the stomach, the cyst will travel to the intestines where it will break open and release the amoebas, causing the infection. The amoebas can burrow into the walls of the intestines and cause small abscesses and ulcers to form. The cycle then begins again.

Bacillary Dysentery

Dysentery may also be caused by shigellosis, an infection by bacteria of the genus *Shigella*, and is then known as bacillary dysentery (or Marlow Syndrome).

Enteroinvasive Escherichia coli may also cause a dysentery syndrome.

Diagnosis

A clinical diagnosis may be made by taking a history and doing a brief examination. Treatment is usually started without or before confirmation by laboratory analysis.

Physical Exam

The mouth, skin, and lips may appear dry due to dehydration. Lower abdominal tenderness may also be present.

Stool and Blood Tests

Cultures of stool samples are examined in order to identify the organism causing dysentery. Usually, several samples must be obtained due to the changing number of amoeba, which changes daily.

Blood tests can be used to measure abnormalities in the levels of essential minerals and salts.

Prevention

To reduce the risk of contracting dysentery the following are suggested:

- Washing one's hands after using the toilet, after contact with an infected person, and regularly throughout the day;
- Washing one's hands before handling, cooking and eating food, handling babies, and feeding young or elderly people;

- Keeping contact with someone known to have dysentery to a minimum;
- Washing laundry on the hottest setting possible;
- Avoiding sharing items such as towels and face cloths.

Treatment

Dysentery is managed by maintaining fluids by using oral rehydration therapy. If this treatment cannot be adequately maintained due to vomiting or the profuseness of diarrhea, hospital admission may be required for intravenous fluid replacement. In ideal situations, no antimicrobial therapy should be administered until microbiological microscopy and culture studies have established the specific infection involved.

When laboratory services are not available, it may be necessary to administer a combination of drugs, including an amoebicidal drug to kill the parasite, and an antibiotic to treat any associated bacterial infection.

If shigella is suspected and it is not too severe, letting it run its course may be reasonable — usually less than a week. If the shigella is severe, antibiotics, such as ciprofloxacin or TMP-SMX may be useful. However, many strains of shigella are becoming resistant to common antibiotics, and effective medications are often in short supply in developing countries. If necessary, a doctor may have to reserve antibiotics for those at highest risk for death, including young children, people over 50, and anyone suffering from dehydration or malnutrition.

Amoebic dysentery is often treated with two antimicrobial drug such as metronidazole and paromomycin or iodoquinol.

Prognosis

With correct treatment, most cases of amoebic and bacterial dysentery subside within ten days, and most individuals will achieve a full recovery within two to four weeks after beginning proper treatment. If the disease is left untreated, the prognosis varies with the immune status of the individual patient and the severity of disease. Extreme dehydration can prolong recovery and significantly raises the risk for serious complications.

Epidemiology

The WHO estimates that there are 80 million cases and 700,000 deaths from *Shigellosis* annually. *Amebiasis* infects over 50 million people each year, of whom 50,000 die.

Typhoid Fever

Typhoid fever — also known simply as typhoid — is a common worldwide bacterial disease transmitted by the ingestion of food or water contaminated with the feces of an infected person, which contain the bacterium *Salmonella enterica subsp. enterica*, serovar Typhi.

The disease has received various names, such as gastric fever, enteric fever, abdominal typhus, infantile remittant fever, slow fever, nervous fever and pythogenic fever. The name *typhoid* means "resembling typhus" and comes from the neuropsychiatric symptoms common to typhoid and typhus. Despite this similarity of their names, typhoid fever and typhus are distinct diseases and are caused by different species of bacteria.

The occurrence of this disease fell sharply in the developed world with the rise of 20th-century sanitation techniques and antibiotics.

Signs and Symptoms

Classically, the course of untreated typhoid fever is divided into four individual stages, each lasting approximately one week. Over the course of these stages, the patient becomes exhausted and emaciated.

- In the first week, the temperature rises slowly, and fever fluctuations are seen with relative bradycardia (Faget sign), malaise, headache, and cough. A bloody nose (epistaxis) is seen in a quarter of cases, and abdominal pain is also possible. There is a decrease in the number of circulating white blood cells (leukopenia) with eosinopenia and relative lymphocytosis; blood cultures are positive for *Salmonella typhi* or *paratyphi*. The Widal test is negative in the first week.
- In the second week of the infection, the patient lies prostrate with high fever in plateau around 40 °C (104 °F) and bradycardia (sphygmothermic dissociation or Faget sign), classically with a dicrotic pulse wave. Delirium is frequent, often calm, but sometimes agitated. This delirium gives to typhoid the nickname of "nervous fever". Rose spots appear on the lower chest and abdomen in around a third of patients. There are rhonchi in lung bases.

The abdomen is distended and painful in the right lower quadrant, where borborygmi can be heard. Diarrhea can occur in this stage: six to eight stools in a day, green, comparable to pea soup, with a characteristic smell. However, constipation is also frequent. The spleen and liver are enlarged (hepatosplenomegaly) and tender, and there is elevation of liver transaminases. The Widal test is strongly positive, with antiO and antiH antibodies. Blood cultures are sometimes still positive at this stage.

(The major symptom of this fever is that the fever usually rises in the afternoon up to the first and second week.)

- In the third week of typhoid fever, a number of complications can occur:
  - o Intestinal haemorrhage due to bleeding in congested Peyer's patches; this can be very serious but is usually not fatal.
  - o Intestinal perforation in the distal ileum: this is a very serious complication and is frequently fatal. It may occur without alarming symptoms until septicaemia or diffuse peritonitis sets in.
  - o Encephalitis
  - o Neuropsychiatric symptoms (described as "muttering delirium" or "coma vigil"), with picking at bedclothes or imaginary objects.
  - o Metastatic abscesses, cholecystitis, endocarditis and osteitis
  - o The fever is still very high and oscillates very little over 24 hours. Dehydration ensues, and the patient is delirious (typhoid state). One third of affected individuals develop a macular rash on the trunk.
  - o Platelet count goes down slowly and risk of bleeding rises.
- By the end of third week, the fever starts subsiding (defervescence). This carries on into the fourth and final week.

Transmission

The bacterium that causes typhoid fever may be spread through poor hygiene habits and public sanitation conditions, and sometimes also by flying insects feeding on feces. Public education campaigns encouraging people to wash their hands after defecating and before handling food are an important component in controlling spread of the disease. According to statistics from the United States Centres for Disease Control and Prevention (CDC), the chlorination of drinking water has led to dramatic decreases in the transmission of typhoid fever in the U.S.A.

Diagnosis

Diagnosis is made by any blood, bone marrow or stool cultures and with the Widal test (demonstration of salmonella antibodies against antigens O-somatic and H-flagellar). In epidemics and less wealthy countries, after excluding malaria, dysentery or pneumonia, a therapeutic trial time with chloramphenicol is generally undertaken while awaiting the results of the Widal test and cultures of the blood and stool.

The Widal test is time-consuming, and often, when a diagnosis is reached, it is too late to start an antibiotic regimen. The term *enteric fever* is a collective term that refers to severe typhoid and paratyphoid.

Prevention

Sanitation and hygiene are the critical measures that can be taken to prevent typhoid. Typhoid does not affect animals, and therefore, transmission is only from human to human. Typhoid can only spread in environments where human feces or urine are able to come into contact with food or drinking water. Careful food preparation and washing of hands are crucial to prevent typhoid.

There are two vaccines licensed for use for the prevention of typhoid: the live, oral Ty21a vaccine (sold as *Vivotif* by Crucell Switzerland AG) and the injectable Typhoid polysaccharide vaccine (sold as *Typhim Vi* by Sanofi Pasteur and *Typherix* by GlaxoSmithKline).

Both are 50% to 80% protective and are recommended for travellers to areas where typhoid is endemic. Boosters are recommended every five years for the oral vaccine and every two years for the injectable form. There exists an older, killed-whole-cell vaccine that is still used in countries where the newer preparations are not available, but this vaccine is no longer recommended for use because it has a higher rate of side effects (mainly pain and inflammation at the site of the injection).

Treatment

The rediscovery of oral rehydration therapy in the 1960s provided a simple way to prevent many of the deaths of diarrheal diseases in general. Where resistance is uncommon, the treatment of choice is a fluoroquinolone such as ciprofloxacin. Otherwise, a third-generation cephalosporin such as ceftriaxone or cefotaxime is the first choice. Cefixime is a suitable oral alternative.

Typhoid fever, when properly treated, is not fatal in most cases. Antibiotics, such as ampicillin, chloramphenicol, trimethoprim-sulfamethoxazole, amoxicillin and ciprofloxacin, have been commonly used to treat typhoid fever in microbiology (*Baron S* et al.). Treatment of the disease with antibiotics reduces the case-fatality rate to approximately 1%.

When untreated, typhoid fever persists for three weeks to a month. Death occurs in between 10% and 30% of untreated cases. In some communities, however, case-fatality rates may reach as high as 47%.

Surgery

Surgery is usually indicated in cases of intestinal perforation. Most surgeons prefer simple closure of the perforation with drainage of the peritoneum. Small-bowel resection is indicated for patients with multiple perforations. If antibiotic treatment fails to eradicate the hepatobiliary carriage, the gallbladder should be resected. Cholecystectomy is not always successful in eradicating the carrier state because of persisting hepatic infection.

Resistance

Resistance to ampicillin, chloramphenicol, trimethoprim-sulfamethoxazole, and streptomycin is now common, and these agents have not been used as first–line treatment for almost twenty years. Typhoid that is resistant to these agents is known as multidrug-resistant typhoid (MDR typhoid).

Ciprofloxacin resistance is an increasing problem, especially in the Indian subcontinent and Southeast Asia. Many centres are therefore moving away from using ciprofloxacin as the first line for treating suspected typhoid originating in South America, India, Pakistan, Bangladesh, Thailand, or Vietnam. For these patients, the recommended first line treatment is ceftriaxone. It has also been suggested that azithromycin is better at treating typhoid in resistant populations than both fluoroquinolone drugs and ceftriaxone. Azithromycin significantly reduces relapse rates compared with ceftriaxone.

There is a separate problem with laboratory testing for reduced susceptibility to ciprofloxacin: current recommendations are that isolates should be tested simultaneously against ciprofloxacin (CIP) and against nalidixic acid (NAL), and that isolates that are sensitive to both CIP and NAL should be reported as "sensitive to ciprofloxacin", but that isolates testing sensitive to CIP but not to NAL should be reported as "reduced sensitivity to ciprofloxacin". However, an analysis of 271 isolates showed that around 18% of isolates with a reduced susceptibility to ciprofloxacin (MIC 0.125–1.0 mg/l) would not be picked up by this method. It is not certain how this problem can be solved, because most laboratories around the world (including the West) are dependent on disk testing and cannot test for MICs.

Relapsing Fever

Relapsing fever is a vector-borne disease caused by infection with certain bacteria in the genus *Rickettsia* and *Borrelia*, which are transmitted through the bites of lice or soft-bodied ticks (genus *Ornithodoros*).

Infection

Louse-borne Relapsing Fever: Along with *Rickettsia prowazekii* and *Bartonella quintana*, *Borrelia recurrentis* is one of three pathogens of which the body louse (*Pediculus humanus humanus*) is a vector. Louse-borne relapsing fever is more severe than the tick-borne variety.

Louse-borne relapsing fever occurs in epidemics amid poor living conditions, famine and war in the developing world. It is currently prevalent in Ethiopia and Sudan. Mortality rate is 1% with treatment and 30–70% without treatment. Poor prognostic signs include severe jaundice, severe change in mental status, severe bleeding and a prolonged QT interval on ECG.

Lice that feed on infected humans acquire the *Borrelia* organisms that then multiply in the gut of the louse. When an infected louse feeds on an uninfected human, the organism gains access when the victim crushes the louse or scratches the area where the louse is feeding. *B. recurrentis* infects the person via mucous membranes and then invades the bloodstream. No non-human, animal reservoir exists.

Tick-borne Relapsing Fever: Tick-borne relapsing fever is found primarily in Africa, Spain, Saudi Arabia, Asia, and certain areas of Canada and the western United States. Other relapsing infections are acquired from other *Borrelia* species, which can be spread from rodents, and serve as a reservoir for the infection, by a tick vector.

- *Borrelia crocidurae* – occurs in Egypt, Mali, Senegal, Tunisia; vectors – *Ornithodoros erraticus, Ornithodoros sonrai*; animal host – shrew (*Crocidura stampflii*)
- *Borrelia duttoni*, transmitted by the soft-bodied African tick *Ornithodoros moubata*, is responsible for the relapsing fever found in central, eastern, and southern Africa.
- *Borrelia hermsii*
- *Borrelia hispanica*
- *Borrelia miyamotoi*
- *Borrelia parkeri*
- *Borrelia turicatae*

B. hermsii and *B. recurrentis* cause very similar diseases. However, one or two relapses are common with the disease associated with *B. hermsii,* which is also the most common cause of relapsing disease in the United States. (Three or four relapses are common with the disease caused by *B. recurrentis,* which has longer febrile and afebrile intervals and a longer incubation period than *B. hermsii.*)

Diagnosis

Most people who are infected develop sickness between five and 15 days after they are bitten. The symptoms may include a sudden fever, chills, headaches, muscle or joint aches, and nausea. A rash may also occur. These symptoms usually continue for two to 9 days, then disappear. This cycle may continue for several weeks if the person is not treated. Relapsing fever is easily treated with a one- to two-week-course of antibiotics, and most people improve within 24 hours. Complications and death due to relapsing fever are rare.

Relapsing fever is a candidate etiology for a mysterious series of plagues in late-Medieval and early-Renaissance England. At the time, they were called sweating sicknesses. They have not recurred in epidemic form since the 16th century. The diagnosis of relapsing fever can be made on blood smear as evidenced by the presence of spirochetes. Other spirochete illnesses (Lyme disease, syphilis, leptospirosis) do not show spirochetes on blood smear.

Treatment

Tetracycline-class antibiotics are most effective. These can, however, induce a Jarisch-Herxheimer reaction in over half those treated, producing anxiety, diaphoresis, fever, tachycardia and tachypnea with an initial pressor response followed rapidly by hypotension. Recent studies have shown tumor necrosis factor-alpha may be partly responsible for this reaction.

Vaccine Research

Currently, no vaccine against relapsing fever is available, but research is on-going. Developing a vaccine is very difficult because the spirochetes avoid the immune response of the infected person (or animal) through antigenic variation. Essentially, the pathogen stays one step ahead of antibodies by changing its surface proteins. These surface proteins, lipoproteins called variable major proteins, have only 30–70% of their amino acid sequences in common, which is sufficient to create a new antigenic "identity" for the organism.

Chapter 8

Visceral Leishmaniasis

Visceral leishmaniasis (VL), also known as kala-azar, black fever, and Dumdum fever, is the most severe form of leishmaniasis. Leishmaniasis is a disease caused by protozoan parasites of the *Leishmania* genus. This disease is the second-largest parasitic killer in the world (after malaria), responsible for an estimated 200,000 to 400,000 infections each year worldwide. The parasite migrates to the internal organs such as liver, spleen (hence "visceral"), and bone marrow, and, if left untreated, will almost always result in the death of the host. Signs and symptoms include fever, weight loss, fatigue, anemia, and substantial swelling of the liver and spleen. Of particular concern, according to the World Health Organization (WHO), is the emerging problem of HIV/VL co-infection.

Signs and Symptoms

Response to infection by *L. donovani* varies a great deal, not only by the strength but also by the type of the patient's immune reaction. People with a history of infection by strains of leishmania that cause visceral leishmaniasis show a continuum of immune responses from protective to non-protective. Those who acquired protective immunity (skin test positive) without ever having visceral leishmaniasis have a strong type 1 CD4+ response to leishmania antigens. Antigen specific interferon-gamma and proliferation, as well as the ability to kill intracellular leishmania, are hallmarks of protective immunity. Because visceral leishmaniasis patients lack these responses to leishmania and other antigens, they usually die of secondary infections unless treated. In addition, increased interleukin-10 secretion is characteristic of the disease. Addition of interleukin-12, anti-interleukin-10, or anti-interleukin-4 to peripheral blood mononuclear cells from acute patients sometimes increases interferon-gamma secretion and proliferation. Acute patient peripheral blood mononuclear cells include CD8+ T regulatory cells that decrease interferon-gamma secretion and proliferation responses to leishmania and other antigens and increase interleukin-10 secretion when added to autologous peripheral blood mononuclear cells harvested after successful treatment. Thus, the CD8+ T regulatory cells reproduce the immune response characteristic of visceral leishmaniasis. CD8+ T regulatory cells are also associated with post kala azar dermal leishmaniasis. Addition of interleukin-12 or interferon-gamma does not prevent CD8+ T regulatory activity. The dominance of type 1 CD4+ T cells in skin test positive adults maybe explained by their secretion of factors that inhibit and kill CD8+ T regulatory cells. Successfully treated patients rarely develop visceral leishmaniasis a second time. Their peripheral blood mononuclear cells show a mixed T1/T2 CD4+ and CD8+ T suppressor response but do have the ability to kill intracellular leishmania.

When people develop visceral leishmaniasis, the most typical symptoms are fever and the enlargement of the spleen, with enlargement of the liver sometimes being seen as well. The blackening of the skin that gave the disease its common name in India does not appear in most strains of the disease, and the other symptoms are very easy to mistake for those of malaria. Misdiagnosis is dangerous, as without proper treatment the mortality rate for kala-azar is close to 100%.*L. donovani* itself is not usually the direct cause of death in kala-azar sufferers, however. Pneumonia, tuberculosis, and dysentery are omnipresent in the depressed regions where leishmaniasis thrives, and, as with AIDS, it is these opportunistic infections that are more likely to kill, flaring up in a host whose immune system has been weakened by the *L. donovani* infection. Progress of the disease is extremely variable, taking anywhere from one to twenty weeks, but a typical duration for the Sudanese strain of the disease is narrower, between twelve and sixteen weeks.

Even with recovery, kala-azar does not always leave its hosts unmarked. Some time after successful treatment—generally a few months with African kala-azar, or as much as several years with the Indian strain—a secondary form of the disease may set in, called post kala-azar dermal leishmaniasis, or PKDL. This condition manifests first as small, measle-like skin lesions on the face, which gradually increase in size and spread over the body. Eventually the lesions may coalesce to form disfiguring, swollen structures resembling leprosy, and occasionally causing blindness if they spread to the eyes. (This disease is not the same as cutaneous leishmaniasis, a milder disease caused by another protozoan of the Leishmania genus which also causes skin lesions.) is *L. donovani* and the species found in Europe, North Africa, and Latin America is *L. infantum*, also known as *L. chagasi*.

The insect vectors are species of sandfly of the genus *Phlebotomus* in the Old World, and of *Lutzomyia*in the New World. Sandflies are tiny flies, measuring 3–6 mm long by 1.5–3 mm in diameter, and are found in tropical or temperate regions throughout the world. The larvae grow in warm, moist organic matter (such as old trees, house walls, or waste) making them hard to eradicate.

Life Cycle

The life cycle of *Leishmania* is completed in two hosts, humans and sandflies. The adult female sandfly is a bloodsucker, usually feeding at night on sleeping prey. When the fly bites an individual infected with *Leishmania*, the pathogen is ingested along with the prey's blood. The protozoan is in the smaller of its two forms, called an amastigote, which is round, non-motile, and only 3–7 micrometers in diameter. Inside the stomach of the sandfly, the amastigotes quickly transform into elongated and motile forms called the promastigotes. Promastigote is spindle-shaped, triple the size of the amastigote, and has a single flagellum that allows mobility.

The promastigotes live extracellularly in the alimentary canal, reproducing asexually, then migrate to the proximal end of the gut where they become poised for a regurgitational transmission. As the fly bites, the promastigotes are released from the proboscis and introduced locally at the bite site.

Once inside the human host, promastigotes invade macrophages. Inside the cells they transform back into the smaller amastigote form. The amastigotes replicate in the most hostile part of the macrophage cell, inside the phagolysosome, whose normal defensive response they are able to prevent. After repeated multiplication, they break down their host cell by sheer pressure of mass, but there is some recent speculation that they are able to leave the cell by triggering the exocytosis response of the macrophage. The daughter cells protozoans then migrate to fresh cells or through the bloodstream to find new hosts. In this way the infection is progressive, spreading to the host's mononuclear phagocyte system, particularly the spleen and liver. The free amastigotes in peripheral tissues are then ingested by sandfly to enter another cyle.

Diagnosis

The gold standard for diagnosis is visualization of the amastigotes in splenic aspirate or bone marrow aspirate. This is a technically challenging procedure that is frequently unavailable in areas of the world where visceral leishmaniasis is endemic.

Serological testing is much more frequently used in areas where leishmaniasis is endemic. A 2014 Cochrane review evaluated different rapid diagnostic tests. One of them (the rK39 immunochromatographic test) gave correct, positive results in 92% of the people with visceral leishmaniasis and it gave correct, negative results in 92% of the people who did not have the disease. A second rapid test (called latex agglutination test) gave correct, positive results in 64% of the people with the disease and it gave correct, negative results in 93% of the people without the disease. Other types of tests have not been studied thoroughly enough to ascertain their efficacy.

The K39 dipstick test is easy to perform, and village health workers can be easily trained to use it. The kit may be stored at ambient temperature and no additional equipment needs to be carried to remote areas. The DAT anti-leishmania antigen test, standard within MSF, is much more cumbersome to use and appears not to have any advantages over the K39 test.

There are a number of problems with serological testing: in highly endemic areas, not everyone who becomes infected will actually develop clinical disease or require treatment. Indeed, up to 32% of the healthy population may test positive, but not require treatment. Conversely, because serological tests look for an immune response and not for the organism itself, the test does not become negative after the patient is cured, it cannot be used as a check for cure, or to check for re-infection or relapse. Likewise, patients with abnormal immune systems (e.g., HIV infection) will have false-negative tests.

Other tests being developed include detects erythrosalicylic acid.

Prevention

There are no vaccines or preventive drugs for visceral leishmaniasis. The most effective method to prevent infection is to protect from sand fly bites. To decrease the risk of being bitten, these precautionary measures are suggested:

Outdoors

- Avoid outdoor activities, especially from dusk to dawn, when sand flies generally are the most active.

- When outdoors (or in unprotected quarters): Minimize the amount of exposed (uncovered) skin. To the extent that is tolerable in the climate, wear long-sleeved shirts, long pants, and socks; and tuck your shirt into your pants.
- Apply insect repellent to exposed skin and under the ends of sleeves and pant legs. Follow the instructions on the label of the repellent. The most effective repellents generally are those that contain the chemical DEET (N,N-diethylmetatoluamide).

Indoors

- Stay in well-screened or air-conditioned areas.
- Keep in mind that sand flies are much smaller than mosquitoes and therefore can get through smaller holes.
- Spray living/sleeping areas with an insecticide to kill insects.
- If you are not sleeping in a well-screened or air-conditioned area, use a bed net and tuck it under your mattress. If possible, use a bed net that has been soaked in or sprayed with a pyrethroid-containing insecticide. The same treatment can be applied to screens, curtains, sheets, and clothing (clothing should be retreated after five washings)."

On February 2012, the nonprofit Infectious Disease Research Institute launched a clinical trial of the visceral leishmaniasis vaccine. The vaccine is a recombinant form of two fused Leishmania parasite proteins with an adjuvant. Two phase 1 clinical trials with healthy volunteers are to be conducted. The first one takes place in Washington (state) and is followed by a trial in India.

Treatments

As with many diseases in developing nations, (including trypanosomiasis and malaria) effective and affordable chemotherapy is sorely lacking and parasites or insect vectors are becoming increasingly resistant to existing anti-parasite drugs. Possibly due to the lack of financial return, new drugs are slow to emerge and much of the basic research into potential drug targets takes place in universities, funded by charitable organizations. This may change as a result of infection of members of the armed forces from the developed nations that currently occupy nations such as Afghanistan and Iraq, where *Leishmania* is commonplace.

The traditional treatment is with pentavalent antimonials such as sodium stibogluconate and meglumine antimoniate. Resistance is now common in India, and rates of resistance have been shown to be as high as 60% in parts of Bihar, India. The treatment of choice for visceral leishmaniasis acquired in India is now Amphotericin B in its various liposomal preparations.)

Miltefosine is the first oral treatment for this disease. The cure rate of miltefosine in Phase III clinical trials is 95%; Studies in Ethiopia show that is also effective in Africa. In HIV immunosuppressed people which are coinfected with leishmaniasis it has shown that even in resistant cases 2/3 of the people responded to this new treatment. Miltefosine has received approval by the Indian regulatory authorities in 2002, in Germany in 2004 and in U.S.A. in 2014. It is now registered in many countries.

The drug is generally better tolerated than other drugs. Main side effects are gastrointetinal disturbance in the first or second day of treatment (a course of treatment is 28 days) which does not affect the efficiency. Because it is available as an oral formulation, the expense and inconvenience of hospitalization is avoided, and outpatient distribution of the drug becomes an option, making Miltefosine a drug of choice.

The nonprofit Institute for OneWorld Health has adopted the broad spectrum antibiotic paromomycin for use in treating VL; its antileishmanial properties were first identified in the 1980s. A treatment with paromomycin costs about $15 USD. The drug had originally been identified in the 1960s. The Indian government approved paromomycin for sale and use in August 2006.

Leprosy

Leprosy, also known as Hansen's disease (HD), is a chronic infection caused by the bacteria *Mycobacterium leprae* and *Mycobacterium lepromatosis*. Initially infections are without symptoms and typically remain this way for 5 to as long as 20 years. Symptoms that develop include granulomas of the nerves, respiratory tract, skin, and eyes. This may result in a lack of ability to feel pain and thus loss of parts of extremities due to repeated injuries. Weakness and poor eyesight may also be present.

There are two main types of disease based on the number of bacteria present: paucibacillary and multibacillary. The two types are differentiated by the number of poorly pigmented numb skin patches present, with paucibacillary having five or fewer and multibacillary having more than five. The diagnosis is confirmed by finding acid-fast bacilli in a biopsy of the skin or via detecting the DNA by polymerase chain reaction. It occurs more commonly among those living in poverty and is believed to be transmitted by respiratory droplets. It is not very contagious. Leprosy is curable with treatment. Treatment for paucibacillary leprosy is with the medications dapsone and rifampicin for 6 months. Treatment for multibacillary leprosy consists of rifampicin, dapsone, and clofazimine for 12 months. These treatments are provided for free by the World Health Organization. A number of other antibiotics may also be used. Globally in 2012 the number of chronic cases of leprosy was 189,000 and the number of new cases was 230,000. The number of chronic cases has decreased from some 5.2 million in the 1980s. Most new cases occur in 16 countries, with India accounting for more than half. In the past 20 years, 16 million people worldwide have been cured of leprosy.

Leprosy has affected humanity for thousands of years. The disease takes its name from the Latin word *lepra*, which means "scaly", while the term "Hansen's disease" is named after the physician Gerhard Armauer Hansen. Separating people in leper colonies still occurs in countries like India, where there are more than a thousand; China, where there are hundreds; and in the continent of Africa. However, most colonies have closed. Leprosy has been associated with social stigma for much of history, which remains a barrier to self-reporting and early treatment. World Leprosy Day was started in 1954 to draw awareness to those affected by leprosy.

Signs and Symptoms

Leprosy is primarily a granulomatous disease of the peripheral nerves and mucosa of the upper respiratory tract; skin lesions are the primary external sign. Left untreated, leprosy can be progressive, causing permanent damage to the skin, nerves, limbs and eyes. Contrary to folklore, leprosy does not cause body parts to fall off, although they can become numb or diseased as a result of secondary infections; these occur as a result of the body's defences being compromised by the primary disease. Secondary infections, in turn, can result in tissue loss causing fingers and toes to become shortened and deformed, as cartilage is absorbed into the body.

Cause

Mycobacterium Leprae

Mycobacterium leprae and *Mycobacterium lepromatosis* are the causative agents of leprosy. *M. lepromatosis* is a relatively newly identified mycobacterium isolated from a fatal case of diffuse lepromatous leprosy in 2008.

An intracellular, acid-fast bacterium, *M. leprae* is aerobic and rod-shaped, and is surrounded by the waxy cell membrane coating characteristic of the *Mycobacterium* genus. Due to extensive loss of genes necessary for independent growth, *M. leprae* and *M. lepromatosis* are obligate pathogens, and unculturable in the laboratory, a factor that leads to difficulty in definitively identifying the organism under a strict interpretation of Koch's postulates. The use of non-culture-based techniques such as molecular genetics has allowed for alternative establishment of causation.

While the causative organisms have to date been impossible to culture *in vitro*, it has been possible to grow them in animals.

Naturally occurring infection also has been reported in non-human primates including the African chimpanzee, sooty mangabey, and cynomolgus macaque, as well as in armadillos and red squirrels.

Genetics

Several genes have been associated with a susceptibility to leprosy. It is believed that around 95% of people are naturally immune. Recent research suggests that there is a defect in cell-mediated immunity that causes susceptibility to leprosy. The region of DNA responsible for this variability is also involved in Parkinson's disease, giving rise to current speculation that the two disorders may be linked in some way at the biochemical level.

Risk Factors

At highest risk are those living in areas with polluted water and poor diet or people suffering from diseases that compromise immune function. There appears to be little interaction between HIV and the risk of leprosy.

Transmission

Although the mode of transmission of leprosy remains uncertain, many think that *M. leprae* is usually spread from person to person in nasal droplets. Studies have shown that leprosy can be transmitted to humans by armadillos. Leprosy is not known to be either sexually transmitted or highly infectious after treatment. Approximately 95% of people are naturally immune and sufferers are no longer infectious after as little as two weeks of treatment.

Pathophysiology

The precise mechanism of transmission of leprosy is unknown; however, both prolonged close contact and transmission by nasal droplet are thought to be implicated. In addition to humans, leprosy has been observed in the nine-banded armadillo, (which, it has recently been confirmed, is among the primary sources of new cases of leprosy in the population of North America), and three species of non-human primates. The bacterium can also be grown in the laboratory by injection into the footpads of mice. There is evidence that not all people who are infected with *M. leprae* develop leprosy, and genetic factors have long been thought to play a role, due to the observation of clustering of leprosy around certain families, and the failure to understand why certain individuals develop lepromatous leprosy while others develop other types of leprosy. It is estimated that due to genetic factors, only 5% of the population is susceptible to leprosy. This is mostly because the body is naturally immune to the bacteria, and those persons that do become infected experience severe allergic reactions to the disease. However, the role of genetic factors is not entirely clear in determining this clinical expression. In addition, malnutrition and prolonged exposure to infected persons may play a role in development of the overt disease.

The most widely held belief is that the disease is transmitted by contact between infected persons and healthy persons. In general, closeness of contact is related to the dose of infection, which in turn is related to the occurrence of disease. Of the various situations that promote close contact, contact within the household is the only one that is easily identified, although the incidence among contacts and the relative risk for them appear to vary considerably in different studies. In incidence studies, infection rates for contacts of lepromatous leprosy have varied from 6.2 per 1000 per year in Cebu, Philippines to 53 per 1000 per year in part of Western India to 55.8 per 1000 per year in a part of Southern India

Two exit routes of *M. leprae* from the human body often described are the skin and the nasal mucosa, although their relative importance is not clear. Lepromatous cases show large numbers of organisms deep in the dermis, but whether they reach the skin surface in sufficient numbers is doubtful. Although there are reports of acid-fast bacilli being found in the desquamating epithelium (sloughing of superficial layer of skin) of the skin, Weddell *et al.* had reported in 1963 that they could not find any acid-fast bacilli in the epidermis, even after examining a very large number of specimens from patients and contacts. In a recent study, Job *et al.* found fairly large numbers of *M. leprae* in the superficial keratin layer of the skin of lepromatous leprosy patients, suggesting that the organism could exit along with the sebaceous secretions.

The importance of the nasal mucosa was recognized as early as 1898 by Schäffer, in particular that of the ulcerated mucosa. The quantity of bacilli from nasal mucosal lesions in lepromatous leprosy was demonstrated by Shepard as large, with counts ranging from 10,000 to 10,000,000. Pedley reported that the majority of lepromatous patients showed leprosy bacilli in their nasal secretions as collected through blowing the nose. Davey and Rees indicated that nasal secretions from lepromatous patients could yield as much as 10 million viable organisms per day.

The entry route of *M. leprae* into the human body is also not definitively known: The skin and the upper respiratory tract are most likely. While older research dealt with the skin route, recent research has increasingly favored the respiratory route. Rees and McDougall succeeded in the experimental transmission of leprosy through aerosols containing *M. leprae* in immune-suppressed mice, suggesting a similar possibility in humans. Successful results have also been reported on experiments with nude mice when *M. leprae* were introduced into the nasal cavity by topical application. In summary, entry through the respiratory route appears the most probable route, although other routes, particularly broken skin, cannot be ruled out.

In leprosy, both the reference points for measuring the incubation period and the times of infection and onset of disease are difficult to define, the former because of the lack of adequate immunological tools and the latter because of the disease's slow onset. Even so, several investigators have attempted to measure the incubation period for leprosy. The minimum incubation period reported is as short as a few weeks and this is based on the very occasional occurrence of leprosy among young infants. The maximum incubation period reported is as long as 30 years, or over, as observed among war veterans known to have been exposed for short periods in endemic areas but otherwise living in non-endemic areas. It is generally agreed that the average incubation period is between three and five years.

Diagnosis

Endemic Areas

Per the World Health Organization, diagnosis in an endemic area is based on one of the following cardinal signs:

- Skin lesion consistent with leprosy and with definite sensory loss
- Positive skin smears

Skin lesions can be single or multiple, usually hypopigmented although occasionally reddish or copper coloured. The lesions may be macules (flat), papules (raised), or nodular. Sensory loss at the skin lesion is important because this feature can help differentiate from other causes of skin lesions such as tinea versicolour.

Thickened nerves are associated with leprosy and can be accompanied by loss of sensation, muscle weakness. However, without the characteristic skin lesion and without the sensory loss and/or muscle weakness is not considered a reliable sign of leprosy.

Positive skin smears: In some case, acid fast leprosy bacilli, are considered diagnostic; however, it should be emphasized that the diagnosis is clinical

United States

Diagnosis in the U.S. is often delayed because healthcare providers are unaware of leprosy and its symptoms. Early diagnosis and treatment prevents nerve involvement, the hallmark of leprosy, and the disability it causes.

There are many kinds of leprosy but there are common symptoms, including: runny nose; dry scalp; eye problems; skin lesions; muscle weakness; reddish skin; smooth shiny diffuse thickening of facial skin, ear, and hand; loss of sensation in fingers and toes; thickening of peripheral nerves; and flat nose due to destruction of nasal cartilage. There is also phonation and resonation of sound during speech. Often there is atrophy of the testes and impotency.

Prevention

Medications can decrease the risk of those living with people with leprosy from acquiring the disease and likely those with whom people with leprosy come into contact outside the home. There are however concerns of resistance, cost, and disclosure of a person's infection status when doing follow up of contacts, thus the WHO however recommends that people who live in the same household be examined for leprosy and only be treated if symptoms are present.

The Bacillus Calmette–Guérin (BCG) vaccine offers a variable amount of protection against leprosy in addition to tuberculosis. It appears to be 26 to 41% effective (based on controlled trials) and about 60% effective based on observational studies with two doses possibly working better than one. Development of a more effective vaccine is ongoing as of 2011.

Treatment

A number of leprostatic agents are available for treatment. For paucibacillary (PB or tuberculoid) cases treatment with daily dapsone and monthly rifampicin for six months is recommended. While for multibacillary (MB or lepromatous) cases treatment with daily dapsone and clofazimine along with monthly rifampicin for twelve months is recommended.

Multi-drug therapy (MDT) remains highly effective, and people are no longer infectious after the first monthly dose. It is safe and easy to use under field conditions due to its presentation in calendar blister packs. Relapse rates remain low, and there is no known resistance to the combined drugs.

Rabies

Rabies is a viral disease that causes acute inflammation of the brain in humans and other warm-blooded animals. Early symptoms can include fever and tingling at the site of exposure. These symptoms are followed by one or more of the following symptoms: violent movements, uncontrolled excitement, fear of water, an inability to move parts of the body, confusion, and loss of consciousness. After symptoms appear, rabies almost always results in death. The time period between contracting the disease and the start of symptoms is usually one to three months. However, this time period can vary from less than one week to more than one year. The time period depends on the distance the virus must travel to reach the central nervous system.

Rabies is transmitted to humans from other animals. Rabies can be transmitted when an infected animal scratches or bites another animal or human. Saliva from an infected animal can also transmit rabies if the saliva comes into contact with a mucous membrane of another animal or human. Most rabies cases in humans are the result of dog bites. More than 99% of rabies cases in countries where dogs commonly have rabies are caused by dog bites. In the Americas, bats are the most common cause of rabies, and less than 5% of rabies cases in humans are from dogs. Rodents are very rarely infected with rabies. The rabies virus travels to the brain by following the peripheral nerves. The disease can only be diagnosed after the start of symptoms.

Animal control and vaccination programmes have decreased the risk of rabies from dogs in a number of regions of the world. Immunizing people before they are exposed is recommended for those who are at high risk. The high-risk group includes people who work with bats or who spend prolonged periods in areas of the world where rabies is common. In people who have been exposed to rabies, the rabies vaccine and sometimes rabies immunoglobulin are effective in preventing the disease if the person receives the treatment before the start of rabies symptoms. Washing bites and scratches for 15 minutes with soap and water, povidone iodine, or detergent as they may kill the virus also appears to be somewhat effective at preventing rabies transmission. Only a few people have survived a rabies infection and this was with extensive treatment, known as the Milwaukee protocol.

Rabies causes about 26,000 to 55,000 deaths worldwide per year. More than 95% of these deaths occur in Asia and Africa. Rabies is present in more than 150 countries and on all continents but Antarctica. More than 3 billion people live in regions of the world where rabies occurs. In most of Europe and Australia, rabies is only present in bats. Many small island nations do not have rabies at all.

Signs and Symptoms

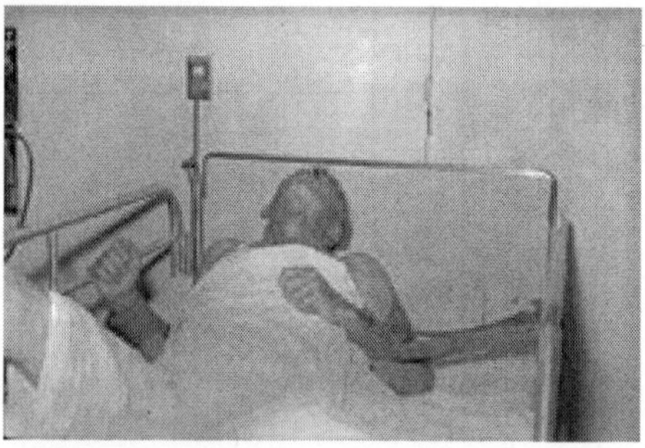

Figure: *Person with rabies, 1959*

The period between infection and the first flu-like symptoms is typically 2 to 12 weeks in humans. Incubation periods as short as four days and longer than six years have been documented, depending on the location and severity of the contaminated wound and the amount of virus introduced. Signs and symptoms may soon expand to slight or partial paralysis, anxiety, insomnia, confusion, agitation, abnormal behavior, paranoia, terror, and hallucinations, progressing to delirium. The person may have hydrophobia.

Death almost always occurs 2 to 10 days after first symptoms. Survival is rare once symptoms have presented, even with the administration of proper and intensive care. Jeanna Giese, who in 2004 was the first patient treated with the Milwaukee protocol, became the first person ever recorded to have survived rabies without receiving successful post-exposure prophylaxis. An intention-to-treat analysis has since found this protocol has a survival rate of about 8%.

Hydrophobia

Hydrophobia ("fear of water") is the historic name for rabies. It refers to a set of symptoms in the later stages of an infection in which the person has difficulty swallowing, shows panic when presented with liquids to drink, and cannot quench his or her thirst. Any mammals infected with the virus may demonstrate hydrophobia.

Saliva production is greatly increased, and attempts to drink, or even the intention or suggestion of drinking, may cause excruciatingly painful spasms of the muscles in the throat and larynx. This can be attributed to the fact that the virus multiplies and assimilates in the salivary glands of the infected animal for the purpose of further transmission through biting, and the infected animal's ability to transmit the virus will reduce significantly if he can swallow his saliva with/without external source of water.

Hydrophobia is commonly associated with furious rabies that affects 80% of the infected people. The remaining 20% may experience a paralytic form of rabies that is marked by muscle weakness, loss of sensation, and paralysis. This rabies form does not usually cause fear of water.

Cause

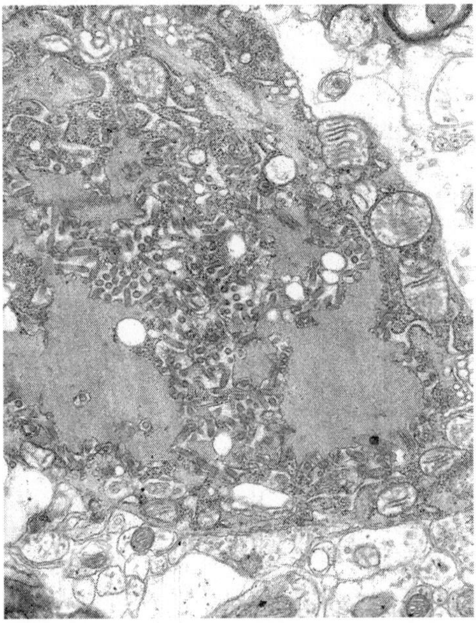

Figure: *TEM micrograph with numerous rabies virions (small, dark grey, rodlike particles) and Negri bodies (the larger pathognomonic cellular inclusions of rabies infection)*

Rabies is caused by a number of *lyssaviruses* including: rabies virus and Australian bat lyssavirus.

The rabies virus is the type species of the Lyssavirus genus, in the family *Rhabdoviridae*, order *Mononegavirales*. Lyssaviruses have helical symmetry, with a length of about 180 nm and a cross-section of about 75 nm. These viruses are enveloped and have a single-stranded RNA genome with negative sense. The genetic information is packed as a ribonucleoprotein complex in which RNA is tightly bound by the viral nucleoprotein. The RNA genome of the virus encodes five genes whose order is highly conserved: nucleoprotein (N), phosphoprotein (P), matrix protein (M), glycoprotein (G), and the viral RNA polymerase (L).

Once within a muscle or nerve cell, the virus undergoes replication. The trimeric spikes on the exterior of the membrane of the virus interact with a specific cell receptor, the most likely one being the acetylcholine receptor, acetyl. The cellular membrane pinches in a procession known as pinocytosis and allows entry of the virus into the cell by way of an endosome. The virus then uses the acidic environment, which is necessary, of that endosome and binds to its membrane simultaneously, releasing its five proteins and single strand RNA into the cytoplasm.

The L protein then transcribes five mRNA strands and a positive strand of RNA all from the original negative strand RNA using free nucleotides in the cytoplasm. These five mRNA strands are then translated into their corresponding proteins (P, L, N, G and M proteins) at free ribosomes in the cytoplasm. Some proteins require post-translative modifications. For example, the G protein travels through the rough endoplasmic reticulum, where it undergoes further folding, and is then transported to the Golgi apparatus, where a sugar group is added to it (glycosylation).

Where there are enough proteins, the viral polymerase will begin to synthesize new negative strands of RNA from the template of the positive strand RNA. These negative strands will then form complexes with the N, P, L and M proteins and then travel to the inner membrane of the cell, where a G protein has embedded itself in the membrane. The G protein then coils around the N-P-L-M complex of proteins taking some of the host cell membrane with it, which will form the new outer envelope of the virus particle. The virus then buds from the cell.

From the point of entry, the virus is neurotropic, travelling quickly along the neural pathways into the central nervous system. The virus usually first infects muscle cells close to the site of infection, where they are able to replicate without being 'noticed' by the host's immune system. Once enough virus has been replicated, they begin to bind to acetyl choline receptors (p75NR) at the neuromuscular junction. The virus then travels through the nerve cell axon via retrograde transport, as its P protein interacts with dyenin, a protein present in the cytoplasm of nerve cells. Once the virus reaches the cell body it travels rapidly to the Central Nervous System (CNS), replicating in motor neurons and eventually reaching to the brain. After the brain is infected, the virus travels centrifugally to the peripheral and autonomic nervous systems, eventually migrating to the salivary glands, where it is ready to be transmitted to the next host.

Transmission

All warm-blooded species, including humans, may become infected with the rabies virus and develop symptoms. Birds were first artificially infected with rabies in 1884; however, infected birds are largely if not wholly asymptomatic, and recover. Other bird species have been known to develop rabies antibodies, a sign of infection, after feeding on rabies-infected mammals. The virus has also been adapted to grow in cells of poikilothermic ("cold-blooded") vertebrates. Most animals can be infected by the virus and can transmit the disease to humans. Infected bats, monkeys, raccoons, foxes, skunks, cattle, wolves, coyotes, dogs, mongooses (normally yellow mongoose) and cats present the greatest risk to humans.

Rabies may also spread through exposure to infected domestic farm animals, groundhogs, weasels, bears, raccoons, and other wild carnivorans. Small rodents, such as squirrels, hamsters, guinea pigs, gerbils, chipmunks, rats, and mice, and lagomorphs such as rabbits and hares, are almost never found to be infected with rabies and are not known to transmit rabies to humans. The Virginia opossum is resistant but not immune to rabies.

The virus is usually present in the nerves and saliva of a symptomatic rabid animal. The route of infection is usually, but not always, by a bite. In many cases, the infected animal is exceptionally aggressive, may attack without provocation, and exhibits otherwise uncharacteristic behavior. This is an example of a viral pathogen modifying the behavior of its host to facilitate its transmission to other hosts. Transmission between humans is extremely rare. A few cases have been recorded through transplant surgery. After a typical human infection by bite, the virus enters the peripheral nervous system. It then travels along the afferent nerves toward the central nervous system. During this phase, the virus cannot be easily detected within the host, and vaccination may still confer cell-mediated immunity to prevent symptomatic rabies. When the virus reaches the brain, it rapidly causes encephalitis, the prodromal phase, and is the beginning of the symptoms. Once the patient becomes symptomatic, treatment is almost never effective and mortality is over 99%. Rabies may also inflame the spinal cord, producing transverse myelitis.

Diagnosis

Rabies can be difficult to diagnose, because, in the early stages, it is easily confused with other diseases or with aggressiveness. The reference method for diagnosing rabies is the fluorescent antibody test (FAT), which is recommended by the World Health Organization (WHO). The FAT relies on the ability of a detector molecule (usually fluorescein isothiocyanate) coupled with a rabies-specific antibody, forming a conjugate, to bind to and allow the visualisation of rabies antigen using fluorescent microscopy techniques. Microscopic analysis of samples is the only direct method that allows for the identification of rabies virus-specific antigen in a short time and at a reduced cost, irrespective of geographical origin and status of the host. It has to be regarded as the first step in diagnostic procedures for all laboratories. Autolysed samples can, however, reduce the sensitivity and specificity of the FAT. The RT PCR assays proved to be a sensitive and specific tool for routine diagnostic purposes, particularly in decomposed samples or archival specimens. The diagnosis can be reliably made from brain samples taken after death. The diagnosis can also be made from saliva, urine, and cerebrospinal fluid samples, but this is not as sensitive and reliable as brain samples. Cerebral inclusion bodies called Negri bodies are 100% diagnostic for rabies infection but are found in only about 80% of cases. If possible, the animal from which the bite was received should also be examined for rabies.

The differential diagnosis in a case of suspected human rabies may initially include any cause of encephalitis, in particular infection with viruses such as herpesviruses, enteroviruses, and arboviruses such as West Nile virus. The most important viruses to rule out are herpes simplex virus type one, varicella zoster virus, and (less commonly) enteroviruses, including coxsackieviruses, echoviruses, polioviruses, and human enteroviruses 68 to 71.

New causes of viral encephalitis are also possible, as was evidenced by the 1999 outbreak in Malaysia of 300 cases of encephalitis with a mortality rate of 40% caused by Nipah virus, a newly recognized paramyxovirus. Likewise, well-known viruses may be introduced into new locales, as is illustrated by the recent outbreak of encephalitis due to West Nile virus in the eastern United States. Epidemiologic factors, such as season, geographic location, and the patient's age, travel history, and possible exposure to bites, rodents, and ticks, may help direct the diagnosis.

Cheaper rabies diagnosis will become possible for low-income settings: accurate rabies diagnosis can be done at a tenth of the cost of traditional testing using basic light microscopy techniques.

Prevention

Almost all human cases of rabies were fatal until a vaccine was developed in 1885 by Louis Pasteur and Émile Roux. Their original vaccine was harvested from infected rabbits, from which the virus in the nerve tissue was weakened by allowing it to dry for five to 10 days. Similar nerve tissue-derived vaccines are still used in some countries, as they are much cheaper than modern cell culture vaccines.

The human diploid cell rabies vaccine was started in 1967. Less expensive purified chicken embryo cell vaccine and purified vero cell rabies vaccine are now available. A recombinant vaccine called V-RG has been used in Belgium, France, Germany, and the United States to prevent outbreaks of rabies in undomesticated animals. Immunization before exposure has been used in both human and nonhuman populations, where, as in many jurisdictions, domesticated animals are required to be vaccinated. Recorded human deaths from rabies in the United States has dropped from 100 or more annually in the early 20th century to one or two per year due to widespread vaccination of domestic dogs and cats and the development of human vaccines and immunoglobulin treatments. Most deaths now result from bat bites, which may go unnoticed by the victim and hence untreated.

The Missouri Department of Health and Senior Services Communicable Disease Surveillance 2007 Annual Report states the following can help reduce the risk of contracting rabies:

- Vaccinating dogs, cats, rabbits, and ferrets against rabies
- Keeping pets under supervision
- Not handling wild animals or strays
- Contacting an animal control officer upon observing a wild animal or a stray, especially if the animal is acting strangely
- If bitten by an animal, washing the wound with soap and water for 10 to 15 minutes and contacting a healthcare provider to determine if post-exposure prophylaxis is required

September 28 is World Rabies Day, which promotes the information, prevention, and elimination of the disease.

Treatment

Treatment after exposure can prevent the disease if administered promptly, generally within 10 days of infection. Thoroughly washing the wound as soon as possible with soap and water for approximately five minutes is effective in reducing the number of viral particles. Povidone iodine or alcohol is then recommended to reduce the virus further.

In the US, the Centres for Disease Control and Prevention recommends people receive one dose of human rabies immunoglobulin (HRIG) and four doses of rabies vaccine over a 14-day period. The immunoglobulin dose should not exceed 20 units per kilogram body weight. HRIG is expensive and constitutes most of the cost of postexposure treatment, ranging as high as several thousand dollars. As much as possible of this dose should be injected around the bites, with the remainder being given by deep intramuscular injection at a site distant from the vaccination site.

The first dose of rabies vaccine is given as soon as possible after exposure, with additional doses on days three, seven and 14 after the first. Patients who have previously received pre-exposure vaccination do not receive the immunoglobulin, only the postexposure vaccinations on days 0 and 2.

The pain and side effects of modern cell-based vaccines are similar to flu shots. The old nerve-tissue-based vaccinations that require multiple painful injections into the abdomen with a large needle are inexpensive, but are being phased out and replaced by affordable World Health Organization intradermal-vaccination regimens.

Intramuscular vaccination should be given into the deltoid, not gluteal area, which has been associated with vaccination failure due to injection into fat rather than muscle. In infants, the lateral thigh is used as for routine childhood vaccinations.

Awakening to find a bat in the room, or finding a bat in the room of a previously unattended child or mentally disabled or intoxicated person, is regarded as an indication for post-exposure prophylaxis (PEP). The recommendation for the precautionary use of PEP in occult bat encounters where no contact is recognized has been questioned in the medical literature, based on a cost-benefit analysis. However, a 2002 study has supported the protocol of precautionary administering of PEP where a child or mentally compromised individual has been alone with a bat, especially in sleep areas, where a bite or exposure may occur without the victim being aware. Begun with little or no delay, PEP is 100% effective against rabies. In the case in which there has been a significant delay in administering PEP, the treatment should be administered regardless, as it may still be effective.

Induced Coma

In 2004, American teenager Jeanna Giese survived an infection of rabies unvaccinated. She was placed into an induced coma upon onset of symptoms and given ketamine, midazolam, ribavirin, and amantadine. Her doctors administered treatment based on the hypothesis that detrimental effects of rabies were caused by temporary dysfunctions in the brain and could be avoided by inducing a temporary partial halt in brain function that would protect the brain from damage while giving the immune system time to defeat the virus. After 31 days of isolation and 76 days of hospitalization, Giese was released from the hospital. She survived with all higher level brain functions, but an inability to walk and balance. On a podcast of NPR's *Radiolab*, Giese recounted, "I had to learn how to stand and then to walk, turn around, move my toes. I was really, after rabies, a new born baby who couldn't do anything. I had to relearn that all...mentally I knew how to do stuff but my body wouldn't cooperate with what I wanted it to do. It definitely took a toll on me psychologically. You know I'm still recovering. I'm not completely back. Stuff like balance and, um, I can't run normally."

Giese's treatment regimen became known as the "Milwaukee protocol", which has since undergone revision with the second version omitting the use of ribavirin. Two of 25 patients survived when treated under the first protocol. A further 10 patients have been treated under the revised protocol, with a further two survivors. The anesthetic drug ketamine has shown the potential for rabies virus inhibition in rats, and is used as part of the Milwaukee protocol. On June 12, 2011, Precious Reynolds, an eight-year-old girl from Humboldt County, California, became the third reported person in the United States to have recovered from rabies without receiving PEP.

Prognosis

In unvaccinated humans, rabies is almost always fatal after neurological symptoms have developed. Vaccination after exposure, PEP, is highly successful in preventing the disease if administered promptly, in general within 6 days of infection. Begun with little or no delay, PEP is 100% effective against rabies. In the case of significant delay in administering PEP, the treatment still has a chance of success. 5 of the first 43 patients (12%) treated with the Milwaukee protocol survived, and those receiving treatment survived longer than those not receiving the treatment.

Smallpox

Smallpox was an infectious disease caused by either of two virus variants, *Variola major* and *Variola minor*. The disease is also known by the Latin names *Variola* or *Variola vera*, derived from *varius* ("spotted") or *varus* ("pimple"). The disease was originally known in English as the "pox" or "red plague"; the term "smallpox" was first used in Britain in the 15th century to distinguish variola from the "great pox" (syphilis). The last naturally occurring case of smallpox (*Variola minor*) was diagnosed on 26 October 1977.

Smallpox was localized in small blood vessels of the skin and in the mouth and throat. In the skin it resulted in a characteristic maculopapular rash and, later, raised fluid-filled blisters. *V. major* produced a more serious disease and had an overall mortality rate of 30–35%. *V. minor* caused a milder form of disease (also known as alastrim, cottonpox, milkpox, whitepox, and Cuban itch) which killed about 1% of its victims. Long-term complications of *V. major* infection included characteristic scars, commonly on the face, which occur in 65–85% of survivors. Blindness resulting from corneal ulceration and scarring, and limb deformities due to arthritis and osteomyelitis were less common complications.

Smallpox is believed to have emerged in human populations about 10,000 BC. The earliest physical evidence of it is probably the pustular rash on the mummified body of Pharaoh Ramses V of Egypt. The disease killed an estimated 400,000 Europeans annually during the closing years of the 18th century (including five reigning monarchs), and was responsible for a third of all blindness. Of all those infected, 20–60%—and over 80% of infected children—died from the disease. Smallpox was responsible for an estimated 300–500 million deaths during the 20th century. As recently as 1967, the World Health Organization (WHO) estimated that 15 million people contracted the disease and that two million died in that year.

After vaccination campaigns throughout the 19th and 20th centuries, the WHO certified the eradication of smallpox in 1979. Smallpox is one of two infectious diseases to have been eradicated, the other being rinderpest, which was declared eradicated in 2011.

Classification

There were two clinical forms of smallpox. Variola major was the severe and most common form, with a more extensive rash and higher fever. Variola minor was a less common presentation, and a much less severe disease, with historical death rates of 1% or less. Subclinical (asymptomatic) infections with variola virus were noted but were not common. In addition, a form called *variola sine eruptione* (smallpox without rash) was seen generally in vaccinated persons. This form was marked by a fever that occurred after the usual incubation period and could be confirmed only by antibody studies or, rarely, by virus isolation.

Signs and Symptoms

The incubation period between contraction and the first obvious symptoms of the disease is around 12 days. Once inhaled, variola major virus invades the oropharyngeal (mouth and throat) or the respiratory mucosa, migrates to regional lymph nodes, and begins to multiply. In the initial growth phase the virus seems to move from cell to cell, but around the 12th day, lysis of many infected cells occurs and the virus is found in the bloodstream in large numbers (this is called *viremia*), and a second wave of multiplication occurs in the spleen, bone marrow, and lymph nodes. The initial or prodromal symptoms are similar to other viral diseases such as influenza and the common cold: fever of at least 38.5 °C (101 °F), muscle pain, malaise, headache and prostration. As the digestive tract is commonly involved, nausea and vomiting and backache often occur. The prodrome, or preeruptive stage, usually lasts 2–4 days. By days 12–15 the first visible lesions—small reddish spots called *enanthem*—appear on mucous membranes of the mouth, tongue, palate, and throat, and temperature falls to near normal. These lesions rapidly enlarge and rupture, releasing large amounts of virus into the saliva.

Smallpox virus preferentially attacks skin cells, causing the characteristic pimples (called macules) associated with the disease. A rash develops on the skin 24 to 48 hours after lesions on the mucous membranes appear. Typically the macules first appear on the forehead, then rapidly spread to the whole face, proximal portions of extremities, the trunk, and lastly to distal portions of extremities. The process takes no more than 24 to 36 hours, after which no new lesions appear. At this point variola major infection can take several very different courses, resulting in four types of smallpox disease based on the Rao classification: ordinary, modified, malignant (or flat), and hemorrhagic. Historically, smallpox has an overall fatality rate of about 30%; however, the malignant and hemorrhagic forms are usually fatal.

Ordinary

Ninety percent or more of smallpox cases among unvaccinated persons are of the ordinary type. In this form of the disease, by the second day of the rash the macules become raised *papules*. By the third or fourth day the papules fill with an opalescent fluid to become *vesicles*. This fluid becomes opaque and turbid within 24–48 hours, giving them the appearance of pustules; however, the so-called pustules are filled with tissue debris, not pus.

By the sixth or seventh day, all the skin lesions have become pustules. Between seven and ten days the pustules mature and reach their maximum size. The pustules are sharply raised, typically round, tense, and firm to the touch. The pustules are deeply embedded in the dermis, giving them the feel of a small bead in the skin. Fluid slowly leaks from the pustules, and by the end of the second week the pustules deflate, and start to dry up, forming crusts (or scabs). By day 16–20 scabs have formed over all the lesions, which have started to flake off, leaving depigmented scars.

Ordinary smallpox generally produces a discrete rash, in which the pustules stand out on the skin separately. The distribution of the rash is densest on the face; denser on the extremities than on the trunk; and on the extremities, denser on the distal parts than on the proximal. The palms of the hands and soles of the feet are involved in the majority of cases. Sometimes, the blisters merge into sheets, forming a confluent rash, which begin to detach the outer layers of skin from the underlying flesh. Patients with confluent smallpox often remain ill even after scabs have formed over all the lesions. In one case series, the case-fatality rate in confluent smallpox was 62%.

Modified

Referring to the character of the eruption and the rapidity of its development, modified smallpox occurs mostly in previously vaccinated people. In this form the prodromal illness still occurs but may be less severe than in the ordinary type. There is usually no fever during evolution of the rash. The skin lesions tend to be fewer and evolve more quickly, are more superficial, and may not show the uniform characteristic of more typical smallpox. Modified smallpox is rarely, if ever, fatal. This form of variola major is more easily confused with chickenpox.

Malignant

In malignant-type smallpox (also called flat smallpox) the lesions remain almost flush with the skin at the time when raised vesicles form in the ordinary type. It is unknown why some people develop this type. Historically, it accounted for 5%–10% of cases, and the majority (72%) were children. Malignant smallpox is accompanied by a severe prodromal phase that lasts 3–4 days, prolonged high fever, and severe symptoms of toxemia. The rash on the tongue and palate is extensive. Skin lesions mature slowly and by the seventh or eighth day they are flat and appear to be buried in the skin. Unlike ordinary-type smallpox, the vesicles contain little fluid, are soft and velvety to the touch, and may contain hemorrhages. Malignant smallpox is nearly always fatal.

Hemorrhagic

Hemorrhagic smallpox is a severe form that is accompanied by extensive bleeding into the skin, mucous membranes, and gastrointestinal tract. This form develops in approximately 2% of infections and occurred mostly in adults. In hemorrhagic smallpox the skin does not blister, but remains smooth. Instead, bleeding occurs under the skin, making it look charred and black, hence this form of the disease is also known as black pox.

In the early, or fulminating form, hemorrhaging appears on the second or third day as sub-conjunctival bleeding turns the whites of the eyes deep red. Hemorrhagic smallpox also produces a dusky erythema, petechiae, and hemorrhages in the spleen, kidney, serosa, muscle, and, rarely, the epicardium, liver, testes, ovaries and bladder. Death often occurs suddenly between the fifth and seventh days of illness, when only a few insignificant skin lesions are present. A later form of the disease occurs in patients who survive for 8–10 days. The hemorrhages appear in the early eruptive period, and the rash is flat and does not progress beyond the vesicular stage. Patients in the early stage of disease show a decrease in coagulation factors (e.g. platelets, prothrombin, and globulin) and an increase in circulating antithrombin. Patients in the late stage have significant thrombocytopenia; however, deficiency of coagulation factors is less severe. Some in the late stage also show increased antithrombin. This form of smallpox occurs in anywhere from 3 to 25% of fatal cases depending on the virulence of the smallpox strain. Hemorrhagic smallpox is usually fatal.

Cause

Smallpox is caused by infection with variola virus, which belongs to the genus Orthopoxvirus, the family Poxviridae and subfamily chordopoxvirinae. Variola is a large brick-shaped virus measuring approximately 302 to 350 nanometers by 244 to 270 nm, with a single linear double stranded DNA genome 186 kilobase pairs (kbp) in size and containing a hairpin loop at each end. The two classic varieties of smallpox are variola major and variola minor.

Four orthopoxviruses cause infection in humans: variola, vaccinia, cowpox, and monkeypox. Variola virus infects only humans in nature, although primates and other animals have been infected in a laboratory setting. Vaccinia, cowpox, and monkeypox viruses can infect both humans and other animals in nature.

The lifecycle of poxviruses is complicated by having multiple infectious forms, with differing mechanisms of cell entry. Poxviruses are unique among DNA viruses in that they replicate in the cytoplasm of the cell rather than in the nucleus. In order to replicate, poxviruses produce a variety of specialized proteins not produced by other DNA viruses, the most important of which is a viral-associated DNA-dependent RNA polymerase.

Both enveloped and unenveloped virions are infectious. The viral envelope is made of modified Golgi membranes containing viral-specific polypeptides, including hemagglutinin. Infection with either variola major or variola minor confers immunity against the other.

Transmission

Transmission occurs through inhalation of airborne variola virus, usually droplets expressed from the oral, nasal, or pharyngeal mucosa of an infected person. It is transmitted from one person to another primarily through prolonged face-to-face contact with an infected person, usually within a distance of 6 feet (1.8 m), but can also be spread through direct contact with infected bodily fluids or contaminated objects (fomites) such as bedding or clothing. Rarely, smallpox has been spread by virus carried in the air in enclosed settings such as buildings, buses, and trains. The virus can cross the placenta, but the incidence of congenital smallpox is relatively low. Smallpox is not notably infectious in the prodromal period and viral shedding is usually delayed until the appearance of the rash, which is often accompanied by lesions in the mouth and pharynx. The virus can be transmitted throughout the course of the illness, but is most frequent during the first week of the rash, when most of the skin lesions are intact. Infectivity wanes in 7 to 10 days when scabs form over the lesions, but the infected person is contagious until the last smallpox scab falls off.

Smallpox is highly contagious, but generally spreads more slowly and less widely than some other viral diseases, perhaps because transmission requires close contact and occurs after the onset of the rash. The overall rate of infection is also affected by the short duration of the infectious stage. In temperate areas, the number of smallpox infections were highest during the winter and spring. In tropical areas, seasonal variation was less evident and the disease was present throughout the year. Age distribution of smallpox infections depends on acquired immunity. Vaccination immunity declines over time and is probably lost in all but the most recently vaccinated populations. Smallpox is not known to be transmitted by insects or animals and there is no asymptomatic carrier state.

Diagnosis

The clinical definition of smallpox is an illness with acute onset of fever greater than 101 °F (38.3 °C) followed by a rash characterized by firm, deep seated vesicles or pustules in the same stage of development without other apparent cause. If a clinical case is observed, smallpox is confirmed using laboratory tests.

Microscopically, poxviruses produce characteristic cytoplasmic inclusions, the most important of which are known as Guarnieri bodies, and are the sites of viral replication. Guarnieri bodies are readily identified in skin biopsies stained with hematoxylin and eosin, and appear as pink blobs. They are found in virtually all poxvirus infections but the absence of Guarnieri bodies cannot be used to rule out smallpox. The diagnosis of an orthopoxvirus infection can also be made rapidly by electron microscopic examination of pustular fluid or scabs. However, all orthopoxviruses exhibit identical brick-shaped virions by electron microscopy. However, if particles with the characteristic morphology of herpesviruses are seen this will eliminate smallpox and other orthopoxvirus infections. Definitive laboratory identification of variola virus involves growing the virus on chorioallantoic membrane (part of a chicken embryo) and examining the resulting pock lesions under defined temperature conditions. Strains may be characterized by polymerase chain reaction (PCR) and restriction fragment length polymorphism (RFLP) analysis. Serologic tests and enzyme linked immunosorbent assays (ELISA), which measure variola virus-specific immunoglobulin and antigen have also been developed to assist in the diagnosis of infection.

Chickenpox was commonly confused with smallpox in the immediate post-eradication era. Chickenpox and smallpox can be distinguished by several methods. Unlike smallpox, chickenpox does not usually affect the palms and soles. Additionally, chickenpox pustules are of varying size due to variations in the timing of pustule eruption: smallpox pustules are all very nearly the same size since the viral effect progresses more uniformly. A variety of laboratory methods are available for detecting chickenpox in evaluation of suspected smallpox cases.

Prevention

The earliest procedure used to prevent smallpox was inoculation (known as variolation after the introduction of smallpox vaccine to avoid possible confusion). Inoculation was possibly practiced in India as early as 1000 BC, and involved either nasal insufflation of powdered smallpox scabs, or scratching material from a smallpox lesion into the skin. However, the idea that inoculation originated in India has been challenged as few of the ancient Sanskrit medical texts described the process of inoculation.

Accounts of inoculation against smallpox in China can be found as early as the late 10th century, and the procedure was widely practiced by the 16th century, during the Ming Dynasty. If successful, inoculation produced lasting immunity to smallpox. However, because the person was infected with variola virus, a severe infection could result, and the person could transmit smallpox to others. Variolation had a 0.5–2% mortality rate, considerably less than the 20–30% mortality rate of the disease itself.

Lady Mary Wortley Montagu observed smallpox inoculation during her stay in the Ottoman Empire, writing detailed accounts of the practice in her letters, and enthusiastically promoted the procedure in England upon her return in 1718. In 1721, Cotton Mather and colleagues provoked controversy in Boston by inoculating hundreds. In 1796, Edward Jenner, a doctor in Berkeley, Gloucestershire, rural England, discovered that immunity to smallpox could be produced by inoculating a person with material from a cowpox lesion. Cowpox is a poxvirus in the same family as variola. Jenner called the material used for inoculation vaccine, from the root word *vacca*, which is Latin for cow. The procedure was much safer than variolation, and did not involve a risk of smallpox transmission. Vaccination to prevent smallpox was soon practiced all over the world. During the 19th century, the cowpox virus used for smallpox vaccination was replaced by vaccinia virus. Vaccinia is in the same family as cowpox and variola but is genetically distinct from both. The origin of vaccinia virus and how it came to be in the vaccine are not known.

The current formulation of smallpox vaccine is a live virus preparation of infectious vaccinia virus. The vaccine is given using a bifurcated (two-pronged) needle that is dipped into the vaccine solution. The needle is used to prick the skin (usually the upper arm) a number of times in a few seconds. If successful, a red and itchy bump develops at the vaccine site in three or four days. In the first week, the bump becomes a large blister (called a "Jennerian vesicle") which fills with pus, and begins to drain. During the second week, the blister begins to dry up and a scab forms. The scab falls off in the third week, leaving a small scar.

The antibodies induced by vaccinia vaccine are cross-protective for other orthopoxviruses, such as monkeypox, cowpox, and variola (smallpox) viruses. Neutralizing antibodies are detectable 10 days after first-time vaccination, and seven days after revaccination. Historically, the vaccine has been effective in preventing smallpox infection in 95% of those vaccinated. Smallpox vaccination provides a high level of immunity for three to five years and decreasing immunity thereafter. If a person is vaccinated again later, immunity lasts even longer. Studies of smallpox cases in Europe in the 1950s and 1960s demonstrated that the fatality rate among persons vaccinated less than 10 years before exposure was 1.3%; it was 7% among those vaccinated 11 to 20 years prior, and 11% among those vaccinated 20 or more years prior to infection. By contrast, 52% of unvaccinated persons died.

There are side effects and risks associated with the smallpox vaccine. In the past, about 1 out of 1,000 people vaccinated for the first time experienced serious, but non-life-threatening, reactions including toxic or allergic reaction at the site of the vaccination (erythema multiforme), spread of the vaccinia virus to other parts of the body, and to other individuals. Potentially life-threatening reactions occurred in 14 to 500 people out of every 1 million people vaccinated for the first time. Based on past experience, it is estimated that 1 or 2 people in 1 million (0.000198%) who receive the vaccine may die as a result, most often the result of postvaccinial encephalitis or severe necrosis in the area of vaccination (called progressive vaccinia).

Given these risks, as smallpox became effectively eradicated and the number of naturally occurring cases fell below the number of vaccine-induced illnesses and deaths, routine childhood vaccination was discontinued in the United States in 1972, and was abandoned in most European countries in the early 1970s. Routine vaccination of health care workers was discontinued in the U.S. in 1976, and among military recruits in 1990 (although military personnel deploying to the Middle East and Korea still receive the vaccination.) By 1986, routine vaccination had ceased in all countries. It is now primarily recommended for laboratory workers at risk for occupational exposure.

Treatment

Smallpox vaccination within three days of exposure will prevent or significantly lessen the severity of smallpox symptoms in the vast majority of people. Vaccination four to seven days after exposure can offer some protection from disease or may modify the severity of disease. Other than vaccination, treatment of smallpox is primarily supportive, such as wound care and infection control, fluid therapy, and possible ventilator assistance.

Flat and hemorrhagic types of smallpox are treated with the same therapies used to treat shock, such as fluid resuscitation. People with semi-confluent and confluent types of smallpox may have therapeutic issues similar to patients with extensive skin burns.

No drug is currently approved for the treatment of smallpox. However, antiviral treatments have improved since the last large smallpox epidemics, and studies suggest that the antiviral drug cidofovir might be useful as a therapeutic agent. The drug must be administered intravenously, however, and may cause serious kidney toxicity.

Prognosis

The overall case-fatality rate for ordinary-type smallpox is about 30%, but varies by pock distribution: ordinary type-confluent is fatal about 50–75% of the time, ordinary-type semi-confluent about 25–50% of the time, in cases where the rash is discrete the case-fatality rate is less than 10%. The overall fatality rate for children younger than 1 year of age is 40–50%. Hemorrhagic and flat types have the highest fatality rates. The fatality rate for flat-type is 90% or greater and nearly 100% is observed in cases of hemorrhagic smallpox. The case-fatality rate for variola minor is 1% or less. There is no evidence of chronic or recurrent infection with variola virus.

In fatal cases of ordinary smallpox, death usually occurs between the tenth and sixteenth days of the illness. The cause of death from smallpox is not clear, but the infection is now known to involve multiple organs. Circulating immune complexes, overwhelming viremia, or an uncontrolled immune response may be contributing factors. In early hemorrhagic smallpox, death occurs suddenly about six days after the fever develops.

Cause of death in hemorrhagic cases involved heart failure, sometimes accompanied by pulmonary edema. In late hemorrhagic cases, high and sustained viremia, severe platelet loss and poor immune response were often cited as causes of death. In flat smallpox modes of death are similar to those in burns, with loss of fluid, protein and electrolytes beyond the capacity of the body to replace or acquire, and fulminating sepsis.

Complications

Complications of smallpox arise most commonly in the respiratory system and range from simple bronchitis to fatal pneumonia. Respiratory complications tend to develop on about the eighth day of the illness and can be either viral or bacterial in origin. Secondary bacterial infection of the skin is a relatively uncommon complication of smallpox. When this occurs, the fever usually remains elevated.

Other complications include encephalitis (1 in 500 patients), which is more common in adults and may cause temporary disability; permanent pitted scars, most notably on the face; and complications involving the eyes (2% of all cases). Pustules can form on the eyelid, conjunctiva, and cornea, leading to complications such as conjunctivitis, keratitis, corneal ulcer, iritis, iridocyclitis, and optic atrophy. Blindness results in approximately 35% to 40% of eyes affected with keratitis and corneal ulcer. Hemorrhagic smallpox can cause subconjunctival and retinal hemorrhages. In 2% to 5% of young children with smallpox, virions reach the joints and bone, causing *osteomyelitis variolosa*. Lesions are symmetrical, most common in the elbows, tibia, and fibula, and characteristically cause separation of an epiphysis and marked periosteal reactions. Swollen joints limit movement, and arthritis may lead to limb deformities, ankylosis, malformed bones, flail joints, and stubby fingers.

Chickenpox

Chickenpox is a highly contagious disease caused by primary infection with varicella zoster virus (VZV). It usually starts with a vesicular skin rash mainly on the body and head rather than on the limbs. The rash develops into itchy, raw pockmarks, which mostly heal without scarring. On examination, the observer typically finds skin lesions at various stages of healing, and ulcers in the oral cavity and tonsil areas. The disease is most commonly observed in children.

Chickenpox is an airborne disease which spreads easily through coughing or sneezing by ill individuals or through direct contact with secretions from the rash. A person with chickenpox is infectious one to two days before the rash appears. They remain contagious until all lesions have crusted over (this takes approximately six days). Immunocompromised patients are contagious during the entire period as new lesions keep appearing. Crusted lesions are not contagious.

Chickenpox has been observed in other primates, including chimpanzees and gorillas.

The origin of the term *chicken pox*, which is recorded as being used since 1684, is not reliably known. It has been said to be a derived from *chickpeas*, based on resemblance of the vesicles to chickpeas, or to come from the rash resembling chicken pecks. Other suggestions include the designation *chicken* for a child (i.e., literally 'child pox'), a corruption of *itching-pox*, or the idea that the disease may have originated in chickens. Samuel Johnson explained the designation as "from its being of no very great danger."

Signs and Symptoms

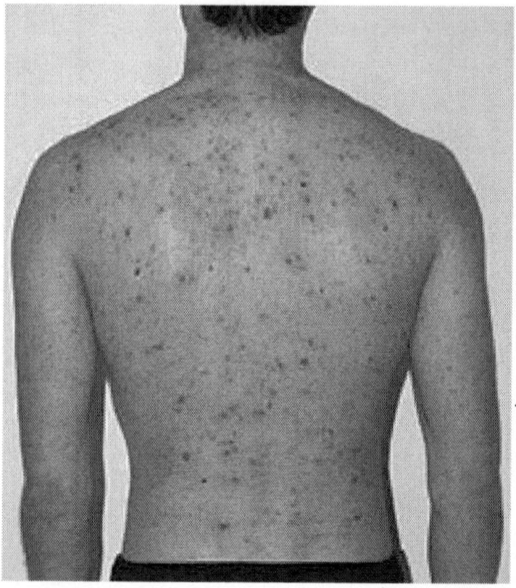

Figure: *The back of a 30-year-old male after five days of the rash*

The early (prodromal) symptoms in adolescents and adults are nausea, loss of appetite, aching muscles, and headache. This is followed by the characteristic rash or oral sores, malaise, and a low-grade fever that signal the presence of the disease. Oral manifestations of the disease (enanthem) not uncommonly may precede the external rash (exanthem). In children the illness is not usually preceded by prodromal symptoms, and the first sign is the rash or the spots in the oral cavity. The rash begins as small red dots on the face, scalp, torso, upper arms and legs; progressing over 10–12 hours to small bumps, blisters and pustules; followed by umbilication and the formation of scabs.

At the blister stage, intense itching is usually present. Blisters may also occur on the palms, soles, and genital area. Commonly, visible evidence of the disease develops in the oral cavity & tonsil areas in the form of small ulcers which can be painful or itchy or both; this enanthem (internal rash) can precede the exanthem (external rash) by 1 to 3 days or can be concurrent. These symptoms of chickenpox appear 10 to

21 days after exposure to a contagious person. Adults may have a more widespread rash and longer fever, and they are more likely to experience complications, such as varicella pneumonia.

Because watery nasal discharge containing live virus usually precedes both exanthem (external rash) and enanthem (oral ulcers) by 1 to 2 days, the infected person actually becomes contagious one to two days prior to recognition of the disease. Contagiousness persists until all vesicular lesions have become dry crusts (scabs), which usually entails four or five days, by which time nasal shedding of live virus also ceases.

Chickenpox is rarely fatal, although it is generally more severe in adult men than in women or children. Non-immune pregnant women and those with a suppressed immune system are at highest risk of serious complications. Arterial ischemic stroke (AIS) associated with chickenpox in the previous year accounts for nearly one third of childhood AIS. The most common late complication of chickenpox is shingles (herpes zoster), caused by reactivation of the *varicella zoster* virus decades after the initial, often childhood, chickenpox infection.

Diagnosis

The diagnosis of varicella is primarily clinical, with typical early "prodromal" symptoms, and then the characteristic rash and oral-cavity sores. Confirmation of the diagnosis can be sought through either examination of the fluid within the vesicles of the rash, or by testing blood for evidence of an acute immunologic response.

Vesicular fluid can be examined with a Tzanck smear, or better by testing for direct fluorescent antibody. The fluid can also be "cultured", whereby attempts are made to grow the virus from a fluid sample. Blood tests can be used to identify a response to acute infection (IgM) or previous infection and subsequent immunity (IgG).

Prenatal diagnosis of fetal varicella infection can be performed using ultrasound, though a delay of 5 weeks following primary maternal infection is advised. A PCR (DNA) test of the mother's amniotic fluid can also be performed, though the risk of spontaneous abortion due to the amniocentesis procedure is higher than the risk of the baby developing fetal varicella syndrome.

Pathophysiology

Exposure to VZV in a healthy child initiates the production of host immunoglobulin G (IgG), immunoglobulin M (IgM), and immunoglobulin A (IgA) antibodies; IgG antibodies persist for life and confer immunity. Cell-mediated immune responses are also important in limiting the scope and the duration of primary varicella infection. After primary infection, VZV is hypothesized to spread from mucosal and epidermal lesions to local sensory nerves. VZV then remains latent in the dorsal ganglion cells of the sensory nerves. Reactivation of VZV results in the clinically distinct syndrome of herpes zoster (i.e., *shingles*), postherpetic neuralgia, and sometimes Ramsay Hunt syndrome type II. Varicella zoster can affect the arteries in the neck and head, producing stroke, either during childhood, or after a latency period of many years.

Pregnancy and Neonates

During pregnancy the dangers to the fetus associated with a primary VZV infection are greater in the first six months. In the third trimester, the mother is more likely to suffer from the adverse effects of the infection. For pregnant women, antibodies produced as a result of immunization or previous infection are transferred via the placenta to the fetus. Women who are immune to chickenpox cannot become infected and do not need to be concerned about it for themselves or their infant during pregnancy.

Varicella infection in pregnant women could lead to viral transmission via the placenta and infection of the fetus. If infection occurs during the first 28 weeks of gestation, this can lead to fetal varicella syndrome (also known as *congenital varicella syndrome*). Effects on the fetus can range in severity from underdeveloped toes and fingers to severe anal and bladder malformation. Possible problems include:

- Damage to brain: encephalitis, microcephaly, hydrocephaly, aplasia of brain
- Damage to the eye: optic stalk, optic cup, and lens vesicles, microphthalmia, cataracts, chorioretinitis, optic atrophy
- Other neurological disorder: damage to cervical and lumbosacral spinal cord, motor/sensory deficits, absent deep tendon reflexes, anisocoria/Horner's syndrome
- Damage to body: hypoplasia of upper/lower extremities, anal and bladder sphincter dysfunction
- Skin disorders: (cicatricial) skin lesions, hypopigmentation

Infection late in gestation or immediately following birth is referred to as "*neonatal varicella*". Maternal infection is associated with premature delivery.

The risk of the baby developing the disease is greatest following exposure to infection in the period 7 days prior to delivery and up to 7 days following the birth. The baby may also be exposed to the virus via infectious siblings or other contacts, but this is of less concern if the mother is immune.

Newborns who develop symptoms are at a high risk of pneumonia and other serious complications of the disease.

Shingles

After a chickenpox infection, the virus remains dormant in the body's nerve tissues. The immune system keeps the virus at bay, but later in life, usually as an adult, it can be reactivated and cause a different form of the viral infection called shingles (scientifically known as herpes zoster). The United States Advisory Committee on Immunization Practices (ACIP) suggests that any adult over the age of 60 years gets the herpes zoster vaccine as a part of their normal medical check ups.

Many adults who have had chickenpox as children are susceptible to shingles as adults, often with the accompanying condition postherpetic neuralgia, a painful condition that makes it difficult to sleep. Even after the shingles rash has gone away, there can be night pain in the area affected by the rash.

Shingles affects one in five adults infected with chickenpox as children, especially those who are immune suppressed, particularly from cancer, HIV, or other conditions. However, stress can bring on shingles as well, although scientists are still researching the connection.

Shingles are most commonly found in adults over the age of 60 who were diagnosed with chickenpox when they were under the age of 1.

A shingles vaccine is available for adults over 50 who have had childhood chickenpox or who have previously had shingles.

Prevention

Hygiene Measures

The spread of chickenpox can be prevented by isolating affected individuals. Contagion is by exposure to respiratory droplets, or direct contact with lesions, within a period lasting from three days prior to the onset of the rash, to four days after the onset of the rash.

The chickenpox virus is susceptible to disinfectants, notably chlorine bleach (i.e., sodium hypochlorite). Also, like all enveloped viruses, it is sensitive to desiccation, heat and detergents.

Vaccine

A varicella vaccine was first developed by Michiaki Takahashi in 1974 derived from the Oka strain. It has been available in the US since 1995 to inoculate against the disease. Some countries require the varicella vaccination or an exemption before entering elementary school. Protection from one dose is not lifelong and a second dose is necessary five years after the initial immunization, which is currently part of the routine immunization schedule in the US. The chickenpox vaccine is not part of the routine childhood vaccination schedule in the UK. In the UK, the vaccine is currently only offered to people who are particularly vulnerable to chickenpox. A vaccinated person is likely to have a milder case of chickenpox if infected.

Treatment

Treatment mainly consists of easing the symptoms as there is no actual cure of the condition. Some treatments are however available for relieving the symptoms while the immune system suppresses the virus in the body. As a protective measure, patients are usually required to stay at home while they are infectious to avoid spreading the disease to others. Also, sufferers are frequently asked to cut their nails short or to wear gloves to prevent scratching and to minimize the risk of secondary infections.

The condition resolves by itself within a couple of weeks but meanwhile patients must pay attention to their personal hygiene. The rash caused by varicella zoster virus may however last for up to one month, although the infectious stage does not take longer than a week or two.

Although there have been no formal clinical studies evaluating the effectiveness of topical application of calamine lotion, a topical barrier preparation containing zinc oxide and one of the most commonly used interventions, it has an excellent safety profile. It is important to maintain good hygiene and daily cleaning of skin with warm water to avoid secondary bacterial infection. Scratching may also increase the risk of secondary infection.

Acetaminophen (paracetamol) but not aspirin may be used to reduce fever. Aspirin use by someone with chickenpox may cause the serious, sometimes fatal disease of the liver and brain, Reye syndrome. People at risk of developing severe complications who have had significant exposure to the virus may be given intra-muscular varicella zoster immune globulin (VZIG), a preparation containing high titres of antibodies to varicella zoster virus, to ward off the disease.

Children

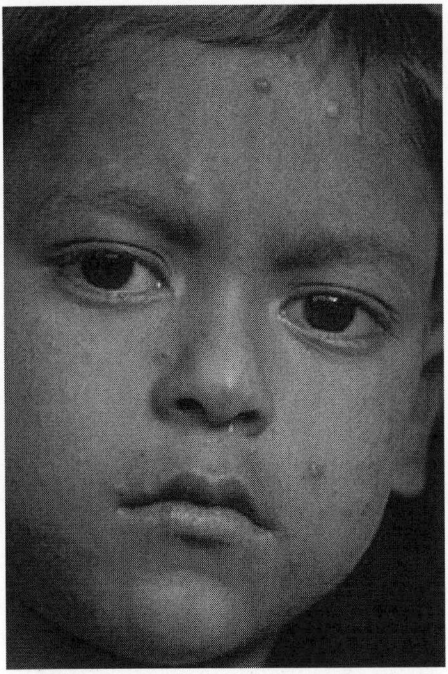

Figure: *An Indian child with chickenpox at an orphanage in Howrah.*

If oral acyclovir is started within 24 hours of rash onset it decreases symptoms by one day but has no effect on complication rates. Use of acyclovir therefore is not currently recommended for immunocompetent individuals (i.e., otherwise healthy persons without known immunodeficiency or on immunosuppressive medication). Children younger than 12 years old and older than one month are not meant to receive antiviral medication unless they are suffering from another medical condition which would put them at risk of developing complications.

Treatment of chickenpox in children is aimed at symptoms while the immune system deals with the virus. With children younger than 12 years cutting nails and keeping them clean is an important part of treatment as they are more likely to scratch their blisters more deeply than adults.

Aspirin is highly contraindicated in children younger than 16 years as it has been related with a potentially fatal condition known as Reye's syndrome.

Some parents believe that it is better for children to contract chickenpox than to get the vaccine, and they deliberately expose their children to the virus, sometimes by taking them to "chickenpox parties." Some doctors counter that children are safer getting the vaccine, which is a weakened form of the virus, than getting the disease, which can be fatal.

Adults

Infection in otherwise healthy adults tends to be more severe. Treatment with antiviral drugs (e.g. acyclovir or valacyclovir) is generally advised, as long as it is started within 24–48 hours from rash onset. Remedies to ease the symptoms of chickenpox in adults are basically the same as those used on children. Adults are more often prescribed antiviral medication as it is effective in reducing the severity of the condition and the likelihood of developing complications. Antiviral medicines do not kill the virus, but stop it from multiplying. Adults are also advised to increase water intake to reduce dehydration and to relieve headaches. Painkillers such as paracetamol (acetaminophen) are also recommended as they are effective in relieving itching and other symptoms such as fever or pains. Antihistamines relieve itches and may be used in cases where the itches prevents sleep, because they are also sedative. As with children, antiviral medication is considered more useful for those adults who are more prone to develop complications. These include pregnant women or people who have a weakened immune system.

Sorivudine, a nucleoside analogue has been reported to be effective in the treatment of primary varicella in healthy adults (case reports only), but large-scale clinical trials are still needed to demonstrate its efficacy. After recovering from chickenpox, it is recommended by doctors that adults take one injection of VZV immune globulin and one injection of varicella vaccine or herpes zoster vaccine.

Prognosis

The duration of the visible blistering caused by varicella zoster virus varies in children usually from 4 to 7 days, and the appearance of new blisters begins to subside after the 5th day. Chickenpox infection is milder in young children, and symptomatic treatment, with sodium bicarbonate baths or antihistamine medication may ease itching, it is recommended to keep new infants from birth up to age 6 months away from an infected person for 10 to 21 days as their immune systems are not developed enough to handle the stress it can bring on. Paracetamol (acetaminophen) is widely used to reduce fever. Aspirin, or products containing aspirin, should not be given to children with chickenpox as it can cause Reye's Syndrome.

In adults, the disease is more severe, though the incidence is much less common. Infection in adults is associated with greater morbidity and mortality due to pneumonia (either direct viral pneumonia or secondary bacterial pneumonia), bronchitis (either viral bronchitis or secondary bacterial bronchitis), hepatitis, and encephalitis. In particular, up to 10% of pregnant women with chickenpox develop pneumonia, the severity of which increases with onset later in gestation. In England and Wales, 75% of deaths due to chickenpox are in adults. Inflammation of the brain, or encephalitis, can occur in immunocompromised individuals, although the risk is higher with herpes zoster. Necrotizing fasciitis is also a rare complication.

Varicella can be lethal to adults with impaired immunity. The number of people in this high-risk group has increased, due to the HIV epidemic and the increased use of immunosuppressive therapies. Varicella is a particular problem in hospitals, when there are patients with immune systems weakened by drugs (e.g., high-dose steroids) or HIV.

Secondary bacterial infection of skin lesions, manifesting as impetigo, cellulitis, and erysipelas, is the most common complication in healthy children. Disseminated primary varicella infection usually seen in the immunocompromised may have high morbidity. Ninety percent of cases of varicella pneumonia occur in the adult population. Rarer complications of disseminated chickenpox also include myocarditis, hepatitis, and glomerulonephritis.

Hemorrhagic complications are more common in the immunocompromised or immunosuppressed populations, although healthy children and adults have been affected. Five major clinical syndromes have been described: febrile purpura, malignant chickenpox with purpura, postinfectious purpura, purpura fulminans, and anaphylactoid purpura. These syndromes have variable courses, with febrile purpura being the most benign of the syndromes and having an uncomplicated outcome. In contrast, malignant chickenpox with purpura is a grave clinical condition that has a mortality rate of greater than 70%. The cause of these hemorrhagic chickenpox syndromes is not known.

Epidemiology

Primary varicella occurs in all countries worldwide. Varicella has a prevalence that is stable from generation to generation. As of 2010 it caused about 6,800 deaths, down from 11,200 in 1990.

In temperate countries, chickenpox is primarily a disease of children, with most cases occurring during the winter and spring, most likely due to school contact. It is one of the classic diseases of childhood, with the highest prevalence in the 4–10 year old age group. Like rubella, it is uncommon in preschool children. Varicella is highly communicable, with an infection rate of 90% in close contacts. In temperate countries, most people become infected before adulthood, and 10% of young adults remain susceptible.

In the tropics, chickenpox often occurs in older people and may cause more serious disease. In adults the pock marks are darker and the scars more prominent than in children.

In the United States, the Centres for Disease Control and Prevention (CDC) does not require state health departments to report infections of chicken pox, and only 31 states currently volunteer this information. However, in a 2013 study conducted by the social media disease surveillance tool called Sickweather, anecdotal reports of chickenpox infections on Facebook and Twitter were used to measure and rank states with the most infections per capita, with Maryland, Tennessee and Illinois in the top 3.

Measles

Measles, also known as morbilli, English measles, or rubeola (and not to be confused with rubella or roseola) is an infection of the respiratory system, immune system and skin caused by a virus, specifically a paramyxovirus of the genus *Morbillivirus*. Symptoms usually develop 7–14 days (average 10–12) after exposure to an infected person and the initial symptoms usually include a high fever (often > 40 °C [104 °F]), Koplik's spots (spots in the mouth, these usually appear 1–2 days prior to the rash and last 3–5 days), malaise, loss of appetite, hacking cough (although this may be the last symptom to appear), runny nose and red eyes. After this comes a spot-like rash that covers much of the body. The course of measles, provided there are no complications, such as bacterial infections, usually lasts about 7–10 days.

Measles is an airborne disease that is spread through respiration (contact with fluids from an infected person's nose and mouth, either directly or through aerosol transmission via coughing or sneezing), and is highly contagious—90% of people without immunity sharing living space with an infected person will catch it. An asymptomatic incubation period occurs nine to twelve days from initial exposure. The period of infectivity has not been definitively established, some saying it lasts from two to four days prior, until two to five days following the onset of the rash (i.e., four to nine days infectivity in total), whereas others say it lasts from two to four days prior until the complete disappearance of the rash. The rash usually appears between 2–3 days after the onset of illness.

Signs and Symptoms

The classic signs and symptoms of measles include four-day fevers [the 4 D's] and the three Cs—cough, coryza (head cold), and conjunctivitis (red eyes)—along with fever and rashes. The fever may reach up to 40 °C (104 °F). Koplik's spots seen inside the mouth are pathognomonic (diagnostic) for measles, but are not often seen, even in confirmed cases of measles, because they are transient and may disappear within a day of arising. Their recognition, before the affected person reaches maximum infectivity can be used to reduce spread of epidemics.

The characteristic measles rash is classically described as a generalized, maculopapular, erythematous rash that begins several days after the fever starts. It starts on the back of the ears and, after a few hours, spreads to the head and neck before spreading to cover most of the body, often causing itching. The measles rash appears two to four days after the initial symptoms and lasts for up to eight days. The rash is said to "stain", changing colour from red to dark brown, before disappearing.

Complications

Complications with measles are relatively common, ranging from mild and less serious complications such as diarrhea to more serious ones such as pneumonia (either direct viral pneumonia or secondary bacterial pneumonia), otitis media, acute encephalitis (and very rarely SSPE—subacute sclerosing panencephalitis), and corneal ulceration (leading to corneal scarring). Complications are usually more severe in adults who catch the virus. The death rate in the 1920s was around 30% for measles pneumonia. Between 1987 and 2000, the case fatality rate across the United States was 3 measles-attributable deaths per 1000 cases, or 0.3%. In underdeveloped nations with high rates of malnutrition and poor healthcare, fatality rates have been as high as 28%. In immunocompromised persons (e.g., people with AIDS) the fatality rate is approximately 30%.

Cause

Measles is caused by the measles virus, a single-stranded, negative-sense, enveloped RNA virus of the genus *Morbillivirus* within the family *Paramyxoviridae.* The virus was first isolated in 1954 by Nobel Laureate John F. Enders and Thomas Peebles, who were careful to point out that the isolations were made from patients who had Koplik's spots. Humans are the natural hosts of the virus; no other animal reservoirs are known to exist. This highly contagious virus is spread by coughing and sneezing via close personal contact or direct contact with secretions.

Risk factors for measles virus infection include the following:

- Immunodeficiency caused by HIV or AIDS, leukemia, alkylating agents, or corticosteroid therapy, regardless of immunization status
- Travel to areas where measles is endemic or contact with travellers to endemic areas
- The loss of passive, inherited antibodies before the age of routine immunization

Risk factors for severe measles and its complications include the following:

- Malnutrition
- Underlying immunodeficiency
- Pregnancy
- Vitamin A deficiency

Diagnosis

Clinical diagnosis of measles requires a history of fever of at least three days, with at least one of the three C's (cough, coryza, conjunctivitis). Observation of Koplik's spots is also diagnostic of measles.

Alternatively, laboratory diagnosis of measles can be done with confirmation of positive measles IgM antibodies or isolation of measles virus RNA from respiratory specimens. In patients where phlebotomy is not possible, saliva can be collected for salivary measles-specific IgA testing. Positive contact with other patients known to have measles adds strong epidemiological evidence to the diagnosis. The contact with any infected person in any way, including semen through sex, saliva, or mucus, can cause infection.

Prevention

In developed countries, children are immunized against measles at 12 months, generally as part of a three-part MMR vaccine (measles, mumps, and rubella). The vaccination is generally not given earlier than this because sufficient antimeasles immunoglobulins (antibodies) are acquired via the placenta from the mother during pregnancy may persist to prevent the vaccine viruses from being effective. A second dose is usually given to children between the ages of four and five, to increase rates of immunity. Vaccination rates have been high enough to make measles relatively uncommon. Adverse reactions to vaccination are rare, with fever and pain at the injection site being the most common. Life-threatening adverse reactions occur in less than one per million vaccinations (<0.0001%).

In developing countries where measles is highly endemic, WHO doctors recommend two doses of vaccine be given at six and nine months of age. The vaccine should be given whether the child is HIV-infected or not. The vaccine is less effective in HIV-infected infants than in the general population, but early treatment with antiretroviral drugs can increase its effectiveness. Measles vaccination programmes are often used to deliver other child health interventions, as well, such as bed nets to protect against malaria, antiparasite medicine and vitamin A supplements, and so contribute to the reduction of child deaths from other causes.

Unvaccinated populations are at risk for the disease. Traditionally low vaccination rates in northern Nigeria dropped further in the early 2000s when radical preachers promoted a rumor that polio vaccines were a Western plot to sterilize Muslims and infect them with HIV. The number of cases of measles rose significantly, and hundreds of children died. This could also have had to do with the aforementioned other health-promoting measures often given with the vaccine.

Claims of a connection between the MMR vaccine and autism were raised in a 1998 paper in *The Lancet*, a respected British medical journal. Later investigation by *Sunday Times* journalist Brian Deer discovered the lead author of the article, Andrew Wakefield, had multiple undeclared conflicts of interest, and had broken other ethical codes. The *Lancet* paper was later fully retracted, and Wakefield was found guilty by the General Medical Council of serious professional misconduct in May 2010, and was struck off the Medical Register, meaning he could no longer practise as a doctor in the UK.

The GMC's panel also considered two of Wakefield's colleagues: John Walker-Smith was also found guilty and struck off the Register; Simon Murch "was in error" but acted in good faith, and was cleared. Walker-Smith was later cleared and reinstated after winning an appeal; the appeal court's finding was based on the panel's conduct of the case, and gave no support to the MMR-autism hypothesis, which the official judgement described as lacking support from any respectable body of opinion. The research was declared fraudulent in 2011 by the *BMJ*. Scientific evidence provides no support for the hypothesis that MMR plays a role in causing autism.

The autism-related MMR study in Britain caused use of the vaccine to plunge, and measles cases came back: 2007 saw 971 cases in England and Wales, the biggest rise in occurrence in measles cases since records began in 1995. A 2005 measles outbreak in Indiana was attributed to children whose parents refused vaccination, as was another outbreak in 2008 in San Diego. Centres for Disease Control and Prevention (CDC) reported that the three biggest outbreaks of measles in 2013 are attributed to clusters of unvaccinated people due to their philosophical or religious beliefs. As of August 2013, three pockets of outbreak, New York City; North Carolina and Texas contributed to 64% of the 159 cases of measles occurred in 16 states. This high number makes it on track to be the most cases since measles was considered eliminated in USA in 2000.

Treatment

There is no specific treatment for measles. Most patients with uncomplicated measles will recover with rest and supportive treatment. It is, however, important to seek medical advice if the patient becomes more unwell, as they may be developing complications.

Some patients will develop pneumonia as a sequel to the measles. Other complications include ear infections, bronchitis (either viral bronchitis or secondary bacterial bronchitis), and encephalitis. Acute measles encephalitis has a mortality rate of 15%. While there is no specific treatment for measles encephalitis, antibiotics are required for bacterial pneumonia, sinusitis, and bronchitis that can follow measles.

All other treatment addresses symptoms, with ibuprofen or paracetamol to reduce fever and pain and, if required, a fast-acting bronchodilator for cough. As for aspirin, some research has suggested a correlation between children who take aspirin and the development of Reye syndrome. Some research has shown aspirin may not be the only medication associated with Reye, and even antiemetics have been implicated, with the point being the link between aspirin use in children and Reye's syndrome development is weak at best, if not actually nonexistent. Nevertheless, most health authorities still caution against the use of aspirin for any fevers in children under 16.

The use of vitamin A in treatment has been investigated. A systematic review of trials into its use found no significant reduction in overall mortality, but it did reduce mortality in children aged under two years. A specific drug treatment for measles ERDRP-0519 has shown promising results in animal studies, but has not yet been tested in humans.

Prognosis

The majority of patients survive measles, though in some cases, complications may occur, which may include bronchitis, and—in about 1 in 100,000 cases—panencephalitis, which is usually fatal. The patient may spread the disease to an immunocompromised patient, for whom the risk of death is much higher, due to complications such as giant cell pneumonia. Acute measles encephalitis is another serious risk of measles virus infection. It typically occurs two days to one week after the breakout of the measles exanthem and begins with very high fever, severe headache, convulsions and altered mentation. A patient may become comatose, and death or brain injury may occur.

Epidemiology

Measles is extremely infectious and its continued circulation in a community depends on the generation of susceptible hosts by birth of children. In communities which generate insufficient new hosts the disease will die out. This concept was first recognized in measles by Bartlett in 1957, who referred to the minimum number supporting measles as the critical community size (CCS). Analysis of outbreaks in island communities suggested that the CCS for measles is c. 250,000.

In 2011, the WHO estimated that there were about 158,000 deaths caused by measles. This is down from 630,000 deaths in 1990. In developed countries, death occurs in 1 to 2 cases out of every 1,000 (0.1% - 0.2%). In populations with high levels of malnutrition and a lack of adequate healthcare, mortality can be as high as 10%. In cases with complications, the rate may rise to 20–30%. Increased immunization has led to an estimated 78% drop in measles deaths among UN member states. This reduction made up 25% of the decline in mortality in children under five during this period.

Reported cases of disease, WHO statistics					
WHO-Region	***1980***	***1990***	***2000***	***2005***	***2014***
African Region	1,240,993	481,204	520,102	316,224	12,125
Region of the Americas	257,790	218,579	1,755	19	3,100
Eastern Mediterranean Region	341,624	59,058	38,592	15,069	2,214
European Region	851,849	234,827	37,421	37,332	2,430
South-East Asia Region	199,535	224,925	61,975	83,627	1,540
Western Pacific Region	1,319,640	155,490	176,493	128,016	34,310
Worldwide	4,211,431	1,374,083	836,338	580,287	55,719

Even in countries where vaccination has been introduced, rates may remain high. In Ireland, vaccination was introduced in 1985. There were 99,903 cases that year. Within two years, the number of cases had fallen to 201, but this fall was not sustained. Measles is a leading cause of vaccine-preventable childhood mortality. Worldwide, the fatality rate has been significantly reduced by a vaccination campaign led by partners in the Measles Initiative: the American Red Cross, the United States Centres for Disease Control and Prevention (CDC), the United Nations Foundation, UNICEF and the WHO. Globally, measles fell 60% from an estimated 873,000 deaths in 1999 to 345,000 in 2005. Estimates for 2008 indicate deaths fell further to 164,000 globally, with 77% of the remaining measles deaths in 2008 occurring within the Southeast Asian region.

In 2006–07 there were 12,132 cases in 32 European countries: 85% occurred in five countries: Germany, Italy, Romania, Switzerland and the UK. 80% occurred in children and there were 7 deaths.

Five out of six WHO regions have set goals to eliminate measles, and at the 63rd World Health Assembly in May 2010, delegates agreed a global target of a 95% reduction in measles mortality by 2015 from the level seen in 2000, as well as to move towards eventual eradication. However, no specific global target date for eradication has yet been agreed to as of May 2010.

On January 22, 2014, the World Health Organization and the Pan American Health Organization declared and certified Colombia free of the measles while becoming the first Latin American country to abolish the infection within its borders.

In Vietnam, in the Measles Epidemic in the beginning of 2014, unto April 19 had 8,500 measles cases, 114 fatalities.

Bibliography

Bray RS: *Armies of Pestilence: The Effects of Pandemics on History*, James Clarke, US., 2004.

Connor, Linda; Samuel, Geoffrey; Geoffrey Samuel: *Healing powers and modernity traditional medicine, shamanism, and science in Asian societies*, Greenwood Publishing Group, Westport, Connecticut, 2001.

Conrad, Peter: *The Sociology of Health and Illness Critical Perspectives*, Macmillan Publishers, UK., 2008.

Gratz NG.: *The Vector- and Rodent-borne Diseases of Europe and North America: Their Distribution and Public Health Burden*, Cambridge University Press, London, 2006.

Hays, JN: *Epidemics and Pandemics: Their Impacts on Human History*, Santa Barbara, California, 2005.

Hermalin, Albert: *The Well-being of the elderly in Asia a four-country comparative study,* University of Michigan Press, US., 2002.

Kohn, Linda T.; Corrigan, Janet M.; Donaldson, Molla S.: *To Err is Human—Building a Safer Health System*, National Academies Press, Washington, D. C., 2000.

Krauss H, Weber A, Appel M.: *Zoonoses: Infectious Diseases Transmissible from Animals to Humans:* ASM Press, Washington, D.C., 2003.

Lewis, Milton James; Macpherson, Kerrie L.; Kerrie L. Macpherson : *Public health in Asia and the Pacific historical and comparative perspectives*, Routledge, London, 2007.

Lindemann, M., *Medicine and Society in Early Modern Europe*, Cambridge University Press, London, 1999.

Lindemann, Mary: *Medicine and Society in Early Modern Europe*, Cambridge University Press, Cambridge, 1999.

Micollier, Evelyne: *Sexual cultures in East Asia the social construction of sexuality and sexual risk in a time of AIDS*, Routledge, London, 2004.

Mikkeli, Heikki: *Hygiene in the Early Modern Medical Tradition*, Finnish Academy of Science and Letters, Helsinki, 1999.

Nettleton, Sarah: *The Sociology of Health and Illness*, Polity, United Kingdom, 2006.

Ohtsuka, Ryutaro; Ulijaszek, Stanley J.; Stanley J. Ulijaszek: *Health change in the Asia-Pacific region biocultural and epidemiological approaches*, Cambridge University Press, 2007.

Packard, RM: *The Making of a Tropical Disease: A Short History of Malaria*, JHU Press, US., 2007.

Packer, Lester; Ong, Choon Nam; Halliwell, Barry; Choon Nam Ong and Barry Halliwell: *Herbal and traditional medicine molecular aspects of health*, CRC Press, US., 2004.

Phillips, David: *Ageing in the Asia-Pacific region issues, policies, and future trends*, Routledge, London, 2000.

Porter, Dorothy: *Health, Civilization, and the State: A History of Public Health from Ancient to Modern Times*, Routledge, UK., 1999.

Proctor, Robert. Racial Hygiene: *Medicine under the Nazis*, Harvard University Press, Cambridge, Mass.,1988.

Rich SM, Ayala FJ.: *Evolutionary origins of human malaria parasites*, Springer, New York, 2006.

Rozario, Santi; Samuel, Geoffrey; Geoffrey Samuel: *The Daughters of Hariti childbirth and female healers in South and Southeast Asia*, Routledge, London, 2002.

Sallares, R.: *Malaria and Rome: A History of Malaria in Ancient Italy*, Oxford University Press, 2002.

Semmelweis, Ignaz; Carter, K. Codell: *Etiology, Concept and Prophylaxis of Childbed Fever*, University of Wisconsin Press, USA, 1861.

Shah, S.: *The Fever: How Malaria Has Ruled Humankind for 500,000 Years*, Macmillan, United States, 2010.

Taylor, Steve; Field, David; David Field: *Sociology of Health and Health Care*, Wiley-Blackwell, Oxford, England, 2007.

Tomes, Nancy: *The Gospel of Germs: Men, Women, and the Microbe in American Life*, Harvard University Press, Cambridge, Mass.,1998.

Vigarello, Georges: *Concepts of Cleanliness: Changing Attitudes in France since the Middle Ages*, Cambridge University Press, Cambridge, U.K.,1988.

Wear, Andrew: *History of Personal Hygiene*, Routledge, London and New York, 1993.

Webb Jr JLA: *Humanity's Burden: A Global History of Malaria*, Cambridge University Press, London, 2009.

White, Kevin: *An introduction to the sociology of health and illness*, SAGE Publishing, US., 2002.

Willcox, Merlin, Gerard Bodeker and Philippe Rasoanaivo: *Traditional medicinal plants and malaria*, CRC Press, United States of America, 2004.

Willcox, Merlin; Bodeker, Gerard; Rasoanaivo, Philippe: *Traditional Medicinal Plants and Malaria*, CRC Press, US., 2004.

Yang, Guoshu: *Progress in Asian social psychology conceptual and empirical contributions*, Greenwood Publishing Group, Westport, Connecticut, 2003.

Index

I

L

M

O

P

R

S

T

V

W

Y

□□□